Chile Makes Us Brave

Stories of Growing Up in Chihuahua, Mexico

Rogelio Bolivar
with Stephanie Bolivar

CHILE MAKES US BRAVE

Copyright © 2016 Stephanie and Rogelio Bolivar

All rights reserved.

ISBN: 0997750707
ISBN-13: 978-0997750706

Cover Art by Leonardo Moreno

DEDICATION

This book is dedicated to all of the residents of Josefa Ortiz who are no longer here on this earth: Tica's mother Doña Petra; Doña Manuela, Vero la vizca, and Solo Vino the painter; Charritas and Doña Andrea; mis abuelas Mamá Maria and Mamá Chiquita; mis amigos Cremas, Fito, Cruzito, Mateo, and René; and fellow gallero and mentor Pancho la Bruja. But mostly this book is dedicated to my favorite tia, Socorro, and mi papa, who was the most awesome influence in my life. Thank you, Apá, for always showing me I could do anything.

CHILE MAKES US BRAVE

CONTENTS

    Acknowledgments   vii

1. **_Niños Malos_ : Bad Boys**   1
   Adventura en el Bosque; Adventure in the Forest
   El Catecismo: The Catechism
   Vero la Vizca: Blind Vero

2. **_Historias Tristes_ : Sad Stories**   31
   Rene
   Tia Socorro
   Fito

3. **_Locos_ : Crazies**   61
   Los Criminales : The Criminals
   Charritas
   Chupis vs. Moy vs. Alejandro vs. Chispa
   Novias : Girlfriends
   La feria por una cerveza : Beer Money

4. **_Mascotas_ : Pets**   105
   El murcielago : The Bat
   El perro de mis suenos : The Dog of My Dreams
   Paco el Puerco: Paco the Pig

5. **_Problemas y soluciones_ : Problems and Solutions**   127
   Torito
   Drogas : Drugs

6 ***Gallos y Gallinas*: Roosters and Chickens**   151
Gallinas: Chickens
Rambo
The Pinto
La Creacion de un luchador: Creating a Fighter

7 ***Las Gangas*: The Gangs**   187
Moy
Cruzito
Julian and la Miller

8 ***Mirando para frente*: Looking Forward**   221
Aprendiendo: Learning
Saliendo a Chihuahua: Leaving Chihuahua

ACKNOWLEDGMENTS

Thank you to everyone who helped us with the writing of this book. Thank you, Rogelio, for honestly sharing your stories. For all of the dinner dates we went on with my computer and for all of the beautiful stories you shared with me over and over again so that I could turn them into this piece of art. Also, thank you for being open and willing to share everything, even painful details so this could be so real and true. Many thanks to Ama, Maria Elena Garcia, for her praise of the book and for helping Rogelio to resurrect some of the details in even greater detail.

Thank you to our children for the many hours you listened to stories and gave us your honest feedback. I'll never forget the day you took *The Smoking Bat* to school, Emilie, and had your teacher read it to the class. Many thanks to our nieces and nephews and our kids' friends for listening and enjoying these stories, too. You all kept us going.

I also want to thank my fellow teachers at ACHS: Eva Menachof, Jennifer Malinowski, Beth Roshon, Rita Hanneman, and Rachel Robinson for being so excited about the book and for volunteering to read chapters along the way. And to my book club—Mary Blake, Stephanie Nelson, (Jen, Eva, and Rita)— for suggesting we read the book as one of our monthly book choices. I love you for that.

Stephanie Nelson, thank you for your support and acknowledgement of me as an author.

Also, students, thank you for reading chapters, sharing your excitement about the stories and always asking for more.

It was awesome to have teenagers at both ACHS and North as my audience.

Thank you to my friend Audrey Dockins for giving me ideas about publishing and being another cheerleader for us.

And thanks to my Facebook friends for helping us to decide on a title. Rogelio and I had many ideas but needed you to help us choose just the right one.

Finally, muchas gracias a mi esposo Rogelio. You would never let me quit even though it was so hard to keep writing with four kids to take care of and a teaching job to do. You kept on pushing me and now the day is finally here. We did it!

-Stephanie

1. NIÑOS MALOS
BAD BOYS

Adventura en El Bosque
Adventure in the Forest

On the weekends when I was eleven, I hung out with my friends Fago, Tica and Panchito. We usually went hunting up in the hills, went to the pools at the balneario, went to the campos and chased cows or went to other fields and chased horses. Sometimes we just hung out in the neighborhood, waiting to watch a fight.

But today was different. Today we decided we were tired of all the usual places—we wanted to do something new. So we all got together at la huerta and started making plans to go on a real adventure. Fago wanted to go to los Picos de la Luna, the moon spikes, which were a group of huge, rocky hills we liked to climb. They lay across the periferico (the highway) that ran to the northeast and were maybe a twenty minute walk from our colonia. But Panchito didn't want to go there. He wanted to go to el cerro, the hills, which were not as high and were closer to our houses, close by what we called the bear's cave. There we would hunt pigeons and prairie dogs with sling shots.

"Let's go hunting," Panchito had said, but we did that a lot. Plus, we wanted our adventure to last all day and it was so hot, we would've burned our butts at either los Picos or el cerro. It was already over 100 degrees and it was only eight o'clock in the morning!

Tica, who was the oldest of us, said, "Let's go to the balneario." At that moment, we thought the pool sounded like a great idea. The pool was not just one swimming pool. There were actually seven different pools to choose from. Fago and Panchito were both grounded, so they couldn't ask for money from their parents. I, on the other hand, had twenty pesos because I had worked for my dad in the store that week and Tica also had had a good week. He had sold a lot of newspapers so he had about twenty pesos, too.

We were hopeful so we did the math and that was when we realized we wouldn't be able to go to el balneario. It was nine pesos each just to get in and we would still need to buy food. We didn't want to go to the pools and starve all day.

And then an idea occurred to me, something that I'd been wanting to do for a very long time. "Why don't we just go to el bosque de Aldama?"

"Are you nuts? That's way too far," Panchito said. El bosque de Aldama was about twenty miles from our neighborhood.

But it was supposed to be super fun. We had heard older people in the neighborhood talking about it. This was the Aldama Forest—the river flowed clean and deep and was full of fish and ducks. We had talked before about how it would be really fun to hunt the ducks. And there was an actual forest with many trees, there were pools, and there were even horses for rent.

"That's a good idea," Tica said, smiling. "I've been wanting to go there for a while."

After a fifteen minute discussion, we all agreed. We would go to Aldama. Tica and I said we would combine our money. And who cared if Panchito and Fago were grounded.

We wouldn't ask anyone if we could go, we would just go anyway, and if Tica and I put our forty pesos together we could buy soda, even beer for everyone.

The four of us left the yard of la Huerta and headed down the street toward Cleofas' little store. We went inside and grabbed a loaf of bread, bologna, cheese—we quickly spent every single penny we had. "Having a party?" Cleofas joked. "You sure are buying a lot of food. Your mamás don't want to feed you today?" Cleofas was only about 35 years old, but he was nosy like an old lady and he was as usual asking too many questions. This could be bad for us because Cleofas couldn't keep his mouth shut. "Don't tell our dads that we're buying all of this food," I said to him, even though I figured he would tell our dads anyway.

We lied and told Cleofas that we were going to go to el Cerro since it was closer. We especially didn't want Panchito's and Fago's parents knowing where we were headed since they were "grounded".

When we came out of the store, we saw my brother's friend Gegos. We talked him into buying us a six pack of beer at la paz. We gave him a few pesos for his trouble and now we were completely out of money.

Then we sneaked through the streets back to my house, carrying our food and beer. Luckily, mi mamá was somewhere else in the neighborhood at the time, so we put all of our food into an old ice cooler that we found. The cooler was so full of food that we only had room to dump in one little bag of ice.

Fago and Tica each grabbed one side of the cooler and dragged it down the street and we all plodded across the yard of la huerta to the periferico. We stood at the highway with our heavy cooler, thumbs in the air, sweating and trying to be patient as we waited for a kind driver. No car would stop. We roasted like hot dogs in the Chihuahua sun and after ten minutes of standing there, we were greasy. But we were determined so we must've stood there for over an hour in total, trying to make car after car stop for us.

We were drenched with sweat and stinking by the time someone finally did stop to pick us up. He was a ranchero in a little pick up. He talked funny, either hung over from the night before, or most likely, still a little bit drunk. Smiles formed on our moist faces. We couldn't care less what kind of condition this guy was in. Someone had actually stopped for us! He and his vehicle were the key to our freedom and now Aldama didn't seem so far away.

"Where are you mocosos going? You're kind of young to be hitching a ride."

The guy, who was about twenty years old, wore cowboy clothes and boots. He got out of the truck, walked around to the front, and bent over next to the hood. As we stood beside the little truck near the back of the box, we heard some wretching noises and then saw a little river of burrito debris running toward us, a tiny stream of vomit on the concrete. The four of us smirked at each other, and then laughed out loud. More and more pieces of food debris ran out from under the truck. I couldn't believe that someone could puke so much.

He walked back around the truck and opened his door, then looked at us with a sickly face. "Where are you guys trying to go? The balnearios?"

"No," I said. "We're going to Aldama. El Bosque de Aldama."

"Really. That's cool. I'm going home. The ranchita of my parents is close by Aldama. Jump in the back."

We boosted our cooler into the box of the truck, jumped in, and sat down in the bed. The ranchero gave the truck a little gas and took off from the side of the road. Looking behind us, we saw even more puke on the ground. It was so full of burrito debris that we burst out laughing again. The guy drove and we laughed hard for almost a mile. As soon as the laughter died down, I felt something fly through the air onto my face. "What was that?" Panchito yelled.

Fago was sitting in the box directly behind the ranchero. Chunks of smelly corn flew into his hair and stuck there, and, at the same time, little pieces of red and brown stuck to the back of his t-shirt in clumps. The dude slowed his truck down slightly, but didn't stop. Vomit dripped from the driver's side door all the way to the back of the tail light. "Oh, shit," someone yelled, and we exploded in laughter again, all except for Fago, who looked surprised as he sniffed the air.

In not too long we forgot about the smell; we sat in the truck bed and talked and joked for the rest of the way. Riding in the back of the truck, the breeze felt great.

Before I knew it, we were driving through the little town of Aldama and through a forest of big, beautiful trees like none I had ever seen.

"Are you guys meeting somebody here?" He had parked the truck near a small deserted stream and was standing outside. "In the forest, there are mostly only adults, and it's dangerous for kids alone."

The guy was talking more straight now. But his lips were pale and surrounded by a white powdery film. His mouth stunk like alcohol, like if you lit up a cigarette in his presence, he might explode.

We reassured him that we were meeting Tica's big brother or uncle at the Aldama pool.

He drove a little more and then stopped the truck again a few minutes later on a gravel road with a forest of tall trees and a stream running along one side. We lifted our cooler out of the back of the truck and jumped out. We yelled gracias to the guy, waved wildly, and walked down the road as he drove off. The cooler was loaded and heavy so we took turns lugging it. Soon we passed by an area filled with grills where people always gather together to drink and make carne asada. But the grills were deserted.

There were humongous trees along the river. At least it seemed like a river to me at the time, but it was narrow and didn't contain much water. We parked the cooler so we could throw rocks along the stream and chase lizards and squirrels. It was even hotter now, but at least here in the Aldama Forest, it was a little breezy and it was fun to run next to the trees. It seemed like there was no one in the world but me and my friends—it felt a little scary yet thrilling at the same time to be alone in the nature.

We had been carrying our super heavy lunchera off and on for close to two hours and now we were getting tired. "I'm so hungry," Fago complained.

"I need water," Panchito said, "and I'm hungry, too." It was about twelve or one and I had only eaten cereal for breakfast.

"Mira," Panchito said. He pointed out a group of trees growing close together. Between the trees was a little spot of shade, an oasis in a desert of tremendous heat. We ran over and sat down to eat lunch in the shady spot. Fago, who had been carrying the lunchera for the last half hour, pulled it over toward him and sat down next to it on the dirt and grass. When we opened it up, it was a very ugly sight. The ice was long gone and had become warmish water, the bread was smooshy, and the bologna had turned purplish-orange from the heat. Our six pack was warm, and the chips were smashed. But they were on top, so at least they were dry. "Look at that!" Tica said, pointing to our destroyed food.

"Hey, don't laugh, wei. That shit is our lunch."

The bologna seemed alright, but the bread was wet and inedible. Fago had opened the bread bag so he could eat a piece in the back of the ranchero's truck, I remembered, and I guessed he hadn't bothered to close the package. We hadn't noticed Fago open the cooler or the ranchero driving all swervy. We had just wanted to get to el bosque.

We ate the bologna, which was kind of warm but still good-tasting. And then Tica said, "Come on guys, let's drink the beers."

"O.K." we agreed, our hearts beating faster with a little rush of adrenaline. As I started to sip the warm beer, I cringed. Beer was terrible; I could not understand how mi papá or any other adult could stand it. Warm beer was worse than terrible. I guessed that none of us wanted to say anything about it because we were drinking cervezas for the first time and no one wanted to be the wimp.

I looked around me. Panchito, Tica, and I were having a hard time drinking, almost gagging on one beer. But not Fago. He hurried up and drank one right away and then another.

I was starting to feel kind of weird. And I couldn't understand how Fago could drink more than one without throwing up.

It had become afternoon. We smashed the empty cans with our hands and stood up. We threw rocks in the river and, after a little while, decided to hunt lizards. In the hills, we often hunted them with a sling shot; we looked for them under rocks and on trees. We would carry them home so I could chop them up into little pieces and feed them to my chickens.

Within minutes, we became very focused on hunting—throwing rocks at lizards and smashing them. As we hunted, we waded into the river which was very shallow. We ran around splashing each other in its beautiful water. The water only came up to our waists, but it was clean, unlike the river near our colonia, which was polluted and black.

It was then we realized that Fago wasn't around.

"Hey Fago," we called to him. He did not call back, so we went to look for him. Where was that menso? We laughed as we looked for him. I must've been a little drunk, because I was laughing at everything.

Where could Fago be? We went back to look for him in the little shady spot where we had eaten. It seemed like half an hour had passed by when I heard branches rustling up in the tree above us and then some crazy laughing. "Hey, putos!"

I looked up. Big, goofy Fago was staring down at us from a tree. He had climbed up high into it and now it appeared that he had been trying to hide from us. But he was huge, by far the biggest of us all. There was no way that idiota could hide in a tree.

We all ran to the trunk of it and started climbing up. Fago continued to climb further and further into the tree; maybe he saw a nest, I thought, and was going to throw an egg at us.

But then, suddenly, it happened. We heard him heave and half-digested beer and bologna splashed down on Tica's back. Tica tried to move out of the way, hoisting himself through tree branches, but since he was right underneath Fago, the back of his shirt got covered in barf. And still there, far up in the tree was Fago, who swayed on a branch now, like he was going to fall out.

He clung onto the branch as he swung from side to side. Shit! He had to be like thirty feet up.

"Vamanos," Panchito yelled. "We have to save Fago."

"Pinche pendejo," I screamed at my stupid drunk friend and hurried through the tree, climbing faster. I moved up and up, balancing on a tree branch and grabbed Fago by one arm.

Tica also hurried through the branches, "Stupid puto!" he yelled as he grabbed onto Fago's other arm. We tried to help Fago down from the tree, but that tree was huge. So Tica and I stepped back down, branch by branch, and that's how we finally removed Fago from that tree. Fago was dizzy and heavy. It took us a long time to get him down to the ground.

"Come on, Fago. We need to take you into the water," I said, "until your dizziness passes."

After a while in the water playing and playing, Fago got a little better.

We were feeling so tired. By now we had hauled Fago from the tree, lugged a cooler around in the hot sun, drank our first beers, and run all over el bosque. It had been an hour since we last ate, and we were hungry again and very thirsty, but we had no water. We had forgotten to bring water!

We followed the curve of the river to kill more lizards, but we were so thirsty we couldn't even drink our own spit. I had wittled the end of a stick so it was sharp and pointy, and we impaled every lizard we caught onto it. We probably had ten or twelve dead ones on a three foot long stick. The colorful lizards were anywhere from two to six inches long. They were bluish and brownish and we had broken the tails off some of them, so they hung and dripped blood. Now, after about three hours of running around with them, they were beginning to stink.

We still walked, looking for water and taking turns carrying the lizard stick. Fago mostly carried it around on his shoulder and lizard blood had stained the back of his shirt. The stink of the blood and the barf intertwined, and we all held our noses and laughed. We couldn't believe how, in a matter of a couple of hours, these lizards got so horribly smelly. After about fifteen minutes of walking, Fago started singing stupid ranchera music off key. Dead lizards dripped blood and some kind of milky white liquid onto his shirt. "Look at that menso, carrying those lizards too close to his shirt." Me, Tica, and Panchito all laughed and made fun of Fago.

"Look at the blood on your shirt, cabron. The barf was bad enough, but now you really smell like shit!"

We may have been laughing, but I couldn't stand the thirst. I knew we needed to think of something, and fast. And then I remembered a time when we went camping really far up in the hills and we ran out of water. That time Fago had been designated to carry the water bottles but had lost them somewhere. We were so thirsty then that we were almost fainting. But our leader, Wereque, found a puddle in between two rocks—green, warm and smelly with a lot of nasty goo in it.

He cleaned out some biggish weird-looking tadpoles from the puddle. Then he took off his shirt. He carefully placed the shirt on top of the puddle folding it over and over. He cupped his hands into the water above the shirt and the water that ran through his hands was clean and clear. It was beautiful water and I couldn't wait to drink it.

"I know what to do," I told them and we all ran around looking for a little puddle by the side of the river. When we found one, I was able to do what Wereque had done. Everything was the same except that the water was not in a puddle; instead, the water branched off from the river and was very cold. I started to drink the water, and yelled to the other guys, "I did it, come drink the clean water I made!" but none of them believed me so no one came over.

When I leaned my head back and shot the water out of my mouth like I was a fountain, they came. Fago first, then Panchito, then Tica. The water was good-tasting, full of vitamins and minerals.

Drinking was a humongous relief for our thirst and mini-hang-overs. I think I drank a gallon.

When I had pulled my shirt out of the little stream, the bottom of it was deep green and moldy. I cleaned it on some rocks and put it back on. When I said, "This feels great!" my friends all wet their shirts too and we walked together toward the picnic area. Fago's shirt was finally clean and he smelled much better. By then we decided that it must be about three o'clock.

We arrived at the Aldama picnic area beyond hungry. It was kind of busy that Saturday and now the bosque was full of people, mostly couples. On the outskirts of the picnic area, there were two couples. There was one dude on top of a lady, a furry butt on thick hips doing its thing. "Oh, my God," someone said and we started laughing so hard that we had to run away. There was another man licking a lady's neck and ears; "He's going to eat her like a paleta," Panchito said.

"Gross," said Tica. "Look how he's licking her."

"Ugh," I said. It had to be the grossest thing ever.

Fago threw up. Maybe he threw up from the beer or

maybe from the dude licking all over the lady. I wasn't sure. But Tica was not disgusted. He was thirteen at the time and it looked to me like he had a little tent in his pants. When we saw that, the other three of us made jokes about it for the rest of the day.

Usually, when we went on an adventure and got hungry, we walked over and sat down by the grills, looking distressed. Within thirty minutes, somebody would feel bad and throw us a piece of meat. Occasionally, people left and didn't even leave us bones, but that was rare.

Today was not our lucky day. We stared with our sad eyes at two grills where young couples were eating. We got fed neither time. Today it was extremely bad because we were so starving. I felt like I wanted to cry and I knew Tica wanted to cry, too. Fago was always the first one to give up so he was already crying. Panchito's eyes teared up and he kept saying, "I need to go home." But this was before cell phones so we couldn't call anyone. No one could help us. And no one would even feed us.

"These young putos will never help us," Tica said. "Let's find some viejo." So we got up and walked around looking for older people. As we walked, we saw an older man trying to light a camp fire, but he couldn't do it. It appeared that he had run out of matches.

Earlier that day Panchito had found a lighter that we had been using to burn the lizards' feet and tails.

He handed the lighter over to me.

My hunger was raging when we went up to the man, told him we had a lighter and asked," Do you need some help?"

He at first said no, but after trying many times to light the fire, he finally said, "Sure, can I use your lighter? Where are your parents?"

We had a lot of practice at making fires out of nothing so Tica and I got it going quickly. The guy had a look of appreciation on his face.

Then the wife came over. A short furry brown dog followed her. Fago had been carrying the stick with the lizards on it the whole time, but two of the lizards had slid off from the motion and the heat and the dog grabbed them from the ground, so happy. When he bit down on the first lizard and shook his head back and forth, the legs and tail ripped off and flew through the air.

"You get those stinky lizards out of here," the man scolded us. His dog was running around, carrying a disgusting lizard in his mouth. My friends and I were laughing, but the man came closer. "Keep those lizards away from my dog!"

We worried that he would tell us to go, too, but we needed to get fed, so we sent Fago to dispose of the lizards in a trash barrel about fifty feet away from the grill.

The wife was probably between sixty-five and seventy, a sweet grandma-lady. "Have you kids eaten yet?" she asked, looking concerned.

In chorus, we all sweetly said, "No."

Our mouths were watering now. The older people had some pieces of meat, onions, and tomatoes and all kinds of veggies. They had a big bowl, and they were going to make some kind of deshebrada tacos, the best food ever. We offered to help make the food, but the lady just kept asking us, "Where are your parents?"

"They're at the pool," Tica quickly said. The lady looked at us in disbelief. Like she had caught us in our lie. When I realized this, I added, "Tica's brother is over by the pool."

The husband and wife, Don Ramon and Doña Lola, were supposed to meet some people at the park, but their friends never arrived so they had a lot of extra food. We had found them at just the right time.

I don't know how many tacos I ate. Maybe about six.

We ate and then talked a little while. It was going to get dark soon so we thanked Don Ramon and Doña Lola for the delicious food and walked away from their little camp.

We went back to the trash can to grab the lizards, our trophies of the day, but they stunk so bad, we decided to leave them there.

Don Ramon and Doña Lola had given each of us a can of soda for the road. So we drank our sodas as we walked toward the pool hoping to find someone we knew. It was now far past dinner time in Chihuahua and there were hardly any people left in el bosque. Even worse for us, there was no one we could find from our colonia, Josefa Ortiz. What were we going to do? I knew for sure I was going to get a nasty beating when I got home. I had told my parents I would be home around two and now it was almost seven. We were twenty miles from home, the sun was sinking lower and lower in the sky and now sunset was very close. We were walking and walking, looking for somebody and had found no one.

"What are we going to do? We're going to be stuck here all night."

"I don't know." Fago said, almost crying again.

Then Tica came up with an idea. "Let's go over by the highway and start walking. Hopefully, someone will see us, pick us up, and take us home." We all smiled, hoping that our friend was right.

For the first time ever, I was hoping that the old tattletale Cleofas had told and mi papa would come looking for us. That's how scared I was. I hadn't cried yet, but I was about to. Fago was getting on my nerves. He was crying a lot. Panchito was crying, too, and Tica was the oldest so he was trying to be strong and not cry, but I could see that his eyes were getting watery. I cried silently with tears rolling down my cheeks in the almost dark.

We walked next to the highway and the darkness came. It was pitch dark, darker than I remember darkness ever being. As we walked along the road, we waved wildly to every single car we saw. So many cars drove by and not even one of them stopped. Would we be stranded in that terrible darkness for the whole night?

What seemed like hours later, we saw lights in the distance. Then a car pulled over. Unbelievable. Someone had actually stopped. From behind us, someone got out of a truck and then we heard a familiar voice. "Where are you guys going? What happened? Where is your brother?"

It was Don Ramon. I felt so much relief.

"I can't believe you boys did this," he said. "It's maybe the dumbest thing I've ever seen in my life. Or even heard of. Four boys out in the wilderness unprepared late at night?"

He paused for a moment and then went on, "That wasn't true, was it? Was your brother even here today? Because if he was, he's going to hear from me. That was totally irresponsible to leave you kids alone in the wilderness. He was here, wasn't he?"

When we told him "No" he looked shocked. Then he said, "Get in my truck. I'm taking you all home."

Don Ramon didn't have to tell us twice. We jumped into the big truck behind he and Doña Lola. We now had to tell the truth. But we felt so grateful that Don Ramon had stopped for us, we willingly told him the whole story, everything but the part about the beers and the couples.

He couldn't believe the four of us kids would go out on our own, four kids unprepared having fun in the wild. At first he yelled at us, but later he started to laugh when we told about our day. He seemed to be calming down now that he knew our story.

"But you know what guys," he said. "I'm taking each of you home, and I'm going to make sure you tell your parents exactly what happened."

When we arrived back in our neighborhood, there was a huge group of people waiting. I remember my older brothers acting happy to see me at first, but their little moment of joy was almost immediately replaced by anger, "We're so pissed off at you, Chispa. You don't even know what's going to happen to you. Apa has been looking for you since three o'clock." They told us they had been looking all over the place—at the balneario, even in the hills. But no one would ever have thought of el bosque de Aldama.

And I was the first one to get dropped off. When I saw Apa, he said nothing. I saw there was a moment of joy on his face and then that look in mi papá's eyes that was very frightening. I knew what was going to happen to me.

"Where have you been, Chispa? Were you at the balneario?" he asked and I stayed silent.

Don Ramon said, "Tell him, or I will." I reluctantly told my dad the whole story. Still nobody knew about the beer—my dad would've killed me.

He didn't hit me in front of Don Ramon. Instead, he seemed very grateful. He shook Don Ramon's hand and told him many nice things. I was saved. "He's calm now," I thought.

He said more nice things to Doña Lola and then I saw him give my friends nasty looks. I knew.

After Don Ramon drove down the street, my dad went away for a moment. I hugged my mom and she hugged me. She was crying tears of joy; I was crying tears of terror.

Apa came back holding the most frightening device that I had ever experienced...la jarilla. This type of tree grew by the river. Its branches were about a half inch in diameter, about three feet long, and very flexible. My dad held the jarilla behind his back.

"I'm going to Doña Andrea. I cannot see this," mi mama said and she left.

I probably got six really good whacks from that jarilla. I cried as my dad prepared for the first hit, "I promise. I'll never do it again."

It didn't matter what I said. My dad said, smugly, "After I hit you, I'm sure you will never do this again," and then whack. Then five more. I instinctively tried to cover my butt after the first whack and my hands were bruised in a nasty swollen line. I couldn't sit down comfortably for a couple of days. This was the worst whacking I ever got, but because of it, I never ran off a whole day for at least a year afterward.

Tica and I got grounded for a week each, but Fago and Panchito, who were already in trouble, couldn't come out of their houses for three weeks and they got horrible whoopings. After that, none of us ever went far from Josefa again without our parents knowing.

El Catecismo
The Catechism

My brothers and I all knew that when we turned ten, Amá would make us go to el catecismo. Of course, since we were Mexican, we were Catholic. And we weren't just a little bit Catholic; mi mamá and mi papá were very Catholic. Mi madrecita lit the candles to her saints and prayed to them for the different things she needed. She said the rosary at meal times and before bed. Mi papá went to our neighborhood Catholic church, Perpetua Socorro, every Saturday or Sunday and mi madrecita went every day and told us about what God would want us to do in every situation.

I was ten and Bombin was thirteen and there we were sitting in the kitchen one morning eating breakfast when mi mamá placed her hands gently on our backs and said, "Bombin and Chispa, it's time that the two of you start going to the catecismo. You are going to join the Catholic church." She said it so cutely and then she smiled and whisked across the room as if she were dancing, like she always did when she got excited about something.

We looked at each other knowingly. Moy and Chentito had told us stories about how horribly boring the catechism was and they teased us that our day would come, too.

El catecismo would start the next Saturday at ten o'clock in the morning. We would go sit in a room and learn about God and the church. Moy and Chentito warned us that Senora Terrazas would be our teacher and we would definitely hate it. The two of them had never made it through. They had been caught on the streets hanging out with their boys while they were supposed to be at church. Amá had tried with them, but after weeks of their ditching, she had finally given up.

Now she was ready to try again with her new hopefuls, me and Bombin. On that Saturday, mi mamá woke us at eight and we took our showers. She laid out our best clothing: white button-down shirts and navy blue pants. These were our uniforms to go to the piñatas, the quinceañeras, everything. Truly our Sunday best.

After I pulled on my clothes, mi mamá rubbed a thick layer of lotion all over my face and poured the hair gel into her hands. She rubbed her hands together, and, with a big smile, pasted the goo on my hair. Bombin knew what was coming. "I'm not getting that Benito Juarez peiñado," he said to her. Since he was a teenager, he cared how he looked more than I did.

"Oh yes you are," she said, and in one quick motion, she smiled and rubbed the gel through his hair. Then she parted it on the side and combed it back, so he looked just like Benito Juarez. She did the same to me.

After she fed us a breakfast of juevos con frijoles and her own flour tortillas, kissed us on our heads, and told us, "Listen to the Señora, m'ijos," we walked down the hall and out the front door.

Bombin was already jogging down the street, "I'll meet you at Cleofas', Chispa. I've got to get this crap out of my hair." There was a water faucet outside the store, and every time mi mama gelled and combed Bombin's hair back, he ran over and washed it out in that faucet. Then he went on to wherever he was going.

When we got to the church, the catechism lady greeted us and took us to a basement room where she taught us songs and told us stories from the bible. Chela Terrazas was the catechism lady. She had three sons who all loved talking about the bible. Miguel was the oldest son and he was fully loaded with freckles. He was extremely white but had more freckles on him than I had ever seen on any other person in my entire life. The middle son was Omar and he was very tall and goofy. And then there was the youngest, Juan Carlos, but we called him Juan Pelos. He was the furriest boy I have ever seen. He had a complete mustache and beard when he was twelve. He had gobs of hair on his back, too. The amount of hair he had already made him a freak of nature, but what was really strange was the fact that his father was barely 5 feet tall and Juan Pelos grew to be about 6'6.

Señora Terrazas was a very good Catholic. She was highly respected by my parents who were also good Catholics. So every Saturday, like good boys, we sat in pews in a room the size of a small classroom. There were fifteen of us from ten to fourteen years old and Señora Terrazas who was giving us a constant sermon.

She told some of us that we were going to go to hell for stealing an apple or a banana from Cleofas' store. But Cleofas often shorted us change so we thought it was only fair to take an occasional piece of fruit. I ate some of the stolen fruit but never nabbed it myself because Cleofas was some kind of cousin to mi papá. That would have been disrespectful.

Senora Terrazas, with her curly boyish hair-do, would read the same verses of the bible and the same parables over and over to us. She loved Daniel and the lion's den and the parable where the demons went into the pigs. She loved Noah and his ark and David and Goliath. She would tell us the parables and make us pray two dozen hail Marys while she went to the restroom. But she loved the Virgen de Guadalupe the most.

Bombin was not a favorite of the Señora because of his crazy antics. She was always enthusiastic as she read the word of God, but Bombin was not. During her readings, Bombin would make faces or fart or talk behind her back.

When Bombin did these things almost everybody in the class laughed. Thanks to him, every single Saturday we had fun only because he made us laugh so hard. Señora Terrazas would say something like, "Virgen Maria" and Bombin would look at us and say, "Yo quiero tortilla" and rub his stomach, bending at the waist looking hungry and silly. Then Tica, Fago, and I would laugh and hardly be able to stop.

Señora Terrazas would then say, "Boys, cáyense. God and the priest are not pleased with your behavior." That comment would bring on the laughter even more so that we shook in our seats as we tried to hold it in.

Bombin also did gross things. We would bring snacks to eat during our break so Bombin would be drinking a can of soda. Then he would spit a big gross wad of saliva into it. When the teacher came back in the room, he would ask, "Who wants a drink of soda?" trying to get her to say yes.

"Ughh!" we would say, and again we would all laugh.

I was not a favorite of the Señora, either, but for a different reason. I have always had a very curious mind and so I asked a lot of questions. I mean A LOT of questions. Catechism was five hours of learning about basic bible stuff, and purely Catholic stuff like learning about Saints and how the Virgin Mary is the mother of God. "How is the Virgen the mother of God? Isn't she the mother of Jesus?" I also asked, "Why should I pray to the saints and the Virgin Mary when the bible says not to do that?"

"You need to pray through the Virgin, Chispa. She is the mother of God." She never had good answers and when I asked all of those difficult questions, she got angry.

"Why does the bible say don't pray to the saints? They have eyes but they can't see you. They have ears but they can't hear you."

She was red and angry.

"You can talk to God directly," I said. I always did.

She said to me, "Chispa, no. You have to have intermediaries. Stop asking these questions."

Her favorite intermediary, like most Mexicans, was the Virgen de Guadalupe. We were supposed to love her. I always respected Mary, because she was Jesus' mama, but the

Senora loved the Virgin Maria so deeply that she made us memorize the story of when Juan Diego met her. How the Indian Juan Diego went to el cerro and the Virgin appeared to him there. He found her at the top of this hill and the Virgin told him to tell the priest that she wanted an iglésia built on that very spot. So Juan Diego rushed to the priest to tell him the Virgin's wishes.

After Juan Diego had told the priest the story at least three times, the priest told him that he was full of shit and to make the Virgin send a signal so they would know he wasn't just making it up and the Virgin really wanted this church built.

At the priest's request, Juan Diego went again to the hill to talk to the Virgin and the Virgin said, "Go down there again. On your way back gather these roses de castilla in your robe and show them to the priest so he won't think you're lying and will believe that I am here." Even though it was winter (not the season for roses), Juan Diego listened to the Virgin.

He went down there and gathered all of the roses. Then he went back to the priest and said, "Is this enough proof for you?" and threw the roses out of his robe. After that, poof, the image of the Virgin was miraculously imprinted on his robe. Because of the roses and the Virgen de Guadalupe's image on the robe, all of the Mexicans believed in the Virgen de Guadalupe and the robe can be seen in her church on a hill in Mexico D.F.

I guess I would've liked catecismo better if it would've been more interesting, if my questions had been answered or if Señora Terrazas would've at least tried to understand me. Instead, she preached to me and said, "Our religion is habit, Chispa. Don't worry about it." That response didn't satisfy me.

Many Saturdays, we got sent out of the catechism room. "I'm telling Nena," Señora Terrazas would say to me and Bombin. Or else the Señora would say to Tica and Gegos, "I'm telling Petra." Later, when she saw our mothers on the street, she would tell them that we were behaving badly at the catecismo, and we would get spankies. But none of us really cared because the Catechism was so long and we were making it fun. All of the laughs we were having were worth getting in trouble for.

We were afraid to find la Señora Terrazas in the streets when we were without our parents because she would give us sermons. She would say "be good boys and finish the catecismo. God will love you and then you will enter heaven." According to her, catechism was indispensable for our salvation.

You might think we went to the catechism just because we were good boys, but if you thought that, you would be wrong. We eventually learned that there was more at Perpetua Socorro on Saturdays then Señora Terrazas and el catecismo. On Saturdays, there was something great—called bolo.

While we attended catechism in the basement of the church, babies were being baptized in the sanctuary. Lucky for us, catecismo let out at about the same time that the baptismos got over.

When Señora Terrazas let us out of the basement room, she led us to the front doors so we wouldn't interfere with the people attending the baptismos.

Some actual good kids from other neighborhoods were afraid of getting in trouble, so they went out where she instructed. But me, my brother, and our friends from Josefa waited and when we saw that the Señora wasn't looking, we would sneak down another hallway and out the back door, where the baptism attendees came out of the church. As we hurried out the doors, we scanned the crowd for padrinos, the godfathers of the baptized children, who had the bolo.

The bolo was money, coins that the padrinos would throw high in the air into the street so the kids at the baptism could collect it. We would pretend we knew the families and chase after it, too. Sometimes one of us would make as much as fifty pesos on one Saturday morning.

It was well worth attending the catechism for some serious dinero. It was kind of like our pay day for having to sit there for those five long hours. And for fifty pesos we could buy a shit load of candy for ourselves and a bunch of our friends. We bought sodas or lunches at Cleofas', or we played arcade games. If you had to be tortured, you'd might as well earn a few pesos for it.

We were supposed to attend catechism for two years, but after about a year, the bolo was no longer enough for us. Bombin and I started ditching.

One day we went to the church and just hung out outside. I saw Señora Terrazas come out the front door.

"Let's run!" I yelled to Bombin. We took off down the street.

"You boys get back here!" The Señora hurried after us. But we only heard her in the distance yelling, "I'm telling your parents."

She did this a few times but after a while, she stopped. She probably got tired of chasing us.

On the days we escaped, we would go to la fantasia, a store in la Hacienda de la flor, to play the arcade games. Or we would just hang out in Josefa or the surrounding colonias. Sometimes we went to the campo to play soccer. Other times we went to the cantina to play pool or smoke cigarette butts which we found on the ground outside. Bombin usually didn't let me smoke, but when he wasn't with me, I did it. My friends and I would pick up the cigarettes that were burned down to the filter. We lit them and smoked just the filters until they burned our lips.

We usually never skipped the whole catechism, because we couldn't miss the bolo. And Senora Terrazas wasn't there every week—some days there were different ladies in charge.

It was hard for the other ladies to remember kids from one week to the next, so usually a few of us ditched one week and a few others the next. That way, it was less noticeable if we were gone.

One day, Bombin and I escaped Perpetua Socorro with a few other kids. Bombin, Gegos and I thought we might hang out in the neighborhood until it seemed like not much was going on. I found Fago and the four of us headed to this cave on the edge of the cerro that we called the bear's cave. We waded through the river, laughing. Bombin and Gegos had cigarettes. "Let's go smoke in the bear's cave," my brother said. As soon as we got there, they entered the cave. "You mocosos go away," Bombin said. "You're too young to smoke."

"Let's go hunt some lizards, Fago," I said, disappointed and we headed further up into the hills.

Mi papa got home from work early some Saturdays so he could coach his baseball games. He owned a pair of high-powered binoculars that he had bought in California and he used them for finding his naughty boys up in the hills. I didn't know at the time that's how he found out. But later, when I was twelve or thirteen and my brother Pedro was missing, I would see my dad at la huerta, smiling. scouting with the binoculars. "There's Pedro, running in the hills," he would say. And later, when Pedro came home, he'd say, "How are you doing, Pedro? Where were you?"

"Playing baseball at the campo."

And then wham, Pedro would get hit with the jarilla smack in the ass. The next day, my little brother would have the swollen wrists from putting his hands over his cola to try and stop the stick.

Catechism was over at two o'clock so I got home around three. I don't know what happened to Bombin but Fago and I had gotten sidetracked playing in the hills. "Why are you home so late?" My dad asked, glaring at me.

"I was playing arcade games," I lied.

"Where did you get the money for those?" An hour was a

long time to play when you were broke.

So I quickly thought up an explanation my dad would believe. In Mexico, a way to make money is to go pick up tortillas from the tortilla factory for some neighbor lady. When you returned with them, she would pay you a little money for the fifteen minute trip.

"We got tortillas for the ladies."

Mi papa must not have believed me. He smiled with his hands beind his back, a horrible sign. "Are you sure about that?" he asked a couple of times.

"Someone told me that you and Bombin were not at the Catechism today." He drove by the church every day—it was his route in and out of the colonia. Probably Chela had told him! She was at the church every Saturday and some days during the week. I was sure she had told him when he was passing by.

I got hit with the jarilla that day. And I'm sure Bombin got hit, too, when he got home later.

Bombin and I didn't stop ditching even though we got more beatings at home. The second year, we ditched almost every week and got beaten by my dad a lot. Finally, Señora Terrazas came to our house and told our parents that me and Bombin were a lost cause. That was the end of the catecismo for me forever, but Bombin had to take it again. Fifteen years later, he became engaged to Ana and had to go to Catechism classes in order to marry her in the Catholic church. I laughed at my brother because by that time, I had left the Catholic church and was free from the catecismo forever.

Vero la vizca
Cross-eyed Vero

Vero la vizca had glasses with lenses as thick as pop bottles. She and her little sister Pati lived with their grandmother, Doña Manuela, in a house of pure adobe. Let me explain. Some houses in my neighborhood, like my house, were finished with concrete inside and out to make them look nice, but this particular house had no finish. It was simply adobe. Dona Manuela's house had dirt floors and a wooden ceiling made of two by fours.

Doña Manuela had been the caregiver of her granddaughters since they were little, when Luli, Vero's beautiful mother, ran off with a guy and left the girls with her. Not too long after she left, Vero's father, who was a drunk, left, too. So Doña Manuela had been the "mother" of the girls since I had first known them.

Doña Manuela was old and had long hair that protruded from her nose and hair on her face that was so long it looked like a peach fuzz beard and moustache. She also had heavy wrinkles etched into her face.

Her house was very rugged outside, not because she liked it that way—people who had more money would finish an adobe house with dry wall. But Doña Manuela could not afford to do anything to fix her house.

By the time Vero was about thirteen, her boyfriends were thirty-year-olds. Her sister, Pati, had a crush on me when we were young and although she was kind of cute, I didn't like her. I thought she was weird because she hung out with much older boys just like her sister Vero.

Doña Manuela was in her 80's and she was often sick and in the hospital. Sometimes she was in the hospital for weeks at a time and the girls were left alone to do what they wanted. Vero was home alone with Pati during those weeks because Dona Mañuela had no other family around. Some older guys, it appeared, were in the house all of the time with Vero and Pati, taking care of them, I thought.

"Dona Mañuela isn't at home." The word would spread around the neighborhood, and soon guys would show up at the house looking for Vero. After I figured out that no one was taking care of Vero and Pati, I just thought they were bad girls, letting all of the guys into the house when their grandma was gone. Girls weren't supposed to do that. But now I realize something very different—the older guys could do whatever they wanted with these two young girls—the guys in my neighborhood were pigs, and there was no one there to protect Vero and her sister.

When Vero and Pati were smaller, Dona Mañuela had been very strict with them. She had made sure the girls went to school every day. Sometimes I would go over and ask, "Can Pati come out and play?" I was seven or eight at the time, so Pati was about the same. Always, Dona Mañuela would refuse to let Pati come outside and play with me and my friends.

But by the time Pati was eleven or twelve, Dona Mañuela had been in the hospital a few times, and now Pati hung out only with older kids. Neighborhood chisme included stories of Vero messing around sexually with older boys and even grown-ups for money. But I never thought all of the gossip was true.

On many days, Vero had come to my house, asking mi mamá if she needed help with small tasks. "Nena, can I do a little job for you for a little money?" she would ask. "Can I maybe sweep the street or wash some clothes for a few pesos?"

"No, I'm sorry Vero." Mi mamá knew Vero needed help, but she didn't have the money to pay someone to do the work. In fact, most people in my neighborhood didn't have extra money to pay for housekeeping or odd jobs, so Vero had no luck finding work this way. Often Vero would say that she needed something like a shirt, a skirt, another piece of clothing or even food while her grandma was in the hospital. "I'm sorry, Nena," she would say to my mom as she got up from the table, "I just need some money to buy something to eat."

One day Memo came to my house. "Chispa, mi'jo, are you ready to do your first communion?" he asked me. "Vero la vizca is charging 50 pesos today, and you get to do whatever you want with her."

"Today's my day," I thought. "I get to mess with a real girl." Fago must've thought the same. We were both jumping around and playfully punching each other as we followed Memo to Vero's house.

"Vero's gonna do stuff to you," Fago said. He snort laughed and shuffled quickly down the beat-up street.

We didn't fully comprehend what was going on, but whatever it was, Memo was going to pay for it. I was only twelve years old; I wasn't even capable of doing what everyone else was going to do to her. I was short and undeveloped.

But still Fago and I walked along, goofy and shy. Within the block we had to walk, Fago turned red and spoke loudly, nervously. "I'm not kissing Vero all over," he said. He smiled a crazy smile and shook his head. Then he ran back down the street and ducked into the corner by Cleofas', kind of hiding. I kept following Memo.

Memo was a very short dude who was my brother Moy's friend. For most of the year, Memo was a busboy at a restaurant in Texas. He would go there, make some money, and then come home. He came home about twice a year—in summer and at Christmas. He knew Moy was working in California, but he hadn't come to my house to see my older brother that day; he had come to my house specifically to get me.

We continued walking down the street toward Vero's. When we got out in front of her house, I saw a bunch of adults and teenagers standing in a line. Dios mio, what were they doing inside that house? A guy would go in and about five or ten minutes later, he would come out smiling.

"What are they doing?" I asked Memo.

"What do you think, Chispa?"

"Oh, wow, they're doing IT!" I yelled out and everyone stared at me. I was in shock.

Now my hands and feet were sweating. I asked Memo, "What am I supposed to do?"

"Don't worry. She's gonna take care of you." Oh, God. Now my mouth was completely dry and I could barely breathe. My eyes were bulging, I'm sure, and my face was getting hot and red.

Right then Fago came back. He had his hands stuck down the front of his pants. He said to me, "You should grab her boobs, Chispa." Even though he was thirteen, his mind was like nine. He was only thinking about Vero's boobs. I agreed, switching my weight from one foot to the other. Touching her boobs sounded like a good idea to me.

My heart was pounding in my ears a little now.

I looked up and noticed Guero. He was standing in front of my neighbor Juanito, looking expectantly at the little house. Guero was about thirty years old and was a little slow. He also had thick glasses and was dirty and frumpy. He delivered newspapers on his bike and was always deeply in love with Vero. He was third in line and Juanito came right after him. The first two were done so Guero hurried in for his turn.

A little bit later, he came out grinning. Then I watched Juanito go in. What would he do? I had an idea, but I wasn't really sure. Every single one went into the house, did their business, and came out.

"I'm afraid," I told Memo then. "I don't want to do it."

When Juanito came out, Memo said something to him

about condoms and Juanito responded, "Don't worry. Just go in and have fun."

But Memo still waited outside. He didn't move toward the door at all.

Vero must've noticed that no one was coming in so she came out. She moved slowly, closely, up to Memo. She smiled shyly and said something to him that I couldn't hear. When I looked at her again, I saw that she had on a really tiny skirt—without any underwear. Then I noticed her culo hanging out a little. My face was getting hot again.

I always thought Vero had a cute body; she was slim with nice little boobs. Her face wasn't terrible but at the same time, wasn't great. She had a piggish nose on a chubby face. Her hair was short, pitch black and straight and she wore pop bottle glasses. But no one cared about her face. I watched the other guys just checking out her body. Here was Memo talking sexually to her. She told me and Fago to look away, but out of the corner of my eye, I saw her bend over for Memo. I guess she was trying to convince him and her other clients to "buy" the merchandise. I felt sick.

In Mexico, we have a saying that goes like this "who doesn't show, doesn't sell." So she showed that place under her skirt to her potential clients. When I saw this, I froze.

Memo might have talked dirty to Vero, but he could not be convinced. He had been in the states where condoms were the way so Memo didn't go in. He walked away and Vero took the next guy in line inside with her to test out the product Memo had recently been shown. Vero must've earned something like three-hundred pesos that day.

And by then, I knew what was happening.

Fago and I never stood in that line again. After we freaked out in front of Vero's house that day, no more kids were invited. Vero may have had sex for money a lot of times, but it was only once more that I saw it. And that time, I noticed that the guys waited in line inside the porch. They no longer waited in the street.

2. *HISTORIAS TRISTES*
SAD STORIES

René

In the first and second grade my best friend was René. René was my neighbor. He was one year older than me, but because he had to repeat, he was in my first grade class. In first grade, René and Chuy mudito (the mute) helped me to learn my colors and how to count. Since René had been in the first grade once before and this was the third time for Chuy, they knew what to do. And since I was so little, they helped me to fight off the abusive bullies who picked on me. Chuy was little but was older, so he was very brave and René was smart about how to deal with the mean boys. For a tiny boy like me, these two were very important; they were mis amigos and they always helped me out.

At that point in his life, Chuy was a good boy. He lived across the street from me. A lot of boys picked on Chuy because something was wrong with his speech and he couldn't talk. He could only make noises.

There were a lot of bullies in my school. One of the main ones was named Miguel and he lived right behind la huerta. We called Miguel pantalones cagados or shit pants, because he always smelled like poop. Miguel was a big boy and was probably about eight in the first grade; maybe that's why he was such a horrible bully. To me, he had to have been the worst ever. My friend Chuy mudito was brave and tough, but even he was afraid of Miguel. In fact, Shit Pants was so bad that the bigger kids in the third and fourth grades were even afraid of him. Everyone was afraid, except for René. And René was only a little tiny bit bigger than me! Maybe René, in a fit of his bad temper, forgot to be afraid. René was almost always calm, but you had to watch out when you really pissed him off, because he would hurt you.

On many days, we played marbles and on those days Miguel cemented his name. When Chuy, René or I were shooting our marbles, Miguel would walk a few feet away from our game. It would seem as if he were concentrating on something. Then he would shake the top of his pant leg and grab down and down the leg as if he was letting something out at the bottom. Was there something in the pocket that he was getting out? If he had shaken something important out of his pants, wouldn't he reach down to pick it up? But he never reached down. So one day, after he left, I went over to see what the thing was. My eyes grew huge when I saw it. There, on the ground where he had been shaking his pant leg, were little balls of poop! Miguel must not have worn underwear. He just pooped in his pants and let the poop fall out of them onto the ground. He was really and truly Shit Pants.

One day we were all playing a nice game of marbles and we were playing on teams. I was with Chuy and Shit Pants was with René. Shit Pants probably had already gone a few feet away to relieve himself, but, no matter, we were having fun playing until Chuy Mudito beat him in the game. After Chuy and I won, Chuy started making fun of René and Shit Pants, because we hardly ever beat them and he was really excited. With his weird little mute language of hissing and robotic beeping sounds, he was making noises and laughing.

Shit Pants immediately and without any warning, yelled, "Fuckin mute, you didn't beat me!" and then punched Chuy in the nose. Chuy bled. I had watched Miguel punch Chuy in surprise and Chuy didn't even defend himself. I guess he was too afraid.

"That was a lucky shot. That one didn't count," Shit Pants said.

"We beat you fair and square," I said, afraid, but I never could shut my mouth when I was mad. "The problem is you. You don't know how to lose. It's just a game."

Shit Pants looked at me with anger in his eyes, and then he came toward me. "You little freak."

We were standing up facing each other and he kicked me without any warning at all. Then he grabbed me and knocked me over, jumped on me, and started punching me. He got me a couple of times in the side of the head until something must've snapped inside René. I saw René's angry face and then I watched him kick Shit Pants square in the face. He knocked Shit Pants off of me and onto the ground, and then he jumped on him. René pounded him in the face with the kind of passion I'd only seen the big boys have. René was so full of anger, he hurt Miguel. He even made the bully cry.

I don't think Shit Pants had ever been beaten up before and a bunch of neighborhood kids had shown up and were really intently watching and enjoying the fight. Their bully was getting beaten! Shit Pants had been put in his place and our lives would now be peaceful.

When second grade came my life got easier because Chuy mudito and Miguel Shit Pants didn't pass. Now it was just René and me.

I played with René every day after school and on the weekends that year. One day René and I made a weapon that we named the Tiralilas (throw lilas). Lilas are little green marble-sized fruits that grow on trees. A lila is a little bit softer than a rock but harder than a grape. You can't eat them, but you CAN throw them. The weapon that threw them, was constructed using a plastic bottle cut in half with a balloon attached by a rubber band to the spout: either a two liter or a half liter would work because they all have the same-sized hole. Then we used it like a sling shot. We loaded the lilas into the end of the spout through the cut off bottle. The lilas were big enough that they would get stuck in the spout, but not tightly. So the tiralilas worked like a simple gun when the trigger was pulled. When you pulled back on the balloon and let go, the balloon would smack the lila really hard in the spout and the force of the smack would propel the lila out of the cut off part of the bottle very rapidly. A lila could shoot out amazingly far, up to 100 yards. My personal favorite tiralilas was constructed using what I thought was a really cool blue plastic Clorox bottle that I found in the trash.

The tiralilas was capable of shooting anything that wouldn't puncture the balloon. Marbles, rocks, sand.

When René and I went to the field by the river, we would ride the little cows and throw rocks at the big ones. We pulled their tails really hard and we poked at their bodies with sticks until they chased us. We spread the word to the other kids so it wasn't long before all of the neighborhood kids were playing with the animals, too.

Once we had made the tiralilas, we began shooting the little bulls with it. And for a while we shot rocks. The rocks could lacerate the meat of a person and Fago had a nasty scar on him to prove it, but the animals had much thicker flesh and it didn't cut them or anything, but we could still tell that they hurt. Almost instantly after hitting them in certain spots, I noticed that their skin got puffy. But we shot rocks at them anyway.

One day all of us little kids were playing war around the colónia with the tiralilas. After an hour or so, the war got really big and some older kids got involved. Then the little kids got kicked out of the game. Now the big kids who were my brother Bombin's age and up were playing—they were all 10 and over. The big kids were shooting rocks out of their tiralilases but since I was only seven, I was out of the game. One of the kids who was playing was from another neighborhood. He was this bratty little kid named Paco who was about my age, but Paco was stubborn and refused to leave the game. About ten minues after the game got crazy, Paco got hit in the eye with a rock. He got hurt, got taken to the hospital, and he lost his eyeball.

After the eye incident happened, we stopped loading rocks into the tiralilases. Now René and I were careful about only shooting lilas, since the lilas were softer than rocks and even though they hurt if they hit, a person couldn't get cut or injured by one. Of course, I didn't realize how horrible we were to the animals just by shooting at them in the first place. We didn't think of what we were doing as animal cruelty; we were just having a lot of fun.

In Chihuahua in the early 80's our teachers stayed with the same students for a few years. My teacher was Domatila, and she was with us from first through fifth grade. Domatila was about four feet ten with short, bobbed black hair. She was very strict and never let us go to the bathroom during class; instead, she always asked us to use the bathroom before entering class in the mornings and then after recess, too.

One morning in the spring of my second grade year, Domatila was in a very bad mood. Several kids were missing that day. I guess she must've been tired of students being absent because that morning she said, "I'm going to go to the direccion (principals' office). If somebody comes, you'd better not let them in. If you open the door and admit even one student into the classroom, NONE of you will go outside for recess today." That said, Domatila rushed out of the classroom, shutting the door behind her.

A few moments later, there was a knock at the door. My friend René and another boy had come late. Our classroom leader, cross-eyed Vero, walked to the door, eager to follow

Domatila's orders and turn the late student away. Vero had been put in charge of the class in the teacher's absence because she was twelve or thirteen and had repeated the second grade many times. She was always trying to please the teacher and had become Domatila's little pet. That's how she got to be the leader of the room.

I looked out the door and saw my friend René as he stood there in the hallway. Vero, who had opened the door ever so slightly, said to him in a whisper, "You'd better go away. If I let you in, we won't get recess. La maestra said so."

René looked worried. "I really want to come in. I don't want to be in trouble at home." He was a very studious little boy who never missed school. This was the one time the whole year that he hadn't arrived to school on time. And he was being punished. My teacher, Domatila, was not aware of the big mistake she was making by not allowing a student to walk through the door.

René wasn't a pushover. He tried to force his way in. His mama was very strict and he didn't have a daddy. Rene had lost his papá a couple of years earlier; I was never sure what had happened to him, but I guessed he had died, because people always called René's mom Martha la biuda (the widow).

Rene was always afraid of his mom; I understood because I was very afraid of my parents, too. If he went home early, his mama would hit him with the belt. "Please," Rene begged Vero over and over, "Let me come in."

A bunch of kids tried to persuade her. "Come on, Vero, let him in. He can sit all the way in the back. La maestra will never know he's here." I thought I could convince her since she was my neighbor down the street. So I asked her to please let René in, and she actually thought about it for half a minute. But then she said, "No. I can't." and, "Shut up," to all of us.

When he saw we were arguing, he gave up and left school on his own. He must not have wanted us to get into trouble.

Poor René. I could see his face; he was mad. He couldn't believe he couldn't get in the school because of Vero the brown-noser.

A few moments later, Domatila re-entered the classroom with her irritated look. Domatila was often angry. She often raised her voice to us and she did it again this time. "Who came in?" she demanded. She had to have heard all of the noise when she was on her way back to the room. She was probably trying to find an excuse to keep us from recess because in the couple of years I had been in her class, she had kept us from recess more times than I could count. That was her favorite punishment besides smacking us on the hands with a ruler.

And then Vero told her that she had turned two boys away. La maestra smiled to her and her mood seemed to lighten. She patted Vero on the back, as if to say to her, "Good job."

But she shouldn't have been smiling. Today Domatila's order had caused one little boy to be afraid to go home— today he would choose anything before he would confront and disappoint his mother, while the little girl in the classroom would sit down at her desk feeling as if she had done the right thing. Pleasing the teacher was surely more important than any other choice she could've made.

It was a long day at school without René. Every other day, he sat in the seat in front of me. Many times Rene and I got into trouble for talking because we were busy making plans for our after school activities.

In the first grade, he had helped me more than I had helped him, but now, in second grade, we were pretty much at the same level. Every day after school we met and did our homework really quickly so we could go and play.

Today it was a long walk home from school without René. Every other day we walked home discussing our plans for new adventures. The two of us would check in at home and then we would do our homework either outside my house or outside his house.

When I walked into my house after school that day, my mom was working in the kitchen. She was crying. When she saw me, mí mamá rushed over and gave me an enveloping hug. As she hugged me, she began crying harder. Scared, I asked, "What's going on?"

She said, choking down sobs, "René...René...What happened, m'ijo? Why wasn't he at school?"

I told her that he had come late and cross-eyed Vero had sent him home at Domatila's request.

"Why was René not at school? Is he becoming a bad boy?" mí mamá asked.

"No," I said. "René is not a bad boy. He's a good boy."

"Oh," she said. "People said that he was ditching school." Mi mamá still was unusually quiet and serious. She was not sweet and funny today.

Why did mi madrecita think Rene was a bad boy? And why was she acting so strange? I told her the story I knew to be true. I wanted her to believe that my best friend was still a nice boy. He was nice. He had tried to come into the classroom, but Vero had wanted to impress the teacher so she had refused to let him in the door.

My mother could hardly speak, though she tried many times, starting to say something and then stopping. "René," she would say, and then stop. My mind whirled already as I sat at the table and waited for her to explain through her tears. Finally, she stopped crying, "René," she said, "René got hurt by the horse." But she didn't explain. She didn't say any more and I could not understand why she was crying so much. Maybe she was having a bad day.

"Is he O.K? What happened?" I asked her. "Is René O.K?" I kept thinking my friend was fine. He might be hurt a little but tomorrow, as always, we would be out in the field, shooting lilas at the little cows and trying to ride on their backs.

Mi mamá did not answer. As young as I was, I knew that

she was holding something back. She sat at the table and when she lifted her head out of her hands and looked at me, she said quietly, "René got hurt."

"I want to see him," I said again and again.

As I begged my mother to let me see my friend, my dad quietly walked through the door to the kitchen. He knelt down in front of me, gripped my shoulders with his thick hands, and looked at me very seriously. "This is going to be very hard on you," he said. "I know René is your best friend." Mi papá told me that he knew René had been sent home from school. Then he said, "You need to understand this has nothing to do with you. We know someone sent him home, but we know it wasn't you. Did the teacher send him home?"

I was the only kid in the room who lived in René's neighborhood besides Vero. Vero, strangely, lived on the same street. So did René. They each lived three houses from me, but in opposite directions.

"Who sent him home?" mi papá asked again.

"It was Vero," I said. "The teacher wouldn't let anyone in late." I was starting to worry. What was happening? Would my teacher be sad? Would Vero be sad? How hurt was René? After he thought I was a little more prepared, mi papá spoke again. "René got in an accident. He's gone."

"What do you mean gone? You mean gone to the hospital? Is he O.K?"

My dad was always smiley, but not today. Today his face was very serious. He said, "He got killed by the horse near el rastro." El rastro was part of the meat packing company, the place where they shoot the cows in the head and the cows fall to the ground. As the cow goes rolling, they cut her in the throat and then cut her up.

When my dad told me René died at el rastro, I felt lost. I felt this huge knot in my throat that wouldn't go away, and I was immensely sad. There was a humungous burden where there once was the extreme love for a friend. René was my best friend. And even though I knew what death meant, I didn't think about how I could never ever play with him again.

In my lost moments, I began to cry very hard. The tears fell from my eyes onto the kitchen table. I sobbed to my father, "This can't be true. He's mí amigo. We play every day." What was I going to do? How would I walk home from school? How would I play marbles? Who would defend me against my bullies? Who would be my best friend?

In my mind I saw René alive, in the hospital hooked up to a bunch of tubes and machines. I wanted so bad to go there now and see my friend. I thought he was dying, but I didn't think he was dead. The rest of that day and all that night I kept thinking of my friend and his image never left me—I even dreamed of him lying in a hospital bed with whiteness all around him.

The first thing I said to my dad when I woke up the next morning was, "I want to see René."

"I think they're going to bring him over today." My dad meant in a box, a coffin, while in my little mind I thought my dad meant a stretcher. They were bringing my friend to the colónia on a stretcher. René was in a coma. Now, I could talk to him and he could hear me and I could wake him up. He was hurting and was in a coma. And I thought, "If I see him on a stretcher in his house with all these tubes, I can wake him up." I wanted to see him. I knew this to be true. I couldn't wait to help him!

I hurried to his house to see him and that was when I saw it through the door. A little light blue coffin. René wasn't on a stretcher. He was in that coffin...And I ran, and I refused to look inside at my friend. Later I found out I couldn't see his lifeless face anyway; no one would get to see his face. He had been trampled and his face was no longer the beautiful face of my young friend, René.

Kids in my neighborhood had always chased the cows. A few days later mí papá explained what had happened on the day René died. "René wasn't chasing the cows," my dad said, and I came back to him from my thoughts. "He was chasing the horses."

When René left school, he hadn't gone home. Instead, he went down by the river with some older boys from another neighborhood. In the field at el rastro, there were a couple of horses. One of the older boys held one of the horses while the other jumped on the horse's back. He held onto the horse's mane and tried to ride, but the horse went wild and tried to buck the boy off. In an attempt to help his new friend, René grabbed the horse by the tail. Of course the horse didn't like having his tail pulled so he kicked René. In the head. Then the horse stomped all over him and he died there, in that field.

Three weeks later, I went over to René's house. I knocked on the door and his sister Ana answered.

"Can René come out to play?" I asked.

His sister could not even look me in the face. "René's not here," she said, barely able to get the words out. At that moment, I remembered. René would never be here again. But my eight year old mind had not been able to process the finality of my friend's death. I couldn't perceive death as permanent.

Now I realize the senselessness of René's death. If someone had explained to René how to deal with the horses, had explained to him the nature of horses and how they spook when they are surprised, he might be alive today. If someone had told him never to pull a horse's tail, or that a horse weighs fifteen hundred to two-thousand pounds, he may have dealt with this horse as if he could be dangerous. But he didn't. And my small friend René died that day.

Mi tia Socorro
My Aunt Socorro

Mi mamá's father, Papá Pancho, was a huge man, very light-skinned, with a chubby face and a big bald spot on the back of his head. He and my Mamá Chiquita, his tiny, native-Mexican-looking, feisty wife lived in Sinaloa. They had ten children and my mother was number two.

Pancho's youngest brother was named José. When Pancho was a teenager, he had made a promise to his parents that he would send their youngest son to college. And when José graduated from preparatoria, Papá Pancho fulfilled his promise.

José went to the university in Chihuahua since Chihuahua happened to have the most prestigious University for what he had chosen to study. After graduating from la Universidád with a degree in Agronomy, José got a job in Chihuahua, married and built a beautiful house on the outskirts of the city.

By the time my mother turned fifteen, Papá Pancho had been growing more and more abusive to his wife and daughters. It just so happened that at this same time, her tio José needed help. He and his wife owned a big grocery store where his wife worked so they needed someone to clean their big, fancy house. After asking for Papá Pancho's blessing, Mamá Chiquita arranged that her daughter, Maria Elena, mi mamá, would leave on the train for Chihuahua the following week to work for her uncle. This was lucky for my mother who had no freedom at home. Even though her uncle would pay her very little, at least she would not be beaten or belittled by her father. She could have some days off and live in a nicer, calmer place.

After mi mamá left home, Papá Pancho continued with his crazy ways. At that time he belonged to a gang that was fighting for some land near his rancho. His gang was very violent. Often they went to attack a nearby neighborhood with rifles and incited fear in the rancheros surrounding them. Papá Pancho fought to protect his land and to rule his part of Sinaloa through fear. His violent behavior bled into his home life, too. In his casa he continued to beat his wife and his two other daughters who were younger than mi mamá.

Mi mamá had been in Chihuahua almost a year and was now sixteen. One day she was in her uncle's backyard hanging up laundry. A boy rode by on his bicycle. When he saw her, he called her over to the fence so he could talk to her. After that conversation and a few more from over the backyard fence, mi mamá and the boy, Vicente, started dating. But it wasn't long before José mentioned it to Papá Pancho. When Pancho found out his girl had been dating without his permission and, even worse, without an escort, he demanded that his brother return her to Sinaloa. She would be replaced with her younger sister, Rosa.

Vicente went to the house of my tio and found out his love, Maria Elena, was gone. When he inquired, he learned that my mother had returned home to her parents, but nothing was going to stop him. He was determined to marry her. He decided to go to her himself. He first discussed his plan with his parents and they agreed—if he loved her, he should definitely go. And soon.

It was only a few weeks after mi mamá had been sent back to her parents' house in Sinaloa when mi papá left Chihuahua on the train. He asked around about the rancho of Senor Garcia, and was led there by a small man named Ruben who knew the family. Mi papá Chente (Vicente) arrived at the rancho in the dark of night and waited outside. When my grandmother came near to the door, he got her attention. "I am Vicente. Dona Maria, mucho gusto. It is so wonderful to finally meet the mother of Elena. I have come for your daughter. I love her and want to take her back to Chihuahua and make her my wife. Would you please honor me with your blessing?"

My grandmother was pleased with his manners, but she feared for her daughter's safety. Her husband would be returning home soon. Mi mamá had already told her that Vicente would be coming for her, and it had been their secret which they had kept carefully hidden from Papá Pancho.

"Yes, Vicente. You may take my daughter with my blessing. Take care of her and love her. You seem like a decent man, and she has told me of her feelings for you, too."

My mother's bags were packed and she left with my father quickly and quietly. About two weeks later, my parents were married in Chihuahua, with the blessing of mi papá's parents.

When he found out that my mother was gone, Papá Pancho raged and beat Mamá Chiquita.

Ten years had passed since my mother had escaped Sinaloa and Papá Pancho. Her sister, who had been a tiny baby at the time, was now ten years old and needed a place to go where she would be safe, too.

So, when I was about two years old, my tia Socorro came to Chihuahua to live with us. My mother was very busy; my brother Chentito was eight, Moy was seven, and Bombin was about five when Socorro came.

My favorite aunt by far was Socorro. Socorro was always helping my mom without any malice. When my mom was pregnant with my two youngest brothers, Pedro and Oscar, she had a lot of problems and there was tía Socorro helping to cook, clean, and take good care of us.

Tia Socorro had a beautiful face, a beautiful smile, and beautiful hazel eyes. In Mexico, where almost all of us have brown or black eyes, Socorro had ojos de miel, and so for some, she was considered exotically beautiful.

Socorro helped my brothers, my sister, and me with things that my mom couldn't, like homework; tia Socorro had attended secundaria, middle school, and my mom had not. So we would sit at the kitchen table with Socorro for hours and there she would help us to solve math problems and study spelling words.

She would also cure us when we were sick. When no one knew what to do about what was ailing one of us, Socorro would call her mother, and every single time Mamá Chiquita would know of some amazing home remedy. A lot of times, Mamá Chiquita was creative and everything that she prescribed actually worked! If you had a stomach ache, Coke and lime. For a cough, honey and lime. And when you had a foot injury, you put your foot in the hottest water you could handle with salt.

Mama Chiquitá even had a remedy for you if you had been forgetting things. After you drank the strange tea she prescribed, sure enough, you would wake up the next day and you would be able to remember again.

Tia Socorro was a hard-working girl. She would feed us and then she would go to help our cousins' families. Chentito's friends were always hitting on her, because she was only about two years older than him, and like I said before, she was beautiful.

I often talked to mi tia about my friends and she would give me her wise advice. "I think that guy's a jerk," she would might say and then advise me not to stay away from him. And she would always have a reason to explain why she felt that way. "Somebody told me that they saw him with the glue at the baseball field." Socorro was always very careful about talking bad about somebody, only telling me things she was sure to be true, not just spreading random gossip like most of the people in my colonia.

Mi tia gave me advice about girls, too. She once said to

me, "I saw that girl, Paula, with an older boy. She was going out with him at the same time she was hanging out with you." At this time, Socorro was twenty years old and was working at the maquilas (factories). She would not get home until two o'clock in the morning. Late at night, when she was walking home from the bus, she would see boys and girls having sex or doing drugs at the campos because the neighborhood boys always went into the dugouts to make out with girls late at night. And she would use what she saw in order to warn us about who to stay away from.

I had a beautiful relationship with mi tia. What a wonderful woman she had become. Now that she was twenty years old, she had reached the age for marriage. Socorro had had some boyfriends, but one day she came home and said to mi mama, "I've been dating this guy named Martín, Nena. He is different than the others. Unlike the other guys I've known, he's very responsible."

"Really," my mother said. "Why are you telling me this?"

"Because, Nena, I think Martín is the one."

Mi tia Socorro had fallen in love.

Socorro saw Martín as a responsible, trustworthy, and loving man, but my mother saw him as something completely different. "You know, mi'ija," I heard my mom say to Socorro one day. "I'm sorry to say this, but there's something about Martín that I just don't trust. I don't think he's an honest person. I really believe this man is not a good person for you, but if you want him, I will respect your decision."

Socorro listened to my mother with respect, but she didn't consider my mother's wisdom and she didn't ask any questions of my mother, either; she decided to marry Martín anyway.

Since my parents loved my tia so well, they gave their word to support her choice, even though my dad was skeptical, too. "We are going to keep a close eye on Martín," I heard him say to my older brothers, "but Socorro really loves him, so she'll have to find out for herself." My dad was somewhat of a philosopher, full of wise comments and phrases. He once said about Socorro, "You know what? A lot of times people believe they're in love, but it's really something else. And there is nothing in the world that can change the minds of the love-blinded. Unfortunately, there's only one way they can open their eyes. Often it is with a broken heart. I'm afraid that this is what will happen with Socorro."

Sometimes a person gets blinded because she's been recently hurt and then some bull shitter comes along and sweeps her off of her feet. In Mexico we believe, "Un clavo saca otro clavo" or a nail can only be removed by another nail. I guess a person needs a deeper hurt to remove a more shallow, initial pain.

Martín was so sweet with Socorro, so disgustingly sweet, that my dad could see right through his disguise. About a month before the marriage, there was a bad exchange of words between my dad and Martín. Since my dad was very protective of Socorro, he probably said something like, "If you dare hurt her in one single way, I promise you will regret it for the rest of your life."

Martín must've been afraid of mi Papa, because two weeks before the wedding, he abruptly stopped coming over to my house. And Martín had many excuses for Socorro as to why he couldn't come in.

Then, just one week before the marriage, my older brothers Moy and Chentito came home angry. "Pinche, Martín," Chentito said to me. "That bitch was hanging out on the avenida with some chicks in a car."

Later I heard Moy tell my mom, "He is a cheater, Amá. I was with Bombin on the avenida and we saw Socorro's Martín with a bunch of girls in a car." In Mexico when a guy is hanging out with a bunch of cute girls it is never innocent. Most of the time guys hang out with guys and girls with girls. If not, there are always other intentions. When I heard what my brothers had said, I realized my mom's instinct about

Martín was right. She didn't need to see him with the girls.

Now no one trusted Martín. Except for Socorro. And because of her deep trust, the wedding happened anyway.

The first few months of the marriage, Martín was a surprisingly good husband to Socorro. And then one day mi tia excitedly told us that she was pregnant. But sadly, once she was pregnant, Martín changed. Martín and Socorro lived on the other side of Chihuahua, about thirty minutes away and now Martín would not allow Socorro to come to visit us. At this time, I found out why my dad never liked or trusted him. I couldn't see it before, but now it became clear. Martín had always been incredibly jealous.

Since Socorro had become pregnant, Martín's jealousy had become overwhelming and now it even overwhelmed her. If she went to the store, he would question her. "Why did you go out alone? I'll bet you were meeting a guy there." When he was with her at the grocery store and she smiled to someone, he never failed to question her intentions. "Why were you looking at that guy and smiling at him?" he would ask her right there in the aisle. "You have something going with him. I know you do."

Martín was mean, but still, Socorro couldn't help smiling at people. She was by nature a kind person.

My neighbors did not like Martín either. Every time Martín and Socorro came around the colonia, the neighbors noticed how he treated mi tia. Many people mentioned to my parents and brothers what they saw as blatant disrespect for Socorro. "How can he treat her like he owns her?" "I heard him call her puta." "What is Socorro doing with that pendejo? Have you seen how he orders her around?" Many of the younger cholos talked about how they would beat Martín with their fists if they ever saw him. I listened to what they said and my anger grew inside me, too.

"Martín is making Socorro unhappy. I wish I could kick his ass," I told my mom one day.

But my mom said, "No, Chispa. You need to stop saying

these things. They just got married. Don't judge Martín for something you're not even sure about."

A few weeks later, Socorro's baby, Martincito, was born. Before long, the baby was a year old and after less than two years with Martín, Socorro just couldn't stand his jealousy anymore so she told him she was going to leave him.

Martín, in that one instant, decided that he was deeply in love with Socorro and he became obsessed. He told her he would do anything to stay with her. I think no one had ever broken this little man's heart, so when Socorro announced that she was leaving, he was in shock. He couldn't believe that his Socorro could leave him and at that time, maybe he finally realized that he had been a jerk. He tried everything to persuade her to stay.

But it was too late and she was mad. She had been mistreated and now she realized it. Martín could do nothing to win his Socorro back.

Socorro had owned their house. Before she married Martín, she had saved enough money to buy a cute little house for herself. But when she and Martín got divorced, he would only agree to sign the divorce papers if she agreed to give him the house.

Of course she gave him her house; she was more than willing. That's how bad she wanted out.

Once Socorro was single, Martín tried to sweep her off her feet again. But my family wouldn't let it happen. I, for one, never left my tia Socorro alone with Martín. I would see him coming through the gate to our house along with his cocky attitude. He would say to me, "Chispa, here's money. Go buy a pop." I knew then that he was trying to get me out of the house so he could be alone with my tia. But I would never go. I knew he was trying to get her to go back with him and I wanted to make sure she would never do that.

She never did go back with him, she kept her son and when she lost her house to Martín, Socorro came back and lived with us. And she stayed with us for two more years until the day she decided to go back home to Sinaloa to live with her mother. By then, Papá Pancho had been dead for several years and Mamá Chiquita was almost sixty years old. Socorro missed her mother and wanted to help her.

I was very sad to hear that Socorro would be leaving us. Still, I understood how she would want to be with her mother.

At the time I was sixteen. I had just bought a brand new cassette tape of Los Temerarios and loved listening to it. Two nights before Socorro left, she heard me playing the music. "I really love that music," she said. "Can I borrow the tape for a while? I don't have time to go buy one."

"I just bought it and I would really like to listen to it for a while." She looked at me, very disappointed.

Socorro only stayed for one more day. We were still close, but I could tell she was disappointed. Hours before she left on the train back to Sinaloa, she told me something strange, and when she said it, I could see the fear in her eyes. "You know what," she said, "You might think I'm crazy, but I had a dream last night, and in it, I saw a big coffin in the hall. It was light colored."

Was she seeing something that had value? Did the coffin signify something? I didn't understand why my tia was telling me this.

Once tia Socorro got back to Sinaloa, she called us often. She said that everything was going fine for her. She was working for someone, but I never knew me exactly what she was doing. Socorro often talked about dancing, and like many young Mexican people, she said she went to the dances every weekend.

Every Saturday night there was a dance. Socorro told us that the dances were held at different little towns all over the area. One particular Saturday, the dance was going to be held at another little pueblo near her home. Socorro and her friends planned to go in a convoy because that's how they do it in the little towns. Many cars follow each other in a long line to the dances. That night Socorro was riding in a truck;

there were ten people total in this old, rusty pickup, people who were all dressed up, showered, made-up nicely, and who were eager to dance. At that time in Mexico few people had their own cars, so it was common to travel in a pick-up full of people, three in the front and seven in the back. Just a usual weekend event.

Socorro and her friends rode in the back of the truck down the dirt road, talking and laughing, looking forward to go and dance their problems away. They could feel the breeze around them as they came to a stop and then, quickly, entered the highway. They saw the big truck coming toward them and they assumed it would stop, but it never did...

The impact when it hit them was tremendous and that was all Socorro knew until she opened her eyes and saw nothing, only the night sky above her. She felt the pain throughout her body and wondered what had happened to the others. She hoped they were alright. She heard the sirens and felt herself being lifted and put inside an ambulance. She told the men who helped her, "Call my sister, Irene," and gave them the phone number. "I am Socorro Garcia Castillo."

When Socorro's younger sister, mi tia Irene, arrived at the hospital, Socorro was alive. To this day, I'm not sure what she and Irene talked about. Did Socorro say that she would prefer to die because she was going to live the rest of her life paralyzed? That had to be a horrible fate for her. Now she would never be able to dance. Socorro also loved to go places and although she couldn't drive, she still took the bus everywhere she could. And she would never get to do those things if she were to live.

Three or four hours after the accident, mi tia Socorro died. She was only twenty five years old.

By the time the ambulance had come for her, Socorro was the only one of her friends still alive. She had been involved in the worst accident ever in the history of Wamucilito, Sinaloa. My tia, along with nine of her good friends had died—nine friends who were parents, brothers, sisters, and children.

Shortly after Socorro left us, I wished with all my heart that I had given her the Temerarios tape. I have always regretted not letting her take it with her. I have always thought, maybe if I had given her the tape, she would've been home listening to it, she wouldn't have gone to the dance with her friends, and she wouldn't be dead.

Martincito was about four years old when he lost his mommy, Socorro. He had lived at our house with Socorro before that. He called my dad Papá and he still calls my mom Mamá Nena. Martincito was like a little brother to me.

I think he's in Chihuahua now. A while back he got in a car accident, hit a politician, and went to jail for about three years. Now he's working in the maquilas, like his mother did, and he's in his twenties. He's having a hard time finding a girlfriend.

Socorro was my favorite tia and she will always be my favorite tia. I wish she were still here. I will never understand why she had to go. From time to time, I still ask myself, "Why her?"

There are things we don't understand. But life and death are God's will. And God's will is the most powerful thing.

Fito

Fito was about six feet tall with black, wavy hair and pitch black, kind eyes. He was very popular in my neighborhood and he had a lot of girlfriends. He even dated my very beautiful cousin for a while, but he wasn't ever very "into" girls. Fito loved the drugs much more. He was the total opposite of me. Girls were more important to me than cholo activities and drugs. But for him, girls came last.

Fito was a good fighter and since my brother Moy was his idol, he always did what Moy said. Fito was only one year younger than Moy, he was a Puesto cholo, too, and he had been in many gang fights against other neighborhood cholos with my older brothers.

Fito had one very dangerous obsession—he loved to jump in front of cars on the highway and in the streets. He claimed he loved the sound of squealing tires. He also loved the adrenaline rush of getting in front of big vehicles.

I'll admit that I liked to feel the power of walking in a pack of cholos across la avenida and making the cars slow down so that we could cross. I did that a few times but never alone like Fito did. And I never knew another cholo that got got the adrenaline rush that Fito must've had when a car came to a screeching halt, just missing him.

But Fito loved it.

He once stood on the tracks in front of a moving train. Lucky for him, he dodged it. Lucky for him, it happened during daytime and the engineer saw him so the train had time to squeal to a stop before it hit him.

La Marrana, Fito's brother, was greatly feared in the neighborhood. He was a huge, muscular guy who had been in jail a lot of times. He was an extremely heavy drug user and did heroin before anyone else in the neighborhood even knew how to use it. When he was using, people feared him. He didn't do drugs with anyone else for this reason. He got messed up alone. La Marrana was one of the hardest criminals I ever knew and, at the time Fito was hanging around at my house, was in prison. He had killed at least one person that I knew of.

Fito had many brothers and two beautiful sisters. One was prissy and stuck up and refused to talk to the guys in the neighborhood. She was one of the only girls from my colonia who went on to college so maybe I was wrong. Maybe she wasn't stuck up. Maybe she was just focused on getting her education and she knew that getting involved with a guy from industrial would get in the way of her goals. Or maybe the guys in my neighborhood with their sixth grade education level were boring to her.

Fito's other sister was not quite as pretty and was nicer with the neighborhood guys. It was really weird to me how Marrana was such a mess since Fito's sisters were definitely a step above most of the other girls in my colonia. Also, his mother was a nice lady and his father was a very hard worker.
I always liked Fito because he was friendly and talked to me and because he respected my parents and other adults. He had played baseball for my dad, too, but only for a few years.

One day my friend Raúl and I were riding the city bus, coming from downtown back to our neighborhood. We found a seat and were sitting reading the light porn comic magazines that we liked. I looked up and noticed that some twenty-year-old guys toward the front of the bus were laughing really hard, kind of sarcastically. I knew who they were. The five cholos from las Canchas were our rivals. I whispered to Raúl that I had seen them and we quietly got out of our seats and sneaked toward the back of the bus. We were going to get off unnoticed at the next stop.

Not even one minute had passed before all five of them were looking smug walking down the aisle toward us. We were about to get jumped.

They were next to us. One guy punched me and another punched Raúl in our faces. Some people on the bus screamed and the bus ground to a sudden stop. Now all five tried to throw punches and kick at us. In retaliation, Raúl and I grabbed and hung from the handles along the roof of the bus and kicked the guys over and over, he with his shoes and me with the steel toes of my boots.

They couldn't get to us because even though we were little, we were grabbing those handles and kicking very fiercely. But they were coming closer and I thought for sure we were going to get our asses kicked that day.

Then Fito appeared out of nowhere. He must have been on the bus that whole time and we hadn't seen him.

Fito ran behind one of the rival cholos and whacked him with a large screwdriver. The other cholos failed to notice. They were trying to get to us.

Fito knocked the first guy down and held another cholo in an arm lock. He choked him and stabbed him with the same rusty screwdriver. As soon as the three others noticed, they threw punches at Fito, trying to move toward their friend. But the second cholo went down and now it was three on three, an even fight.

We continued to fight with these guys who were about twenty years old, Fito's age. Raúl and I were only fifteen.

That day, my friend Tica's dad, Don Pantera (Mr. Panther) happened to be riding the bus and when he recognized me, he hurried over toward the fight and punched one of the cholos. Don Pantera was tough. With one punch, Pantera hit the dude in the head and knocked him down.
Then he yelled to us, "Don't be stupid. Why do you guys fight? You guys are almost neighbors and you are fighting all of the time. Stop." We always listened to adults we knew out

of respect and so we immediately stopped. The other cholos listened, too, because Don Pantera was a tall, tough, fifty-year-old man.

He said to the guys from las Canchas, "You guys need to leave now," and to me, "Chispa, you're in trouble, too. I'm going to talk to your dad. Don't you know that fighting is wrong?"

"They started it. We were trying to get away."

Don Pantera refused to listen. "Fighting is always wrong," he said.

The bus stopped and the las Canchas guys left. I could see that the guy who Fito choked was bleeding. Fito had stabbed him in his arm and maybe he was bleeding from some other part of his body, too.

As the bus drove on, Don Pantera gave us a sermon. He was some kind of strong Christian. "Normally I wouldn't interfere," he said. "But these guys were older and you were at a great disadvantage. You are Tica's best friend, Chispa and I feel bad that I hit the young man, but I had to."

After Don Pantera talked to Raúl, Fito, and me, the bus continued on for only about a mile to our stop and we exited. As the four of us walked the ten blocks home, Don Pantera told me he was still going to talk to my dad. I shouldn't be fighting.

Don Pantera's house was closest to the bus stop so he left us and went inside. The three of us kept walking. Raúl and I were talking and talking about the whole episode. I had a fat lip and one black eye, but Raúl was in even worse shape. Both of his eyes were blackened and he was bruised all over. Since I was always very quick, I was mostly kicking, but Raúl was fist fighting. Fito was clean…they hadn't even touched him.

Raúl and I were going on and on about the feeling we had. We were so proud that we had beaten up the older guys. Fito just listened. "We should've been messed up in that bus," I said.

"A la verga, Fito! Without you and Don Pantera, we

would've been fucked."

"Chingao. Puta madre, es la verdad!"

Thanks to Don Pantera, Fito and our own big cajones, we had come out ahead, even though, "Pinche viejo's (the old man's) gonna tell on us. You just wait." My dad was going to be mad. He knew that we always hurt people when we got into fights. But every moment had been so worth it.

I got home and told Moy about the incident. When he saw Fito later he was so gracious, thanking him over and over for protecting us.

Fito was a nice guy, but he sniffed a rubber cement glue called Resistol 5000. Most of the cholos in my neighborhood would take a little plastic bag with the glue inside and breathe in and out into the bag until the glue dried up. A lot of the cholos used Resistol because a can of glue only cost twenty pesos, like two dollars, and it only took a little to get high. I watched so many of my friends sniff from those little bags and Fito did it, too.

When I was about eight, my dad told me that the glue damaged your brain and your ability to remember things and that it made you act like you were super drunk. I told many of my friends what the glue did, but they must not have cared. I guess I was different from them because I was always really into taking good care of my body. Caguama, one of the Centenos, lost eyesight in one of his eyes from sniffing so much glue. He looked so weird. One of his eyes was normal-looking, but the other was completely white. He also had a hearing problem from sniffing. Caguama told us once about all of the damage the glue and thinner had done to him and now I was scared to try it. But I guess the others weren't as concerned as me.

It was always tempting to sniff when my friends said things like, "Don't be such a wimp, Chispa," and I didn't want that label. But thank God for my dad for constantly reminding me of the negative impact drugs could have on my body. I always cared about my future and wanted more than anything to have an impact on a lot of people.

Drugs just wouldn't fit into that goal.

One Saturday night about five o'clock Fito came by our house. Moy was out in the street in front and they were talking. Fito seemed a little high, but it was early so he wasn't in too bad of shape yet. When Bombin and I saw the two of them, we came out and we all stood outside, reminiscing about the day Fito saved Raúl and me in the bus. We went on, remembering and reliving a lot of fights we'd been in as we talked outside my house that night. After about an hour and a half, Fito left.

A couple of hours later, Fago, Tica, and I were hanging out talking to Cleofas in his store when we heard screeching tires. We thought somebody had crashed, so we ran outside to look. But there was no wreck. It was Fito. He was in the middle of the street in front of a car, smiling. The car was less than a foot away from him, and the driver was yelling, "Pinche cholo! You stupid kid!"

Later, he did it again. That night, Fago and I saw Fito dodge two cars in less than an hour.

A little bit after that, I went home and forgot about Fito's car dodging. It wasn't anything new.

I hung out talking in the street in front of my house and didn't hear any more squealing tires. But Fito must've sniffed more glue, because later, close to eleven, he walked down the street in front of my house again. "Hey, Fito," someone yelled out, but he didn't say anything to us. He just seemed lost as he wandered by.

Fito looked like a strung out mess with his Resistol 5000 high, but inside his mind, he probably felt like Superman.

What none of us knew was that moments before we had seen him wandering, Fito had told a friend that he was going to go to la avenida and get in front of more cars. There the cars drove faster—that would be a bigger adrenaline rush for him.

Fito continued his car dodging for years until one night he talked about train dodging. When he told his friend Romulo what he was thinking, Rómulo said to him, "You shouldn't do that, cabron. You were lucky last time. The train is way too heavy...it can't stop. I can't fucking believe you're talking about this."

After that, Fito dropped his talk about the train and instead told Rómulo that he was going home. He was staying with some relatives in another neighborhood.

But Fito didn't do what he said. And because he was too full of glue to listen to his friend's advice, he walked to La Ferro, rival gang territory, by himself at eleven thirty at night. That's where the train tracks were.

Sometime between twelve thirty and one o'clock, the train engineer saw a guy standing in front of the train from about fifty meters away. The engineer was frantically honking, but just like every other time, Fito didn't move. And on that night, insanity met destiny. Fito's crazy habits could no longer cheat death. The train hit him. It hit him hard, too. Two hundred meters after impact the train stopped and the engineer stepped down to see if the guy was O.K. Maybe at the last minute, he had jumped off of the tracks.

But, no.

From beside the tracks the engineer saw it. Half a body from the waist down. And underneath the train—the top half of the body. The halves were separated by about twenty meters. When the men pulled the top half of the body from underneath the train, they saw that Fito's lifeless hands, in their attempt to grab on to the bottom of the engine and somehow hold onto life, had been severely burned.

We all presumed that as Fito got hit, he tried to grab on to something and the only thing for him to hold onto was the undercarriage of the train.

Fito surely died within a couple of minutes.

When we found out that our friend had been cut in half by the train, we couldn't believe it. He loved to play chicken with the cars. But he wasn't supposed to die.

3. *LOCOS*
CRAZIES

Los Criminales
The Criminals

Roberto's grandfather lived in my neighborhood and, like me, owned chickens and roosters. Roberto was very interested in roosters; of course, I was, too so we started to hang out together.

His house was a big house about a block and a half away from my house. Every weekend, laborers worked there, remodeling. They would be fixing the kitchen or painting or landscaping the yard with rocks. Roberto's house always fascinated me. I always wondered how his family could work on making their house so beautiful while every other family in mi colonia just struggled for food.

Our houses were very basic. Made of concrete and painted in bright colors or else not painted at all and not very nice to look at.

Roberto's papá and three other guys owned their fancy house and these guys were all somehow related. They were known as los criminales and were feared by the other adults in the neighborhood because they were considered "nothing but trouble". So much trouble that not even the police messed with them. Everyone knew that the four homeowners sold crystal meth, which was known to us as chiva, along with all kinds of other drugs—marijuana, cocaine, crack, and paint thinner. These men were the main drug distributors in our region of the city.

They worked out of their house—the same house where all of their families lived. Three or four kids and all four wives. The men may have been bad, but they always had money. One day, Roberto's family hired the whole colonia to pour concrete on their flat Chihuahua roof. Afterward, when the work was completed, there was a huge fiesta. Two pigs were killed and roasted and there was cerbeza for all of the adults in the whole neighborhood. The kids were eating chicharrones and the grown-ups were getting drunk on all of that beer.

In the colonia when a family needed massive amounts of labor, they would just hire the whole neighborhood and feed them lunch.

At Roberto's house that day, there were two crews of people mixing the concrete in the street and two other crews carrying the concrete to the roof on a scaffold. For pay, everyone would be fed and their thirst was beyond quenched with beer after beer.

My friends and I enjoyed going to Roberto's house, not because of Roberto, but because all four of los criminales would tell us stories. They were all incredibly proud of their illegal behavior and their children were, strangely, proud of their parents, too.

I could never tell my parents I was over at that house; they had forbidden me to go.

But I went anyway. Roberto and I weren't very close, but if my friends ever decided to go to the house and I refused, they would call me a chicken or a joto.

One day, my friends Tica and Fago came over and asked

me to go to el Víbora's. El Víbora, the viper, was one of the criminals, a fabled pickpocket of the Chihuahua city buses.

Minutes after we entered through the front doors of Roberto's house, we were invited to the kitchen and we sat down around the table. It was there, at the table, where we were about to learn some of the techniques of criminal behavior.

That day when El Víbora sat down at the table, he was really a mess. His chest was heavily bandaged and his eyes were blackened. He was wearing a cast on his hand. When we asked him what had happened, he began to tell us a long story. El Víbora frequently rode the Chihuahua city buses. But, as we knew, not to go anywhere...we had heard he had no destination. Now we would know for sure if he did indeed ride with a different purpose in mind. We would know for sure if he would go into the buses and push up against people as they were getting on and off and if his riding was only a cover for his real intention—to steal the wallets of the riders.

"The bus was loaded with maquila workers, and I was just pushing up next to people and doing my thing," El Víbora said. I listened carefully for proof that the things I had heard about him were true. "I got one, so I moved to the other end of the bus, and then I did it again. Picked the wallet right out of the guy's pocket." The guy who he took the wallet from didn't know it, but another lady saw. The instant she saw him deposit the wallet inside his coat, she yelled and stared at him, her eyes filling with rage. "Stupid rat thief!"

"There's a thief in the bus. HE'S TAKING YOUR WALLET!" the woman yelled out to the victim.

El Víbora continued, "I was afraid of what would happen now, since the woman had announced my guilt to the entire bus."

"Cayate, you old bitch!" I yelled and punched the lady in the mouth to shut her up, but there were a couple of good Samaritans on the bus who fought back. They punched me again and again, punched my face and my stomach in defense of the old bitch (vieja puta, he said)."

When the man who hadn't realized he'd been robbed felt inside his pocket and found no sign of his wallet, he and the other guy ran over to where the fight had ensued and got involved, punching Víbora, too. "So there I was, on the floor of that dirty old bus. Four or five of those bastards punched and kicked me. One of them pulled a knife from my pocket and stabbed me... with MY OWN KNIFE. Es la verdad!"

Víbora lay on the bus floor, bleeding from the stab wound that had torn apart his chest. Minutes passed by and then for some reason, "I guess I had good luck because after those putos on the bus beat me, the driver stopped the bus and threw me outside. I was in the streets for a while, and then," miraculously, someone lifted him from the street and drove him to the hospital. By the time it was all over, El Víbora, who had suffered several stab wounds, a broken nose, and some broken ribs and who had been horribly beaten by almost ten people, somehow managed to survive. "I am alive," he said. "Can you believe it?"

We all sat around the table, impressed. Our mouths had to be dropped wide open, maybe we were even slobbering. In shock and awe, I realized the stories I had heard around the colonia were true!

El Víbora's cousin was Beto. He lived in the same house, but he did not pick pockets. He had a different clandestine operation. He stole cars.

Most of the cars that Beto stole, he sold. But there was one car that he kept as his prize: a beautiful, yellow 1980 Trans Am. Beto did not tell us all of the details of the car theft, merely that he had stolen his beautiful car from El Paso and had managed to drive it across the border with fake papers, unsuspected.

The other guy had knowledge of how to make drugs. He was very proud of his knowledge, too.

Though I listened intently to all of their stories, no stories could match the one Chinaya told.

Chinaya was the most interesting to me of all of the criminals who lived in the big house. He was about sixty-five years old and had a cute forty-year-old wife. He and his wife were the parents of a very beautiful daughter who I had a huge crush on. She was called Lucerito. Lucerito was one year older than me and was a grade ahead of me in school. Like his daughter, I always thought Chinaya was likable and funny.

From the moment I first saw him, I noticed that Chinaya was missing a hand and I was always very intrigued about why his right hand was cut off from the wrist down.

And so on a different day when all of Los Criminales were telling us stories about their adventures, I asked Chinaya, "Why are you missing your hand? What happened to your hand? Were you born like that?" I didn't mean to be nosy. I was just so curious.

Chinaya laughed, somewhat nervously, but he did laugh. "So you want to know, Chispa, how I lost my hand?" He took a deep breath, "Pinche Chispita, I guess I can tell you." He smiled at me through crooked, yellow teeth and began to talk. "This happened about five or six years ago." He paused and took a swig of his beer. He put the bottle down on the table, wiped off his lower lip, and began. "One of our techniques was to study people. So we did. We would find out where they lived, where they worked, when they were alone." Los criminales didn't work, at least not in the traditional sense so I realize now that they had a lot of time to dedicate to examining the lives of others and to wait for an opportunity to get the upper hand.

"A while back," he said, "I went to this other neighborhood and studied this old ranchero." Chinaya went on to say that the guy lived alone with his wife and they were probably in their seventies. Chinaya was waiting for the perfect time. And then one day, it came. "Mi oportúnidad," said Chinaya. "The old bastards were gone from home so I easily opened up the door and crept inside the house. I packed up a bunch of their stuff, mainly jewelry." He knew where to look. He told us behind pictures many people had hiding places for jewelry and coins... "Hijole, I was cleaning out the house. But long before I expected, those old people returned. Holy shit! When I heard the car and voices outside, I hurried up. I wanted to just get the hell out of that house, but that old bastard must've thought that something was wrong," because as Chinaya moved toward the door, the old man saw him through the window and sneaked inside.

Chinaya said he knew he was being greedy. He had seen an antique gun in the bedroom. "You see, I'm a real son of a bitch, and I really wanted the pinche gun." He was stuffing the gun in his bag and losing some time. " I took an extra twenty or thirty seconds, but I should've left. I should've run outside and hid the moment I heard the old folks."

Chinaya paused and looked around at us. None of us said a word.

"As I walked through this little hall that led to the front door, there was the man. I saw him in the blink of an eye, saw him hiding in the corner holding a shotgun."

In Mexico there is no make my day law. A lot of people claim they have guns, but they don't practice shooting them. They have guns only to scare the bad guys. So Chinaya assumed the man was only holding the gun to scare him. He approached the man with a knife poised, ready to stab him. But it was too late for the knife. The gun had already blown off Chinaya's hand.

"I cried for my life. I was bleeding all over the place," Chinaya explained. "I thought I was going to die and I asked the old man to forgive me. I told him 'I repent. I will no longer be a thief. I want to change my life.' The old man must have thought I had learned my lesson, so he didn't turn me in to the police and he even gave me back my horribly damaged hand."

"My hand was gone, but the adrenaline was rushing so hard," Chinaya went on, "I had no idea how bad it was and how close I was to death, but El Víbora did. He was waiting for me in a car about a half a block away. Víbora turned pale when he saw me run, blood rushing from the hole in my arm, to the car. 'Drive!' I yelled with my last bit of strength and doubled over into the passenger seat. On the way to the hospital my life came to me like a movie. I saw myself and all I had done. Had I been a good citizen, a good husband, a good father? No, I had not. At that moment, I seriously thought about changing my life—I was so close to death and didn't want my kids to be without a father."

"And Víbora was in shock," Chinaya told us. "He'd never seen so much blood. He didn't know what to do, but he did what he could. He took a shoelace from his shoe and tied it around my arm, fast. It controlled the bleeding a little. But my arm was still bleeding really badly. Víbora suggested that I put the wound up against the car's muffler to stop the bleeding. So we stopped the car and he dragged me outside to burn my wound. I don't know if it was the shoelace or the burn that controlled the bleeding, but I got to the hospital and I was still alive and very grateful."

"The ranchero never turned me in. He truly believed that I would become a good person for life," Chinaya said with a sly smile on his face.

"For about a month, I seriously thought about turning my life around, but...it's been five or six years since I lost my hand and I'm still robbing houses."

"So Chispa," Chinaya sighed. "There's your story. That's how I lost my hand."

Chinaya sat up in his chair a little taller and rested his elbows on the table. His other hand was clasped to his stub in front of him. He grew serious. "Chispa, I want you to know something," he said. "Most people think that I lost my hand in a machete fight. But I don't lie in front of my kids. I'm not proud of my activities, but it's the only thing I know. I will probably die before I change. I don't want to commit to a job. That's something I'll never do."

And he never did in all of the years I knew him.

Los Criminales always had cash. But they did not have honor. I was amazed that all four men thought it was wonderful that they knew how to make a living by planning and carrying out their illicit activities. They must've thought they were doing my friends and me a big favor by giving us all of their rip-off tactics. But, young as I was, both El Víbora's and Chinaya's stories only led me to look at them and see a couple of fools and their unjust activitie led me to appreciate my dad: his honest and ethical ways, and his pure view of life. Although the criminals were rich, I never thought that they were cool.

Charritas

Charritas was always my next door neighbor. His house was right next to my house and before I was born, from what I've been told, his house, my parents' house and my grandparents' house, la Huerta, were the first three houses within the few blocks of Josefa Ortiz de Dominguez, the little four blocks of colonia industrial where my family lived.

Now that my brother Moy's days in the Puesto 1 gang were over, he and Charritas' daughter, Tere, got serious. When they were about ten and eleven years old, they had been referred to by Moy's friends as la novios de manita sudada (the sweaty hand couple). The two of them had been an on again, off again couple for thirteen years. Moy was Tere's first boyfriend when he was only four!

Now they were eighteen and nineteen and Moy let Charritas know of his intentions. He wanted to marry Tere and be with her for life. Charritas was not happy about this because Moy was not his choice for a son-in-law. Moy had had too many girlfriends and smoked weed. Pot-smoking was not acceptable among adults. My brother was cool for his friends but was a bad choice for Tere.

Charritas gave his blessing because he loved my parents, but he could not stand Moy. And he really disliked Moy's cholo friends.

A lot of couples went to the justice of the peace and said their vows. But in Chihuahua at that time, ninety percent of "respectable" couples got married in the church. Tere was the baby of her family and had been treated as a special little gift from God throughout her life, and Tere's parents, Charritas and Dona Andrea, who were older and greatly concerned with their daughter's honor, insisted Moy and Tere marry in Perpetuo Socorro, the neighborhood Catholic Church. Tere's family was very religious, so Charritas and Dona Andrea saw this as the only option for la boda de Moy and their little princess, Tere.

All of Moy's friends were afraid of Moy's father-in-law to be because Charritas had the reputation for being crazy nuts. His violent behavior in the past had earned him his crazy reputation and, for this reason, Moy's friends feared for Moy's life if for some reason his marriage to Tere ever failed. Moy was so excited to be getting engaged; at the same time his friends warned him, "Be careful. You know Charritas is crazy!"

Several stories were told and retold in my neighborhood and the main character in all of them was Charritas. Charritas shooting people, Charritas blowing things up. He and his explosive temper were the theme of many tales. If an unfortunate rock hit his roof during a cholo fight, he would unload his gun on whoever was responsible. It didn't matter to Charritas where the cholo was from. Even if the guy was from my neighborhood, Charritas would shoot him, too. He was very protective of his property. And for his violence and willingness to go to any extreme to protect himself and his family, he was the most respected older person in my neighborhood. Everyone feared him.

One summer night, two well-known neighborhood drug addicts, el Caballo (the horse) and Chícharo (pea head), were fighting with machetes in the street in front of Charritas' house. As usual, Charritas was sitting on his roof drinking Jose Cuervo from the bottle, smoking, and enjoying the weekend scuffle. The brother of el Caballo, Alejandro el Panzon, the big belly, was standing in the street watching. When it appeared to Alejandro that his brother was at a disadvantage and would be hurt by Chícharo's machete, Alejandro grabbed up a rock from the street and prepared to throw it at the pea-sized head of his brother's opponent. Alejandro el Panzon took careful aim and threw the rock with great force, hoping to knock out Chícharo. But when Chícharo dodged the rock, it missed its target, and whizzed through the air, shattering Charritas' kitchen window.

Dozens of people had been watching. But as soon as the rock hit the window, everyone scattered. Charritas yelled from above, "You're a dead man, Alejandro!" and immediately climbed down from the roof. When they saw him descending, Alejandro and the two drug addicts immediately forgot about the fight and darted across the street to take refuge in Alejandro's house.

My mom hurried outside and yelled to us, "Get in the house, now!"

She knew immediately when she saw Charritas climb down from the roof that he would go into the house to retrieve his gun and then do something crazy.

As predicted, Charritas ran into his house, then back out producing an arsenal of weapons. He climbed back up the ladder to his rooftop and promptly unloaded his shotgun into Alejandro el Panzon's house across the street. He shot out all of the house's windows. Bullets ricocheted off of the cement walls and the sound was like fireworks from inside our house. Luckily, the houses in our neighborhood had such thick walls that no one was hurt. But the exterior of Alejandro's house wore bullet scars for many years.

The next morning, it was unusually quiet on my street. Then at about noon some mediators came to Charritas' house to ask if Alejandro and the two drug addicts would be allowed to come over and ask for forgiveness. Charritas agreed so later that day, the three guys came over and after over an hour of apologies, they were forgiven. After this incident, everyone loved Charritas even more, because now my street, which used to be the scene of a fight every weekend, was the most peaceful street in the neighborhood. The drug addicts had always been the ones fighting. But now, there were no other serious fights on our street for years to come. This incident and the punishment of the drug addicts by Charritas had been a blessing for us. Crazy Charritas was our hero.

Fifteen years prior, when Tere was a little girl, Charritas was involved in another of his incidents. He had been drinking at el mineral, the next neighborhood over, in the cantina. Most weekends he got drunk, but his cousin was visiting from Durango so he had been in the mood to get very drunk. He and his cousin had gone to the bar and by 1:00 in the morning, Charritas was drunk and angry and was arguing with the other borrachos at the bar.

Until the cantinero politely told Charritas that he would not serve him anymore that night.

In the cantinas, it was usual not to serve someone if he was getting overly drunk and it was common for a cantinero to politely ask a very drunk patron to go home. This bartender knew Charritas, and for Charritas' sake, he said again, "Charritas, go home."

But Charritas was not a happy drunk, and he was getting more angry with each second. "I just want to drink one more cerbeza. Come on! I've got the money to pay for it."

Again, the cantinero said, "No, Charritas. Go home."

"If you don't serve me, you are going to regret it," Charritas slurred, stumbling ferociously toward the door. "Come on, Victor," he shouted to his cousin as he made his way out the door and down the street. "We've got work to do. How dare that pinche cantinero kick us out of his bar. He'd better wachale. Nobody kicks Juan Charrasqueado out without consequences! That asshole is going to pay!" With a plan in mind, Charritas headed quickly home with his cousin beside him.

Charritas worked for the government, demolishing and building roads. He was an expert at exploding hills so that the roads could go through. He was the owner and operator of many pounds of TNT so he rushed to his house and, uniquely armed, returned with his cousin to the bar. They walked bravely through the door and Charritas strode up to the bar.

He calmly and politely said to the cantinero, "I would like another cerbeza."

Again, the cantinero boldly answered, "No, Charritas." Charritas turned away from the bar in an unusual state of calm. He walked out of the cantina.

Outside the entrance, Charritas planted three cartridges of TNT. Tactically, he placed the explosives in a little gap between the door and part of the wall. He lit up the pieces and he and his cousin ran to take cover across the street. A few seconds later, the dynamite he had placed in the gap exploded. Chunks of cement blew into the street with a bang that could be heard throughout Mineral and Indústrial. After the dirt and refuse settled, there was a huge hole blown in the entrance of the cantina; the door had been blown off and three people, including the cantinero, had been injured in the blast. Charritas, who had hurried home with his cousin and gone to bed, was turned in by a customer and served a prison sentence of five years.

The stories went on and on. But even if his future father-in-law was about to be crazy Charritas, Moy loved Tere so no one could talk him out of getting married.

Following Moy and Tere's elaborate church wedding with flowers and cholos everywhere, a reception was held at Charritas' house. As planned, very few people were invited to the party. Many of Moy's friends were upset because they wanted to be there to support their homie, but they were not allowed in. So they took to the colonia, to the street in front of the house, anyway. When Moy and Tere returned from Perpetuo Socorro Catholic Church, a group of Moy's friends were waiting in the street to congratulate him and his new bride. After accepting his friends' congratulatory words, Moy told them, "Go home, guys. Charritas is drinking. Please don't make my new father-in-law upset tonight." Moy was happy his friends had come over, but he told them he would see them the next day.

At two A.M., Moy's friends Maca, Jorge, Jaime and Rómulo returned to our street in their car. Now they were drunk; they had been drinking and celebrating Moy's happiness. Since they couldn't come inside to the private family party, they decided to once again express their happiness for the newlyweds outside.

Moy's friends drove through the street singing, "Felicidades, and much happiness!" and honking the horn of their car. When they stopped the car in front of Tere's house, they shouted, "Congratulations, Tere! Congratulations, Moy!" They were surprised to hear a voice from the roof.

"Muchachos, go away. The novios are about to go to sleep. They're tired. They've had a long day. We all want peace tonight. Please, go away. I'm getting tired and my patience is getting thin."

So the guys waved to Charritas and drove off in their car. They returned one hour later, very drunk. This time, aware that the novios were in bed, "sleeping", they yelled drunkenly, laughing, "Arriba, Moy! Abajo, Tere! (On top, Moy, on bottom, Tere!)" Then, "Arriba, Tere! Abajo, Moy!"

On the roof, Charritas sat, still smoking and drinking. "I warned you, cabrones! You have now made me very mad. Now you will suffer the consequences." The friends did not know that every time Charritas was in a celebratory mood he shot his rifle into the air—tonight was one of those nights; the friends did not know Charritas was sitting next to his rifle on the roof; the friends also did not know that their jokes were offending Charritas. His daughter's honor and reputation were extremely important to him. And saving the reputation of Tere was something well worth fighting for.

He grabbed his gun and yelled something to the unwelcome friends. Moments later, Charritas pointed his rifle and shot the car at least six times, shattering the back window. Two bullets lodged themselves in Jorge's back. Maca raced off to the hospital with him.

The following day, the police came to Charritas' house and Charritas was charged with attempted murder. Since the police knew this crazy guy possessed weapons and were aware of his dangerousness, they were afraid that he would put up a fight, but even though he expressed that he was just trying to look out for his daughter's honor, he was taken into custody. He was only in jail for a week because, since Moy's friends were so afraid of him, they pressed no formal charges. The novios were now together and happily married, but Charritas, as usual, had made his craziness known, this time on Moy and Tere's wedding night.

Chupis vs. Moy vs. Alejandro vs. Chispa

Every weekend when I was thirteen and fourteen years old, the whole neighborhood got together, rented a bus, and went to las albercas (the swimming pools).

The bus was horrible—a 1955 school bus. It was white and burgundy and looked pretty decent from far away, but up close you could see that the bus had been painted with a paint roller and acrylic paint. The seats were ripped and some didn't even have cushions so when we rode, many of us had to stand up.

It was a lot of fun to go to the swimming pools because Alejandro, my neighbor, cut up meat and loaded it into ice coolers to cook at the pool. We would carry the coolers into the bus and the bus' owner would drive us. Las albercas were fun.

There were about six different pools together in a park on the outskirts of Chihuahua. The pools were different shapes and depths. My friends and I always went to the largest, rectangular-shaped pool, because there we had space to play baseball.

After we played for hours, using our clasped arms as bats, Alejandro made tacos on his very large grill, and we ate and drank cokes. The men drank a lot of beer.

One particular day it happened that Chupis, who was Alejandro's brother and my tia Cuca's husband, drank a couple of extra beers and my tia Cuca did the same.

We got on the bus to go back to the colonia after having been out in the sun all day and once the bus started moving, Cuca and Chupis began to argue. "You are drunk, Chupis," Cuca laughed, "Your voice sounds so totally stupid when you're drunk."

"Shut up, you stupid whore," Chupis said, "I'm not drunk. And who are you to say anything about how I talk, parrot voice?"

"Tu no sabes nada, cabrona (You know nothing.)!"

"I know a lot more than you, peanut brain. I can't believe I'm even with such a pinche puto!"

The two of them argued harder and harder and got louder and louder and when the bus stopped in our neighborhood, Cuca and Chupis continued to scream at each other as they walked, weaving up the street to tia Lencha's house, where they were planning to spend the evening.

Chupis was still arguing with Cuca about who was more stupid when they got to tia Lencha's. There they went into Lencha's bedroom to argue some more.

In the bedroom, Cuca went after Chupis. She knew he was horribly jealous and they had seen the nice seventy-year-old she used to date at the pool. "You lazy ass. At least that old man I loved was a hard-worker. He was feeding his whole family while you were too busy looking him over and getting wasted at the pool."

Chupis fumed. He couldn't stand her comments anymore, and he slapped her, hard, in the face. With her face burning red, tia Cuca screamed, "If you think you're a real man, why don't you punch your fist into that concrete wall instead of my face, pinche cabron."

Almost instantly he yelled, "Pinche puta!" and slammed his clenched fist into the bedroom wall.

Chupis hit the wall over and over, cutting up and bloodying his fists. Tia Cuca tried to grab him by the waist and pull him away so he would stop. But Chupis continued to hit the wall.

Polin, who was a friend of my older brother Moy, walked back to the bedroom, thinking that the two of them were done arguing.

When he saw Chupis' bloody fists, he thought Chupis was

beating Cuca instead of the hard wall so he ran out of the house and rushed through the streets of the colonia looking for my brother Moy. Polin knew that Moy was a tough cholo so he thought Moy would be the best person to stop Chupis.

He found Moy in the street talking to El Perro.

"Moy, you need to come quick. Chupis is beating up your tia." Polin was winded and gasped for a breath. His voice was shaky. "There's a lot of blood on the wall. There is blood on his fists. You'd better go to Lencha's before he really hurts her."

Moy hurried up and ran to Lencha's house. By then, Chupis and Cuca were coming out of the bedroom, still arguing.

Moy ran into the house, and, when he saw Chupis, without a word he punched him square in the face. Chupis threw a punch back at Moy and the two of them began boxing in the hallway.

My brother grabbed Chupis by the neck of the navy blue fox t-shirt he wore every weekend. "Let's take this outside. There's more room. This is the last time you touch my tia." Moy growled at Chupis, but, at the same time, he couldn't help but wonder what was going on. Cuca didn't have any marks on her.

In my colonia, gossip could be lethal. People had died because of it.

There were a lot of rumors that Chupis had hurt Cuca in the past so, in the street outside Lencha's, Moy and Chupis continued to fight.

Now a big, loud group of people surrounded the fighters in the street. Everyone was cheering for Moy. No one in the neighborhood really liked Chupis, except for his brothers.

Now Alejandro Panzon, Chupis' brother, was in the circle surrounding him. Chupis pleaded to him as Moy brought punch after punch to his nose. "Alejandro, help me. I'm drunk."

By then, Chupis had a bloody nose and a bloody mouth,

and Moy, who was also drunk, was fucking him up. I was watching the fight. It was such a cool feeling. My brother was destroying this jerk. I know he was my tio, but at that moment, I hated him.

Moy then walked a few steps from Chupis and pulled off his shirt. But the moment he wasn't looking, Alejandro came from out of nowhere and hit him in the back of his head with a tree branch.

Moy fell down and Chupis took advantage of the situation. Now both Alejandro and Chupis were kicking Moy. Moy somehow managed to get up and run toward our house to grab a machete. It was an interesting sight: a young, thin cholo was being chased down the street by two thirty-something chubbies. Unfortunately, right before Moy reached our house, he tripped on something and hit his head into the muffler of Polin's car. Moy was now unconscious.

What happened next was totally out of line.

Chupis jumped on top of the unconscious Moy and started punching him. He then grabbed a big rock and held it up above Moy's head, ready to whack him. When I saw Chupis holding that rock, my warrior blood started boiling. I was small, but no man was going to hurt my big brother when he was on the ground.

Moments before Chupis could smash Moy with the rock, I rushed over next to him and kicked him in the head with the steel toe of my boot.

He fell to the ground.

WOW! I couldn't believe it!

I had kicked Chupis so hard, I had knocked him over. Both excited and afraid, I kicked Chupis again and again, bruising his body with the steel toes of both boots. Alejandro looked over and then moved toward me. I thought that he, too, wanted to hurt my brother, but instead, he said to me, "Pinche mocoso, I'm going to fuck you up." I knew he was about to go after me, so, when he drew closer, I kicked him, too.

I thought I kicked Alejandro in the stomach, but I realize now that I kicked him in the balls. Gracias a dios my oldest brother Chentito pulled up in his car just as Alejandro and Chupis were pulling themselves up from the street.

Chentito looked very angry. And he was tough because he was a professional baseball player. Chentito was also in really good shape. So he hurried across the street to where Chupis and Alejandro stood, "What did you do to my brother, cabrones?" Chentito intimidated them with his size and strength, then punched them one after the other, until their faces were even bloodier.

And then the fight got crazy.

More Saucedo brothers came to join Chupis and Alejandro. They were all in their twenties and thirties—Chícharo, el Caballo; this family was the terror of the neighborhood. They were famous for having murdered and beaten up many people and they had all been in jail several times.

Because all of the neighbors were worried for us, many of them stood in the middle of the street between the Saucedos and the teenaged Bolivars. "Moy is unconscious. Let's stop this," Chentito said. It was such an uneven fight that all of the neighbors worked to push the Saucedos away from us. "You're married to their aunt, Chupis," one said. "You're practically related to the Bolivars."

A couple of older neighbor men hoisted Moy up from the concrete and carried him inside to his bed. My brothers and I followed, concerned. But the Saucedos waited outside with rocks and knives.

Moy would not wake up.

Then tia Lupe, who had followed us inside, told us, "Rub alcohol in his nostrils," so we did, and Moy slowly came to. As he lay there on the bed now conscious, my brothers and I looked through the window to see if the Saucedos still waited.

And then I saw it. A welcome sight! My dad was walking down the street confidently, holding a baseball bat in his hands.

My dad was very respected by our neighbors—criminals, thieves, children, women, killers, respectable men—by everybody in the whole neighborhood.

Chupis approached my dad and asked, "Chente, can I borrow your bat?" The whole neighborhood seemed to gasp, wondering what would happen next.

There, as the neighbors watched and listened, my dad asked Chupis, "Are you out of your fucking mind?"

"Do you think I will let you borrow my bat so you can use it to hurt my sons?" he questioned Chupis, and then, to all of the Saucedos, he said, "If any of you assholes come near me, I'll mess you up." I couldn't believe that mi papa had just said the word fuck and then called people assholes. In all of my life, I'd never heard him use bad words.

My brothers and I filed out of the house then. Bombin and Chentito grabbed rocks. Moy carried the big machete. I grabbed a broom, the first thing my hands could find.

We all stood outside in a huddle.

But then Cuco, one of the Saucedos who worked for my dad, said to his brothers, "You guys are crazy. These are your nephews. You guys have never fought them before. Moy was just trying to protect his tia and Chispa was protecting Moy." Cuco's words managed to calm every one of them down.

My dad was very cool and calming, too, "If you guys want to get it on, it's not worth it. But if you guys are hard headed and must fight, let's do it."

Once the fight was stopped, Chupis and Alejandro offered an apology to mi papá. Apá accepted the apology but refused to shake their hands.

The next day, the police came into my colonia, looking for thirteen-year-old Rogelio Bolivar. Chupis had pressed charges against me because I had broken his nose with my steel-toed boots. When my dad heard that the police had come for me, he went to Chupis and said, "What do you think you're doing? Chispa was protecting his brother. Are you crazy?"

And then Chupis asked for money. Once again, I heard my dad say to him, "Are you crazy? Chispa was protecting his brother. If you don't drop the charges, I'll mess you up and then you can bring charges against me. Chispa is only a kid."

For the next couple of days, I didn't leave the house. I was afraid of seeing the Saucedos in the streets.

When the police returned for my testimony, I was too afraid to go outside with them and my dad wisely would not allow them to question me.

Chupis dropped the charges almost immediately. And once I knew, I was no longer afraid. Chupis had initially pressed charges because he only wanted money.

And me? I earned a reputation in my neighborhood because I had officially beaten up an adult. Even the bully Chuy Mudito left me alone for a year or two.

But I am still bitter about one particular part of what happened; after all of the drama and their nasty fight, Chupis and Cuca went home like nothing ever happened, cuddling and hugging.

After that day, Chupis and Cuca fought almost every weekend. Often Cuca asked for help, but each time, my dad told us very strongly not to interfere. Even though Cuca was his sister, he said, "She's crazy. So is he." Almost every weekend one of them injured the other. Cuca might have the black eye or Chupis might have it. Cuca might have nasty bruises on her arms or back. But we never tried to fix the situation for either of them from the day of the fight on.

Fighting was just part of their lives. That was how they showed their love for each other.

Novias
Girlfriends

Even though my neighborhood was rough, there were always lots of girls. There was Marlene who I held hands with in the third grade and then Adriana, a girl from Camargo, who came to industrial only in the summers. The first time I saw Adriana, I swore she was the most beautiful girl I had ever seen; she had light brown hair, white skin, and ojos de miel (hazel eyes). Actually the first summer, when I was twelve, I never saw her. I only heard rumors about how beautiful she was. So I kept walking by her tia's house trying to see the white-skinned beauty people had told me about, but I was disappointed. She never came outside.

The second summer was different. One day, I was walking over to get Fago and there she was in front of the house, her hair pulled up in a red scarf. Oh Dios mio! She was truly a beautiful angel. Somehow, I was blessed to have her as a girlfriend for a few weeks. She was like a doll and I couldn't get enough of looking at her.

Adriana's tia, Virginia, lived on the same street as Fago so Fago often informed me about what Adriana was doing. Fago also was interested in what was going on at that house since he had a crush on Adriana's cousin, Paula. Paula, like her cousin, had a beautiful face but she had a very roundish body. According to Fago, Adriana liked to flirt too much with the other guys in the colónia.

I wanted to know if this was true.

One day, Fago came and got me so we could watch her. Adriana sat in her front yard while me and Fago hid a couple of houses away on Charrito monta piojos' front porch, spying on her. Wow! A few different dudes came over to talk to her in a two hour time period. First she talked to and flirted with Nando the perv who was about twenty. Later she talked with another twenty year old, smiling and giggling and next another guy, Carlos, who was seventeen. She liked to flirt with the older guys. I had a jealous moment at that point.

Next, some other girls came over and talked to her. They seemed to be telling secrets and giggling about something. After she went inside, Fago and I sneaked off the porch and walked back toward Fago's.

"Wow!" I said. "I think you might be right, Fago."

"See, Chispa," he said.

"I'll ask her tonight if I can."

That night I knocked on Adriana's door at seven-thirty. "Would you like to go to the avenida to get some ice cream?" I asked her.

"Sure," she said. At the nieveria, I ordered my favorite, fresas con crema, and she had a peach ice cream. We walked to the parque in front of the nieveria and sat down, eating. "What did you do today?" I asked her. "Did you talk to anyone?"

"No," she said. "I went over to the house of my other tia. It was boring over there." That was a lie. I knew because I had watched her myself.

"Did you talk to any other guys today?" I asked. I was waiting for her to say yes, but...

"No," she said.

I sat there quietly, eating my ice cream and planning what to do next.

I had made my decision. We were walking home when I said, "I can't be your boyfriend anymore, Adriana. Because I hate liars."

"How am I a liar?" she asked.

"I heard you were talking to three different guys today and you refuse to admit it. You are lying and I don't like it."

After watching her flirt with all kinds of guys in the colónia that day, I realized something. A girl like Adriana might be beautiful, but her intense flirting with everyone was a turnoff. And her lying about it made her even more worthy of blame. Her disloyalty ended it for me. Even if she was a doll. That was the first doll I ever dumped. My friends in the neighborhood thought I was crazy, but I dumped her anyway. Poor Fago—Paula had been very nice to him while Adriana was my girlfriend. Now she wouldn't say a word to him.

After my experience with Adriana, I really didn't take much of an interest in the girls in my neighborhood. Probably because most of them never went on to high school and I did. In prepa and even during my final year of secundária, most of the girls I dated were girls I met at school or girls I met when we hung out in the nearby neighborhoods.

I learned early that I would like to be with a beautiful girl, but also one with a brain. I also learned early that girls thought I was nice and fun to talk to. So I used my charm to get to know them. I talked about science, movies, music, and my inventions. I even talked to girls about rooster fighting. By the time I was in high school and started to go on actual dates, I was placing and tightening the knives myself when I fought my roosters. I would tell girls about the rooster fights, but in a way that they wouldn't be disgusted. And weirdly enough, they actually seemed interested. Maybe that's because I loved my roosters and actually trained them for the fights.

I genuinely liked girls as people, loved them, even. I liked to entertain my dates and tell them about my experiences. "I just went to Juarez to play in a baseball tournament and we did well, or we sucked," or I would tell them, "You know I play soccer" because what kind of girl just wants to hear about fighting and who you beat up last weekend? Occasionally, a girl liked violence so I would talk about some martial arts classes I took and sometimes my cholo activities.

Since I had a job, I had an advantage because I always had money to go out. Other guys my age didn't work and never had money, but I worked almost every day and used my money wisely. I didn't just spend it on stupid things. I spent it on my martial arts classes so that I could better protect myself. And I spent it on my dates.

One of my favorite activities from ages fourteen through seventeen was going to the cine. My friends and I would go early and meet girls outside before the show. Often when we saw girls there, my friends would be shy. But they loved to take me with them because I wasn't afraid to talk to the girls and find friends for us. We loved going to the theater, meeting friends and being accompanied by them to the movies. We often picked the scary movies so the girls would hug us, scream, and grab our bodies. I can't tell you about any of the movies.

I was still a gangster. I beat up people and I got jumped myself, but deep down inside of me I was just looking for a beauty I could talk to, hang out with, and love.

If you consider the rough neighborhoods where the girls came from, you wouldn't be surprised that many of the ones I met played with lots of guys or would do anything just to have a boyfriend. Maybe they didn't understand that throwing yourself at a guy would not get them quality.

It was hard to have a faithful relationship in my colónia; there were always sexual indiscretions throughout industrial. One major indiscretion was the godfather, godmother relationship. It was interesting how a good-looking woman would never pick an ugly guy to be the godfather for her child. Likewise, a good-looking man would never be the godfather of an ugly woman's child. Why?

Fago and I came to a conclusion which we later investigated ourselves. One weekend we just started talking about comadres and compadres. We shared many stories with all of our friends. Through our story telling, we figured out that ten out of eleven comadres had had sexual relations with a compadre. And we never just assumed a sexual relationship; we had some evidence to prove each one. (We had actually spied on some people to figure out what they were up to; I cannot say any names. I don't want to get anybody in trouble.)

Obviously it was going to happen in a place like industrial. Come on, people! There were parties every weekend: Fridays, Saturdays, and Sundays. Every single weekend. One of the reasons the comadre, compadre relationships went down was that often one of the compadres was in jail. Probably fifty percent of the adult males in the neighborhood were in jail at any given time. So what do you think the ladies did when their men were locked up? Most of the couples in my neighborhood were not officially married, they just lived together and referred to themselves as married. The only actual married people I knew were my parents, Charritas and Doña Andrea, and el Perro's parents.

One night, Fago, Tica, Julian and me were walking around in the streets as usual—walking around checking out what was going on was part of our weekend entertainment.

There were fights in the streets that night.

We walked by a neighbor lady's house, and she came walking out into the street. "Hey guys, what happened in the streets? " Gertrudis said she'd heard about the fights, talked to us for a little while, and then asked, "Would you guys like a caguama?" Of course we would. Sixteen-year-old boys and beer? What else?

Gertrudis was kind of tall with huge boobs. She was bigger than all of us except for Fago and even though she was a large-built woman, she was still highly desired by many of the men in the neighborhood, mostly because of her enormous boobs. Gertrudis was about forty-five years old. She was large but hot with a big, round, tight ass and a caguama was a lot of beer. A caguama was a forty-ouncer.

"I have some beer here." She smiled. We followed her toward her front door. "Do you want to come inside and have one with me?" She opened the door for us.

We followed her into the kitchen.

All of us knew she was alone. Her husband was in prison and her three-year-old daughter must have been in bed asleep. It was late. "Have a seat," she said, and that's how Tica, Fago, Gertrudis and I ended up at her table where we sat down to drink and play cards. My friends and I drank two caguamas between us as we laughed and played. Gertrudis must've noticed we were getting a little buzzed because soon she asked, "Do you want to play spin the bottle with me?"

We all said, "No, no." She didn't argue with us—she only smiled and brought out one more forty-ouncer. We drank it while we played some more cards. Until we were all really feeling the alcohol. "If you don't play, you're all marricones," she smiled and teased us. Not wanting to be "gay" or wimpy, we complied.

Gertrudis grabbed the bottle limply in her hand and spun it very weakly. "You lose," someone yelled. We all laughed.

She took off her shirt, all the while laughing herself, and sat there in her bra. Her bra was white and lacy but heavy duty. It was huge with metal underwire. Then I lost my shirt, and before too long we were all topless and she was braless.

We were staring at the hugeness of her boobs.

As we walked out the door, she said, "I just wanted to have fun with you guys. I won't tell. Will you tell?" Until now, I don't think any of us ever told about the game with Gertrudis. Shortly after we lost our shirts, we dressed quickly and left.

The next day and every day after that, I couldn't look her in the eye. I never liked to see her on the street.

The ladies in my neighborhood must've told each other that my friends and I would do things with them. And now different ladies would find us on weekend nights. They would tempt us to play the bottle game and after a while, we would give in.

We played the game several times with several ladies.

But we didn't just hang out with grown-up women. We had dates with girls, too. About a block from my house was the baseball field where we had played all of our little league games. We spent a lot of time there during the day playing baseball and soccer with friends and during the late evening hours making out with our dates. We often took dates to the casetas.

People in the neighborhood took advantage of the casetas at night for love meetings. Occasionally they were even used during the daytime. At night, there was always some couple in the dugouts; they functioned as free hotel rooms in a neighborhood where no one had any money for the real thing.

My friends and I would walk around in nearby neighborhoods, meet girls, and bring them to our neighborhood. And guess where we went?

Sammy was about twenty years old. He was married to Leti. For a while there was a rumor going around my neighborhood that he was seeing a friend of mine's sister, Mariana, on the side.

One night Fago and I had brought our dates to visit the casetas when we noticed that Sammy and Mariana were inside one. Since we each needed our own dug-out, we decided to go back to the corner to hang out until both of the casetas became unoccupied. This was probably around eleven p.m.

As we sat talking on the corner by Cleofas' store, a huge group of people formed and began marching down the street—Sammy's wife and mother-in-law took up the lead followed by Mariana's mom, Hortensia. Following them were dozens of other nosy neighbors. Someone must've told on Sammy.

"This is going to be good," I said to Fago and our dates. After the throng of people passed, we hurried down another street, eager to see what would happen at the caseta. Within a minute or two, we were behind the group. As the family members approached the occupied dug-out, the crowd moved silently, almost synchronized behind them.

My friends and I ran up closer to watch the group as it entered through the little doorway. There was Mariana on the caseta's bench with Sammy on top of her. Mariana grabbed onto Sammy's bushy long curls as they made their way through their love session. That was until the group grabbed Sammy's naked body and pulled it off of her.

"Que estás haciendo con esa puta?" Sammy's mother-in-law screamed. She slapped his face with a crack.

"It's not what it seems it is," he said.

"What is it then?"

"Pinche Sammy! How can you do this to me?" Now Leti raised her hand and slapped him.

Next it was his mother's turn. She looked at him with her angry red face and slapped him, too.

The three women were practically beating him up and screaming at him as Mariana sat there naked and silent. Her mother, Hortensia, also stayed silent.

Fago, the girls, and I were all in different places near the dugout, matches in hands, watching the whole drama. Sammy and Mariana sat on the bench naked. I could see that Sammy's chest and neck were covered in hickies; Mariana's breasts were covered, too. Everyone watched and one helpful neighbor had even brought his flashlight to validate the evidence. He quickly handed it off to Sammy's mother-in-law at the perfect moment. So we could see clearly the lovers' moment of public humiliation and even though feeling a little bad for them, we watched and laughed hard anyway.

Most weekends my friends and I went hunting for girls. One of my girlfriends was named Carmen. Carmen had a good friend named Gloria who we called Bigotes because she had a little moustache. Since I was with Carmen, we decided that

Tica would go with Bigotes. I thought that must've been intimidating to Tica because Bigotes had a lot more facial hair than he did.

Rain or shine, we were in the dugouts making out. I usually went to the south side and Tica went to the other one. Those casetas were our love nests. With the light from the moon, it was very romantic inside lying there on the bench. Coincidentally, many nights I ended up being there at the same time as my brother Bombin and his girlfriends.

Why did I take so many girls there? Because I could. And because I was looking for someone who I thought was beautiful and who I enjoyed talking to. I wanted a girl with an adventurous spirit, like me. A girl who was kind and funny and not too easy. Someone who would challenge me. And I only found that girl once in Chihuahua.

But I was young. I wasn't ready to settle down. I knew the ropes with girls. I knew how to talk to them and what to talk about. I knew how to pick them up and how to romance them with my conversation and kisses. On many nights, my friends would take girls to the casetas and only get a tiny kiss, when in the other one, I would get the girl to make out with me. I'm sure the girls had different ideas than I did. I would be thinking about how it was all really fun but she was not for me; at the same time, I'm sure she was thinking about how we would be together and about how she was my girlfriend. And I would not have mentioned the word girlfriend to her at all. Still, these girls were probably creating mental relationships to explain why we were here together.

One weekend, me and Tica went to a neighborhood by la Ferro. We saw this petite, brown-haired girl sitting on a porch. Tica was in instant love. "Oh my God. I like that girl a lot," he said to me.

She was probably about sixteen and he was eighteen. He liked the girl so much, I didn't want to take her away from him so I decided to befriend her. I went and talked to her. She probably thought I was hitting on her, but I had other plans. "Do you think you would like to meet my friend?" I asked, careful not to flirt.

"I want to see what he looks like," she said. "I want to go closer so that I can see him, but I don't want him to see me."

So I took her over to where she could look at him without him seeing.

"That looks like a nice guy," she said when she saw him. He always wore a button up shirt, clean pants and more than enough cologne.

"I'd like to double date with you guys. Do you have a friend for me?" I asked her.

"Yes," she said so I went back and told Tica that she said yes and we were on. He was smiling so hard when we came back walking to pick her and her friend up. The friend, Rosa, was really pretty, probably twenty years old, but there was something weird with her teeth. We talked and, after a closer examination, I knew that I didn't really like her. But we walked toward the casetas anyway. Rosa was cute and young, but she had these yellow and brown teeth plus a forty-year-old body. She was kind of chunky with pistolas—too big through the hips for me.

The four of us walked through the streets of my neighborhood, looking at the stars. We talked about our lives. Rosa was such a kind person. She liked animals and soccer and like me, she loved Pumas. I could always tell when girls liked me and she liked me.

We walked on to the casetas. Tica and his new friend sat and talked on the bleachers. I took Rosa into a caseta and we immediately starting kissing. Rosa was one of these girls that thought that once we passed some time talking, we were instantly in a relationship.

Having my car, Motoraso, gave me a great advantage. I could drive around and quickly find the girls I knew. I could also drop them off quickly when necessary. When Rosa asked,

"Would you like to come and meet my parents?" I freaked out. I had to quick think of a reason to drop her off at home without having to go inside. Meet her parents? No, way. I barely even liked this girl. So I said, "Sorry. I need to go to bed early. I have to work in the morning."

Yeah, I had to work. Work on getting another girl. I had brought Tica and his new friend with me when I dropped Rosa off. Coincidentally, Tica's new friend had another friend who wanted to meet me. So we went and talked to her. Her name was Betty. Betty was cuter than Rosa—really cute, actually. She had light hair, a slim, nice body and a cute face.

We all went back to the baseball field and hung out talking on the bleachers. I was talking with Betty on the back row for about an hour while Tica and his new friend talked together in the first row. We had a lot of attraction for each other and as we talked, we touched and kissed. And throughout all of it, she managed to talk a lot. She was pretty, but she talked and talked. Would she ever stop?

Betty and I were on the bleachers for awhile, but when the caseta was free, we hurried to it. Betty was older and she was fast so things happened quickly.

Afterwards, Betty was talking non-stop. Again. She talked on and on about her work, then she talked about how all these guys wanted to go out with her.

I'm sure they did. She was really hot. Maybe they didn't know how much she talked.

"I'm playing soccer tomorrow," I said, "so I need to take you home."

"That's O.K. It's getting late and I need to go home, too. I have so much to do tomorrow y voy a ir a mimis, you know beauty sleep is really important for..."

Yeah. I dropped her off.

When I left with Betty, who was still talking, Tica and his friend were on the bleachers, still talking. When I got back to the ball field, there they were, still talking and now they were giggling. "I'm out of here," I said and decided to go for a little cruise in my car. I didn't want to bother them.

While cruising, I spotted a friend who had just gotten off of the bus. The late shift at the maquilas was from three to one-thirty. It was my old friend with benefits, Diana. She waved at me and I pulled my car over. She was with two other nineteen-year-olds. "Do you girls want to go get some nieves?" I asked them, but only Diana said yes. "Que padre," I said, "but I need to go to the house and park my car first."

"Can we go hang out at the baseball field?" she asked me.

"OK." I said, a little surprised. Diana was cute, nice and slutty. She had once told me, "You know I only date guys with cars, Chispa. When I go to the club, the first thing I look at is a guy's shoes. If he has dusty shoes, forget that chulo."

Diana and I hung out under the moon on the bleachers. I enjoyed sitting there just talking with her. I really was OK just talking. But the next thing I knew she was all over me. And she was getting aggressive. Tica and his friend were hugging now and looking at the stars. "Muy romantico," I thought. The caseta was open the whole time because it was after one-thirty and Tica and his muchacha sat there just talking, enjoying each other's company.

I wasn't trying to be horrible to girls. But what was I supposed to do when Diana attacked me? Run away? Call the cops? Yell, "Ayudame! Come and save me, Fago!" Hell, no. Mexican pride, wuey.

I really wanted to find the right girl. But always something was missing.

And maybe I was too picky, but maybe I wasn't meant to be with a Mexican girl.

I remember talking to my mom under the stars many nights at la huerta. "When will you find a girlfriend, Chispa?" she would ask me.

I told her, "Amá, my girl is not in Chihuahua. I haven't found her. My girl is going to have glasses and really light hair." I also knew that someday I would come to the states and have a little huerita, a blonde little girl. And I do.

I found my lady, too. In fact, when I met her, we would spend hours and hours just talking and laughing, like Tica did on the bleachers that night with the girl who later became his wife.

La Feria por una cerveza
Beer Money

It was a Friday afternoon like many others. As usual, Camelia was standing out in front of Cleofas' little store asking everyone who came by for enough money to buy a cerveza. It didn't matter who walked past. Camelia would ask anyone for 100 pesos to buy a cajuama of beer, which was like a forty-ouncer.

Camelia was tall and dark with pitch black hair and a lot of pits in his face. Camelia, who was Chupis' brother, was one of only two good Saucedo brothers and was actually my favorite of all of them. There were eight brothers in that family; Camelia was number four. Unlike his other brothers, Camelia never messed with us and he loved and respected my dad. He had played baseball with my oldest brother, Chentito.

He had begged for beer money on that corner for many years. But it wasn't because he didn't have a job. He worked with his brother, Alejandro, texturing walls of houses. He was around twenty-five years old, and he was so tight with the money he earned, he didn't want to spend it. He would rather stand outside the neighborhood market and hit other people up for money to buy beer than spend his own.

It was after work, five or six in the afternoon. And, like I said before, it was a Friday. Construction people usually worked from six to six Monday through Thursday and on Friday, pay day, they worked only half day. On Fridays they got out of work at twelve o'clock.

Camelia stood on the corner wearing his golf shirt with the varying width stripes of gray and black and his black dickies pants—his cholo suit. He had already been drinking at the corner all afternoon, drinking off of other people's money.

He wasn't the only one to beg on the corner. It was common for the neighborhood cholos to go to this one corner to ask for money from anyone who passed by. Since everybody in the colonia was afraid of them, people would typically just stop and give them what they wanted. Beer money. Strangely enough, the cholos didn't directly ask people to give them money. Instead, they'd say, "Hey. Let me borrow one-hundred pesos, so I can buy a cerveza." If someone didn't cooperate and didn't hand over enough cash for a cajuama, Camelia or one of the other guys would get violent. If the person said, "No, I don't have money," the cholo pulled a knife or other weapon out of his pants and demanded, "Give me some money, or I'll stab you with this knife."

He'd been standing there for a couple of hours drinking beer and sniffing glue when Platanito walked toward the store to buy something for his family. Platanito was a real life Tarahumara Indian who was married to a neighbor girl. He was short and dark with thick, black, medium-length hair. He was passive-looking, like he wouldn't fight with anyone. He was one of those people who appeared peaceful unless you looked for a couple of seconds into his eyes. Those eyes were intense and proud and could show you that Platanito was a man who would fight for what he believed in. But you had to look carefully.

Platanito spoke mainly the Tarahumara language and could only speak a little Spanish. His wife was only part Tarahumara and she was very pretty but very dark.

Camelia proceeded to ask Platanito for money. But Platanito was known for not letting anyone take advantage of him. Just recently, he had been involved in another fight with Polo Saucedo, Camelia's brother, and he had won, kicked ass, actually.

In Chihuahua when you fight with someone in a clean, one-on-one fight, if you win, the person you beat up along with their family members will respect you and, therefore, leave you alone. But the Saucedo's didn't play by the same rules that every other family in my neighborhood did. The unwritten code of ethics did not belong to them.

A couple of months before, Platanito and his wife had been walking in the street near Cleofas' store and the Saucedo brothers were standing there. It was normal that a bunch of bachelors at the corner would whistle at pretty girls when they walked by.

That day, the Saucedos, including Camelia, took the liberty of whistling at Platanito's wife as she passed by. "Mamacita, quiero," they said. "Que buena estás!" (Hey baby, I want you. You're so fine!) True, Platanito didn't know exactly what they were saying, his Spanish being limited, but he didn't need to understand Spanish to know that the Saucedos were messing with his wife.

Platanito, with his honorable Native American nature, marched up to the group. "What you say not very nice. Would you like if I whistle at your mother and tell her she beautiful? If I call her mamacita…is this nice for her? You think I do not know what you say. I not speak Spanish good, but I know what you say to my wife."

The five Saucedo brothers all laughed, and then someone said, sarcastically, "I'm sorry." Of course, none of them were sorry, but, for the moment, their insincere apology worked, and Platanito and his wife turned around and started walking away. They hadn"t walked more than a few steps away when the Saucedos started in again, this time with, "Mi'ja…mamacita..tu estás una chica buena."

This time Platanito could not hold his anger. He may have been a little man but, when he turned to face the Saucedos, his pitch black eyes were filled with fury. His feet were set fearlessly, "Why you say these things to my wife? My people do not show bravery by insulting a woman. We show through fight with machete or other weapon, man to man. I will fight one of you. You choose who fight."

The brothers talked and chose Polo. He took boxing classes, and they were certain that because he was much larger and thicker, he was going to take Platanito easily in the fight. There was a lot of commotion and a big gathering of people— the whole neighborhood was showing up to watch the fight on this already stifling Saturday morning.

Like a cold-blooded asshole would, Polo hit Platanito before he was ready. He punched him in the chin with so much force that he went down. Polo was on the ground ready to jump on Platanito and pound on him when Platanito surprisingly recouped, jumped up, and went for Polo's legs. He dove, grabbed, and brought Polo down in one swift motion, then moved effortlessly on top of him. On the ground, size no longer mattered.

I watched, impressed and shocked. Platanito was a good fighter. Although his moves were nothing fancy, he had learned how to compensate for any disadvantages of his short stature. He held Polo down and punched him over and over until his face was a pile of meat and blood. It was a good old-fashioned ground and pound. Nothing fancy, just effective. The other Saucedo brothers were shocked.

The entire time they stood around their brother looking as if they were ready and wanting to jump in. But, no, this was a real fight of honor, one-on-one. And the whole neighborhood was there, so this time, the Saucedos had no choice but to be honorable. Jumping in would not have been acceptable.

As he lay on the ground, bloody, Polo sighed, "Ya estuvo (I've had enough)" and asked to be let go. Platanito told him, "I will not stop until you ask forgiveness." Polo didn't say anything, so Platanito beat him more. About thirty seconds later, Polo, even more bloodied, asked forgiveness.

Platanito stood up proudly and calmly, and turned to go. "I do not like to fight," he said to the brothers, "but if that is the only way you leave me alone, I will fight any one of you." He turned and walked away with his wife at his side, embracing her.

Platanito was lucky on that day that none of the five Saucedos were either drugged up or drunk. Just two weeks before, the brothers had gone crazy and had sent someone to the hospital. It had been the worst beating I had ever seen in my whole life.

As Fago and I watched Camelia more, we noticed he was now terrorizing the neighbors who walked by with a small knife in the front of his pants. He pulled it on Patanito and said, "I need one thousand pesos."

Platanito's rage from the month before seemed to return. He said in response, "If you want money, you get job!"

Camelia said, "I have a job. I make more money than you."

"Why do you abuse? Why you need my money if you have job? If you want my money, be like man and take it."

"You bet I will." Camelia grabbed a machete from the back of his pants. In the front of his pants was a short knife. Fago and I saw him pull the small one out at the same time and casually throw it to the ground.

At this point, Fago and I had been at the corner having fun watching Camelia take people's money for an hour and a half. During that time, he had taken money from about ten people, and he had shown the knife to about eight of them. We had known that at some point there was going to be a fight, as soon as someone refused to give him the money. Every time he did this, we always knew it was just a matter of time. And we were always curious to see who it would be. Fago and I didn't anticipate that Platanito would be the one to resist, and now we were impressed with the big cajones he had.

Camelia had pulled the big machete out of the back of his pants. But Platanito had a surprise for him. We always knew that the Indios carried knives, so this was going to be a fun fight to watch. We were just waiting, our adrenaline rushing, to see what kind of a knife Platanito would pull. Without a word, he pulled it and there it was. A short machete, about one and a half feet long. This knife had a piece sticking out in front at a right angle—we called it az (oz).

Now that Camelia and Platanito had seen each others' knives, they pulled their shirts off and wrapped them around their left forearms to protect their exposed skin from the sharpness of each others' weapons.

For the past hour or two, me and Fago had been standing about five feet from Camelia, but now we cleared out of the area. We hurried across the street to stand on the opposite sidewalk. By then there were a bunch of people filling up the street to watch, so we walked up behind them, standing room only, to watch, too.

Camelia clearly hated Platanito because he had kicked his brother Polo's ass. He wasn't ever mean to us, but there were certain people he didn't like and those people were the ones he messed with and tried to beat without mercy. But his brothers were complete jerks. Most of them tried to fight everybody.

Camelia's knife was much larger than Platanito's. With it, he ran in close and tried to slash Platanito in the chest, but Platanito avoided the knife with his agility and quickness. Camelia was actually quite skilled with the machete, and he wanted to get Platanito at all costs, so after returning to his corner for a moment, he attacked again, slashing Platanito's forearm. At that moment I realized that Platanito had been trying to avoid the fight. That was until he got cut. The moment he got cut, his eyes wore a new type of look, and his movements were violently clad as he clearly attempted to slash Camelia.

As they ran in and out of an imaginary ring attacking each other over and over, their knives crashed like swords a few times. There were actually sparks. Before too long, each opponent had several slashes on his hands. Camelia was a good machete fighter—he had won several fights and injured some people, but because Platanito was a natural fighter, he was even more skillful and deliberate and was able to get the upper hand by waiting patiently for his chance.

The next moment was almost surreal. It is in my ears still today, a sound like I had not heard before...as if a large chunk of human meat was being sliced. I kept looking at Fago and then back at Camelia.

Platanito's knife had done its job.

I never thought a knife could do that to a person, cut through the skin so clean. Camelia then made a grunting noise that seemed to come from deep within his gut. He dropped the big machete with a clang into the street, grabbed his stomach, and said, "I give up."

Within seconds he fell backward, showing a huge, bleeding gash in his stomach.

Platanito seemed immediately aware that he had inflicted a mortal wound. He looked down at his hands as if he couldn't believe they had done it, then at Camelia, and then he turned and ran.

Nobody seemed to notice when Platanito fled.

The neighbors were all standing still in shock, too busy gazing in horror at Camelia. Somebody, I can't remember who, tried to help him up, and I watched his guts fall out of his stomach. Some others laid him down carefully in the middle of the street. His whole body convulsed in spasm after spasm. Cuco had been the only one of his brothers there watching the fight, and now the rest of the Saucedo's closed in on the crowd.

"Who did this to my brother?" one of them demanded of the crowd, who stood in shocked silence. Cuco calmly beckoned to his brothers, calling them all together, and they talked in quick shouts. Moments after, they split up, searching around the area, most likely for Platanito.

Cuco then left running and came back driving his truck. Camelia lay there on that slab of street until his brothers placed his intestines back into his stomach cavity, lifted him with blood-stained hands into the back of the truck, and took off down the street at high speed, leaving only a bloody smear on the concrete.

No one bothered to call an ambulance. It would've taken at least an hour for it to arrive.

Camelia could never have lived through that devastating

wound. He forgot to respect the code of honor, and he died three hours later. Platanito left the colonia. We never saw him again.

CHILE MAKES US BRAVE

4. *MASCOTAS*
PETS

El Murcielago
The Bat

When I was a kid, I loved animals and I was always messing with them—doing experiments on them and interacting with them. And since my dad was a baseball coach in my neighborhood in Chihuahua, I spent a lot of time at the baseball fields.

One night, when I was about eleven years old, I saw some murciélagos near the field. They would fly around as it got dark, but I was disappointed that I could never get close enough to really examine one.

I would climb around in the trees looking for birds, but one evening I was excited when I found no birds, just a little bat. He looked like a little tiny mouse; he was actually the size of a small hamster. His wingspan was about five inches long and his wings were flat with opaque brownish skin holding visible bones inside. The bat was stuck in a little hole in the tree trunk. I thought he must be injured. And, when I looked at him closer, one of his wings appeared to be broken. I picked him up, held him, and petted his soft fur.

When Fago saw me with the bat, he came over. "Look what I have." I came down from the tree and opened up my bare hands. There was the bat, trying to escape. I had to grasp and ungrasp my hands to keep him from getting away and at the same time allow my friends to look at him. He looked ugly, like a wet mouse with a lot of balding spots.

"Estas loco? They have teeth. That bat's gonna' suck your blood out!" my friend Jose Luis said.

"Don't touch it, pinche Chispa!" some other boys told me, but I was so fascinated with my new pet, I refused to listen to them.

I noticed my dad looking over at me as I was showing people my bat. Later, as I stood proudly near the dug-out with my new pet in my hand, my dad said, "Chispa, put the bat down. They carry diseases. I told you before not to play with them."

So I walked away and put my bat in a safe place where mi papa couldn't see him. Then I hurried back to my house and looked around for a shoe box. I carried the box the two blocks back to the baseball fields, found my bat, and put him inside. By then it was getting dark so I took the bat home without my dad seeing anything. At home, I grabbed a screwdriver from my box of tools, poked holes in the cardboard so the bat could breathe, and hid the box in my room under my bed. Once I pushed the box underneath the bed, I could hear the bat's wings flapping around inside. So I grabbed a blanket from a pile in the corner and wrapped it around the box; hopefully no one would hear my bat inside of there.

During the day when my parents weren't aware, I would bring my friends into my room to show them the murciélago. They all thought it was cool to have a bat for a pet. And my bat's wing was getting stronger because every day I put a feast of crickets and huge cockroaches inside the box with him. At first when I tried to feed him in the daylight, he refused the yummy insects, so later, after someone told me to keep him away from the light because he could go blind, I fed him in semi or complete darkness. In darkness he happily ate.

I took care of his wing, too. When my chickens were hurt, I put a purple ointment on their wounds and, after a few days, they healed. Now, I gave the same treatment to my bat. After about a week of applying the methiolade both morning and night, my bat got better. His wing was healed. The bat's fur was still ugly; he definitely wasn't beautiful and he never would be. But he grew more active in his box and I thought he was muy chingon (super badass) anyway.

One day I packed him into my school bag inside his box. Except for how hard he beat his wings inside the box, he was a quiet pet. The quietest; that's why I was able to hide him away for so long. He only made a tiny, almost inaudible, high-pitched squealing sound.

At recess, I carried my bat in his box out onto the playground. I carefully placed the box on the ground underneath a shade tree and opened it. My bat looked tired and groggy in the middle of the day. I lifted him out of the box and held him. Some kids came over and looked. "OH, A VAMPIRO!" one kid yelled and ran off. Word got around that I had a bat in my hands and then other kids came to see him. One hundred percent of the kids at school that day had never seen a bat up close before. Most of the boys thought he was really cool but it wasn't the same for the girls.

I tried to show him off to some of the cute girls I liked, but they thought he was the grossest thing that they had ever seen. "No quiero ver el animál feo," they would screech and run off all angry.

In the yard at la Huerta, my friends and I experimented with him since we wanted to find out everything we could about bats.

I fed my bat pop with a syringe. My friends and I gave him water, beer, even blood. He drank everything. But, of course, he was forced.

One day, my friend Ramon Pelos Quietos (fuzzy hair)

came to la Huerta. He had a cigarette in his pocket. We had been experimenting so much with my bat, I always thought, "I wonder if the bat can do this, I wonder if the bat can do that," about everything. This time I thought, "I wonder if a bat can smoke a cigarette." So we tried. My friend lit the cigarette with his dad's lighter and the end burned hot and red. I carefully placed the cigarette in the bat's mouth, and he took a real puff of it. He actually smoked it just like a person would and then coughed afterward.

I was able to hide my bat for about three weeks. But because my friends and I had been pulling him out of the box so much to perform our experiments on him, I became afraid my dad would find out. So when my friend Tica offered me five pesos in exchange for my bat, I didn't turn him down. I sold my murcielago, afraid that my dad would be disappointed in me for not listening to him.

El perro de mis suenos
The Dog of my Dreams

One Saturday I was playing with my friends Matteo, Tica, and Julian by the river. The river was about three blocks from my house along the edge of my colonia. We called it rio de aguas negras, the black water river. When I was a tiny kid, the river was clean and people fished there, but now waste from factories and humans was being dumped into the water and the river was ugly and polluted. People now used the banks of the river as their own big garbage dump and since Chihuahua had so little rain, the river bed was usually dry. When it did rain, the water level would rise and fresh water would seem to cleanse the blackness for a week or so. But we hadn't had rain in days so the river was its usual black color and the water barely flowed.

My friends and I left our houses in the late morning and walked to aguas negras to search for glass bottles. We were going to play our usual game. In this game, we threw bottles up in the air, fighting them as if they were roosters. Whichever bottle shattered in midair first was the losing "rooster".

That day we walked and then ran beside the river, choosing the best bottles—the less likely to shatter the better. Since I had decided the tequila bottles with thick bottoms were the best, those were the ones I always looked for, and again today, I was hunting for one. The four of us had been breaking bottles for a couple of hours when Julian said, "Listen! What is that?"

We all got quiet. A whining sound was coming from somewhere close by. None of us could figure out exactly what this sound was, but it sounded like the crying of some kind of baby animal. None of us said anything else; we were focused on finding bottles, so we ignored it and just walked on next to the river.

The sound was getting louder—I noticed some boxes and bags piled up nearby.

"Why don't you look through the boxes, Chispa?" my friend Matteo said when he noticed just how distracted I was.

So I walked over to the pile.

I picked through boxes while my friends stood close by, holding rocks to throw. In the past, we had found huge rats living in the trash piles by the river. When they ran out from under boxes or lurched from their homes in the piles of trash, we pounded them with rocks until we killed them. After the rats stopped breathing, we would dangle their corpses from sticks and bring them home to show off to friends and to prove our bravery to pretty little neighborhood girls who we hoped to impress.

Our rats were our trophies. And our trophies could also include snakes, lizards, and sometimes even skunks.

After I had rummaged through several bags and still had found nothing, the whining became much louder. I was puzzled. My friends stood close to me, watching and waiting to pound the mystery animal with the rocks they held in their hands. We all wondered out loud about what we might find. "I think it's a mangy dog," Julian said.

"Maybe it's a squirrel," Tica laughed.

"What kind of sound does the zorillo (skunk) make?" he asked me, laughing. Zorillo was the name my friends had given to me because I wet the bed so much.

Many times people abandoned dying dogs with missing eyes or worms crawling in their wounds down by the river. Aware that I might find something disgusting, I carefully picked up bags and boxes and dropped them back down in another pile. I picked up one more dirty box from the pile and that was when I saw him. He was fragile-looking and appeared to be very hungry. He was digging through the bags with his front paws and sniffing the ground, most likely trying to find something he could eat.

Strangely, the hungry, dirty animal that we found that day by the river turned out to be the cutest yellow dog I had ever seen in my life. And even though he was tiny, his feet were humongous. He was skinny, probably from malnutrition, but he looked to be about one month old. When I looked closely at him, I could tell this puppy was going to become a very big dog.

My friends and I all talked at the same time. "Oh, this dog is really nice," we agreed.

This dog was unusual to us. All of the dogs in our colonia were weird mixtures and none of them were nice to look at. They were all strange sizes and shapes. Most were not well cared for so their coats were matted and dirty.

But this dog was special. He was a pure breed, it was obvious. We all agreed that even though skinny and dirty, this was the most beautiful dog we had ever seen.

"I want to take him to my house," I said, "I think mi papa will let me keep him."

"No. I want him," Matteo said.

We all wanted that dog, the one who was so different and special.

Tica, Matteo, Julián and I all argued for a while until, finally, we agreed that bottle fights would settle who would win the perrito and earn the honor of taking him home. We "fought" our bottles until only Matteo and I were left.

Now hundreds of tiny butterflies fluttered their wings inside my stomach. The winner would get this special dog. Even through my butterflies, I still felt confident, since I had been fighting my big Tequila bottle. That bottle had brought me to the finals. But Matteo, who had a smaller bottle, requested time to look for a new, stronger bottle so he had a better chance of taking home this most beautiful dog.

Matteo walked away and moved along the edge of the

river; I prayed to my God that my friend would not find a bottle larger and stronger than mine.

About ten minutes later, Matteo returned to us with a new bottle. It was a glass water bottle, the kind that you refilled at the big supermercado. It was as big and as strong as my Tequila bottle. I started to worry.

We went to our places and uno, dos, tres, threw our bottles up to clash in the air. When the two bottles collided, my bottle cracked on contact and fell onto the blackened ground. I bent over and picked up my cracked bottle and almost cried because I knew it would break in the next "fight". And, just as I had feared, in the next bottle collision, the worst possible happened. My bottle broke into a thousand little pieces.

I cried out loud.

I had prayed to Dios to let me be the one to take the little dog home. But now I guessed that my God had other plans; I had lost the fight and the dog was Matteo's. And now Matteo was the happiest kid in the neighborhood. Not me.

By the time our bottle fight was over, it was getting late, so we all decided to go home. My friends and I had played at the river all day long.

As I trudged home, I couldn't believe how much sadness I felt. "My dog," I thought. I had had so many plans for that dog.

And I was the one who had found him. But in my family, I had learned to always play fair and my brothers and I weren't allowed to take things from others that didn't belong to us. Matteo had won the dog fair and square and now el perrito wasn't mine to take.

"I want you guys to know that I'm going to take really good care of this dog," Matteo told us. I guess since he was a couple of years older than the other three of us, he understood that we needed to be reassured that he rightfully deserved the perrito.

Matteo's familia had a reputation for being cruel to animals. His big brothers fought roosters against my big brothers. If their rooster lost or ran before his fight was over, they would kill the rooster with a baseball bat.

Matteo's big brother Polo Patas de Atole (thick, clumsy feet) was in his twenties. He killed pigs and made them into carnitas for a living. It was well-known that he killed the pigs cruelly by hitting them over the heads with a baseball bat. Pigs have very thick skulls so their skulls do not crush easily. Many times, when Polo killed the pigs, we could hear them screaming throughout the neighborhood for long minutes before they finally died. I was understandably worried for the puppy.

But Matteo took us to his house and showed us where he was going to keep the dog. Matteo had a chicken house that he was going to convert into a house for el perrito. The house would include carpet for the dog to sleep on—the dog would have a nice place to live in. I now felt a little better. I really hoped the dog would be O.K.

I had managed to reach Matteo's house without showing all of my disappointment, but after leaving my friends, I began to cry out loud.

By the time I got home, I was crying very hard. I had always wanted a dog, but my dad would never get one because he would only accept one that was pure-bred. And there was never a pure-breed dog available that my family could afford.

So I knew that my dad would have approved of that dog. But I had failed to win him and bring him home. Now I had lost my only chance at the dog of my dreams.

The very next day I was still completely sad, but when I told my dad about the dog and how I had found him, then lost him to Matteo, he surprised me. "Chispa, if you really want the dog, maybe we could trade something for him."

That was a great idea! I had eight chickens, and my dad said that possibly we could trade the family Centeno some of my chickens for the dog. I loved my dad's idea and I was hopeful. What a smart papá I had. I had never considered that with a little creative thought and a good trade the dog might be mine.

That day was Sunday. Curious about what the day would bring, I walked to Matteo's house to ask him how the dog had slept. When Matteo opened the door for me, he was crying hard. My heart sank. Had something bad happened to the perrito?

"Why are you crying?" I asked my friend.

"When my father got home yesterday, I got in trouble for bringing the dog," he said through sobs, his mocos rattling as he sniffed them in, hard. "I got whipped by mi papá. He won't let me keep the puppy."

I knew Matteo's dad was strict and I guessed that bringing a dog home without talking about it first was not acceptable behavior. I could identify. If I had brought the dog home without my dad's consent, I probably would've gotten whipped or hit by the stick, too. I was sorry, but when I heard the news, I couldn't help it. A huge smile came on my face.

"It's not funny. Why are you laughing?" Matteo asked looking angry, although he continued to cry and sniff in his mocos.

I wasn't trying to smile and I was sorry. "I really wanted the dog and you knew it. I'm not trying to be mean, Matteo. " I couldn't believe it. I knew the dog was mine. And mi papá had already given his consent.

I tied a shoelace loosely around mi perrito's neck and led him home. That was the luckiest Sunday ever. The little dog was mine and I hadn't even had to trade any of my chickens for him. I walked through my neighborhood leading the puppy home with a huge smile, the happiest kid in the world.

Since I already had chickens, I emptied out one chicken house for my puppy. And since we had no carpet in my house, I found some old clothes to cover the floor and keep him warm. In the late afternoon, I tied the puppy up on the patio.

My puppy would be safe and my dad would like him, I knew. This dog was so cool! His bark was not a puppy bark. It was a big, deep, adult woof, which was good for me.

I knew the history of my dad and grandpa when it came to dogs. The two of them would throw female puppies in the river because female dogs are so difficult—they are always in heat and are getting pregnant. Other male dogs are always hanging around. My dad just thought female dogs were a nuisance so he would never keep one. But this big, deep bark ensured that my dog was male, my dad would accept him and we would keep him.

I think the moment my dad saw the beauty of my dog and heard his deep, male bark, he immediately fell in love with mi perrito.

All day I had been thinking about a name for my dog. Finally, I remembered that there was a T.V. show that had a dog on it just like mine so I decided to call him "Pipo". That evening I asked my parents about the name and they approved it right away.

My friend Pachito's father, Francisco, had a chicken farm in my neighborhood. Francisco killed the chickens and sold the parts from his 1950's Chevy truck, "Pechuga de pollo. Pierna de pollo. Rica y sabrosa, la pechuga de pollo!" He would advertise the chicken breasts and legs that he sold, shouting into a loud speaker as his wife drove through the neighborhoods in their little white truck with a camper on the bed.

When neighbors heard Francisco's voice announcing the great flavor of his chicken, they hurried out of their houses and headed to the truck with their cash. Dona Amelia would stop the little truck, and Don Francisco would sell whole pollos or cut up pieces from his spot at the back of the camper. There were always parts of the chicken that Pachito's father couldn't sell, like feet and organs. My dad would buy those parts at a discounted price and my mom would make them into wonderful smelling soups for my Pipo.

It wasn't long before Pipo was getting huge. By then, he and I were having so much fun together. We ran around the neighborhood or went hunting and Pipo took René's place as my best friend.

Soon Pipo was getting big and we played and wrestled every day after school. But, by then my beautiful yellow lab Pipo had developed a reputation—he was known to some neighbors as the teror of colonia Josefa.

Since he was so huge and full of energy, many neighbors were afraid of him. And they claimed he hunted their chickens and ducks. Berta and Charritas, our next door neighbors on either side, insisted that when their animals disappeared, Pipo had killed them. But my dad swore it wasn't Pipo. Pipo was such a good dog; we just couldn't imagine that he would kill anything. I often caught him chasing the neighborhood animals, but I knew he was only playing.

At that time, I had ten chickens and three roosters of my own and Pipo never bothered them. But my chickens lived a block away at la huerta and were fenced in. The other animals ran all over the streets—easy targets.

One day mi mamá complained that she smelled something awful outside her bedroom window. In that spot, my mom had a cute little fenced in garden with rose bushes, an apricot tree and several other plants. After she complained of the smell, I walked into the garden and dug up a little dirt, hunting for the source of the odor. There in the garden, I found Pipo's buried treasure.

It was strange. Every time I wanted to play with Pipo, I

whistled for him and he came to me from God knows where. That day in the garden, I found what appeared to be one of his several hide-outs. Under the window were four or five gutted bird carcasses; one duck, three or four chickens, one huge rabbit and one cat.

The minute I found them, I thought of throwing the dead animals away so Pipo wouldn't get into trouble. But I couldn't lie to my dad. I knew that he would find out later and I would get whipped with the stick or get spanked.

When my dad got home, I told him what I had found. I hated every bit of it, but I said, "I think it was Pipo," anyway. Really, I knew it was Pipo. He was always interested in the chickens and he chased them a lot. And chickens had always been a problem in my neighborhood. Many of them ran all over and destroyed gardens. In fact, neighbors who tried to keep nice gardens were happy when chickens would turn up missing. The neighbors whose chickens were vanishing were the only ones complaining.

After having admitted to mi papá that my Pipo was to blame, I was very concerned that my dad might get rid of my dog. I knew my dad was so assertive that he would never ask me. One day, my Pipo would just disappear.

But mi papá surprised me again when he said, "You know, it's actually a good thing that Pipo killed those animals. The chickens dug holes in both Amá's and Doña Andrea's gardens and ate the plants, and the ladies were very annoyed by it." Because Pipo killed the animals who were pests, my dad decided to give him another chance.

Chuy el mudito (the mute) was a small boy. But he was tough. I once saw Chuy fighting with Chucas who was twenty-five years old when he was only fifteen, and Chuy had beaten up Chucas! Chuy may have been short, but it didn't matter because he was very strong. He would wrestle people to the ground and then beat them up once they were down.

I was very afraid of Chuy.

Chuy was nice to me in elementary school, but after that, I don't know what had happened. He was now about fourteen and was again terrorizing all of the kids in the neighborhood. Since I was the smallest eleven-year old, he was especially abusive to me.

When I was on my way to Cleofas' store to buy galletas, he would slap me with his open hand on the back of my head as hard as he could. Any time I was at the store or anywhere else in the colonia, Chuy mudito was looking for me, waiting inside or outside just so he could hit me. He would ambush me and smack me in the front or the back of the head really hard and then run away. Chuy did that to most every kid my age—he did it to Fago, too.

By the time Pipo got older, he followed me everywhere I went – to my friends' houses, to the store, and down all of the streets. So wherever I was, there was Pipo. And now Pipo wasn't a puppy. He was two years old—a huge eighty-five-pounder with paws bigger than most other labs.

One day, a bunch of kids were out in the street between my house and Irma Cabeza de Oso's (bear head's) house playing some games. None of us liked Chuy mudito, so when he asked us if he could play, we all said no. Of course Chuy got mad, and as he walked away, hit me in the back of the head as usual. Then he tried to run off, but Pipo was there. Something must've snapped inside of mi perro, because as Chuy ran, Pipo chased after him and bit him hard on his back.

Pipo wouldn't let go of Chuy's pants—it almost looked like my dog was trying to rip his pants off. Pipo had bitten him in the back. Now, Pipo dug his strong jaws into Chuy again. Chuy was bleeding and crying. He had to be hurting so bad; plus, he was afraid of dogs. He always was afraid of my Pipo, but he hadn't been careful and he hadn't seen Pipo start running after him. Pipo just did what dogs do. When you run, they chase you. So Pipo chased Chuy and Pipo must've been angry, too, because I was his person and Pipo had seen Chuy hit me over and over again, so many times.

I was slow to help Chuy because I was too busy enjoying the moment. Chuy had been terrorizing me for many years. But after a couple of minutes of Pipo attacking, I went and retrieved him. He let go of Chuy at my command and Chuy limped away to his house.

The next morning Chuy's grandparents came over seeking reimbursement from my mom and dad. "Your dog bit Chuy yesterday," Chuy's grandma said.

"I know," my dad returned, "and I'm very sorry."

"Has your dog had his shots? We weren't sure, so we took Chuy to the hospital. We had to pay two-hundred pesos for that shot."

"Yes, he has." We took care of Pipo well, unlike many other dog owners in the colonia.

"We need you to pay for the shot, or we will have to turn your dog in to the city." My dad knew that if he gave them nothing, Pipo would be captured and put to sleep. So he agreed to give them the money which he paid them at the end of the week.

People in the neighborhood started to talk again. Earlier, they had been complaining about Pipo killing the small animals and now they were talking about the "vicious attack" on Chuy mudito. Of course they never mentioned how Chuy was a bully to all of the neighborhood kids.

The next week, when the neighbors had finally forgotten about how Pipo had bitten Chuy so violently, we were playing games again in the same place in the street. That day Juana, Chuy's sister, came to play with us. Somehow Pipo got really upset again and this time bit Juana in the butt and on the leg. When Pipo went after her, I tried to grab him, but it was too late.

Once again Chuy's parents came and asked for money, a lot of money this time. When mi papá told them, "There's no way I can pay," they responded saying they would call the city. That week I cried and worried that the city truck would come and capture my dog.

But before that could happen, my dad sat me down for a talk. "I don't want your dog to be put to sleep, Chispa," he said. "I've found some people on a farm that will take him. You will never see him again, but I want you to know that your dog is not going to die."

I couldn't believe I was going to lose my Pipo.

I had worked so hard for him and spent so many hours playing with him. I loved him and he loved me. What would we do without each other? I cried and cried until I couldn't.

It was three o'clock the next afternoon when mi papá told me it was time. I hugged Pipo for the last time as he looked at me with his trusting brown eyes and his tongue hanging out, panting. The tears covered and stained my face as my dad loaded him into the back of his little truck and drove slowly down the street. Pipo stood looking at me as they rounded the corner heading toward the highway. My dog did not know he would never see me again. It was devastating to lose him but at least mi perro would be allowed to survive.

Over the next few years, I would sometimes mention to my dad that I wanted to go to the farm where Pipo lived so that I could see him. But my dad would always put me off. "Maybe next month", "next weekend", or "another time". That went on until I was fourteen or fifteen. I missed Pipo; I loved my dog so much and he was my all-time favorite pet.

Right before I left Chihuahua for good, I asked my dad what happened to Pipo. I knew something wasn't right with what he said. "At the time I knew it was best to tell you he went to the farm," my dad had said, "but actually, I took Pipo to the city and they said they would probably have to put him to sleep."

Back then, my dad just didn't have the heart to tell me that Pipo would die, and although it was possible that he was quarantined and set free, mi Pipo, the dog of my dreams, had most likely been put down the day after my dad drove him away. He was only three years old.

Paco el Puerco
Paco the Pig

One summer when I was about ten years old, my grandma, Mamá Chiquita, came from Sinaloa on the train. When she climbed down from the beat-up train car, she carried in her hands a wooden banana box. "What is that?" I asked. "Is it a chicken?"

"No, Chispa. It's a puerco." I thought a chicken was cool, but a PIG! That was even cooler. When my Grandma got to our house, she opened the box and out walked the cutest thing you've ever seen in your life.

He was black and furry like a little cat or dog and was very shy at first. He walked around the yard looking all over and when I tried to pick him up, he shook slightly. He squealed and sniffed when I held him in my arms and carried him all over the yard.

The pig we named Paco became immediately famous in my colonia. I would bring my friends Fago, Julian, and Tica over to la huerta and we would play with him, chasing him around the yard and petting him, as if he were a dog. Paco was only a month old when my grandma brought him so we fed him milk from a baby bottle. From that time until he was about six months old, we played with him.

But by six months, Paco had gotten big. Really big! He weighed about seventy pounds and he started to bite a lot. A pig has a very strong mouth, strong enough to chop your fingers off and because we knew this, we played with him a little less roughly now. None of us wanted to lose a finger. Before we had played with Paco at least once a week, but now we saw him very little and played with him only once in a while.

As Paco got bigger, I overheard my parents talking. "He should be very fat in a few years," my mom had said, "Nice and fat for the quínce."

By this time, I was about twelve, and I knew the plan was to eat Paco at my only sister's quinceanera. After that conversation, I learned that being eaten was Paco's main purpose in life; that was why my abuelita had brought him to us.

It didn't matter to me if he was going to be carnitas someday. Paco became our family pet and I seldom thought about what his fate would be when he fully matured.

Every night after dinner, Amá sent me outside with scraps to feed Paco. Paco ate mostly corn, frijoles, sopa and tortillas. He would put his little nose into the small bowl, snorting and gobbling up the food in seconds. As Paco grew, his appetite grew, too. Since I raised gallos, I always had many chicks running all over the yard eating corn and grasshoppers.

One day, when Paco was about one year old, he was in the yard eating the chicken feed out of the tire feeder. Gertrudis, my favorite chicken, had just had a new batch of chicks. They were cute, fluffy, all different colors: red, white, yellow, and black. Nearby was huge Paco and he was too interested. He watched the little chicks toddling around the yard, pecking at the ground for tiny pieces of food and insects.

It seemed his eyes focused in on one, a black one, and he ran off across the yard. He chased the chick for about twenty seconds, opened his mouth, and an "oof" and a few quick bites later, swallowed the chick and went over to the shade of the chicken house and lay down for his afternoon nap. This was the first of many chicks that Paco ate for dinner.

I loved Paco a lot, although I didn't love his chick-eating habit.

Often, he escaped from his little house. The little house

at la huerta was about eight feet by eight feet with a concrete floor, brick walls, and a sheet metal roof. The house had a gated door where we could let him in and out, but the door wasn't very tall. If Paco stuck his head into the latch in a certain way and jiggled it around, he could get free.

Strangely, there were only certain times he must've wanted to get out because it seemed to me he could've escaped every day if he had wanted. Because Paco loved to eat eggs and little chicks, the moment he got through the door, the chickens at la huerta went crazy. They would balk and balk and carry on, alerting all of the close neighbors. Then some neighbor would run over and yell, "Your pig is out AGAIN!"

Minutes later my brothers and I would be running around the neighborhood looking and calling for Paco. Although he wasn't very tall, he was a buff, tough pig of three-hundred pounds. He was about the height of a Rottweiler but weighed as much as four of them.

It was really fun to chase Paco. He was so huge that he couldn't run very fast. When we chased him, sometimes he would turn around and snort at us. The snort almost sounded like he was barking.

As Paco ran, a teenaged-guy could jump on his back and he would carry him around. My neighbor, Chuy Mudito, once jumped onto Paco's back, but Paco didn't like it. He ran next to the corner of a building, slamming Chuy into a wall. Chuy fell off Paco's back onto the cement and cried like a baby, which made me laugh. After the Chuy incident, if anyone would jump onto Paco's back, he would get viciously slammed into a wall. But some stupid kids never learned so we had to remind them over and over.

Even though Paco was huge and could easily carry us, we just chased him around and around until he got tired and then we steered him back into his little house.

Paco was very popular in the colonia. Everyone knew my pig and thought that his life would be spared because he was such an important part of my family. But while Paco was outside the house every day snorting and eating scraps or resting in whatever shade he could find, mi mamá and mi papá continued making plans for my sister's quinceañera. It was only going to be a neighborhood party at our house because my family didn't have that much money.

Instead of the traditional quinceaeñera, with the big party in the rented hall, the dance with D.J., the wedding-like quince dress, a huge wedding-like cake and tons of food, my sister had asked Apá for a new dress and a party at home to celebrate her fifteenth birthday.

Two days before the fiesta, as Amá was busy buying food and getting my grandma's house at la huerta clean, a man from our neighborhood knocked on the door with a big knife.

It was Polo, the neighborhood butcher. "I'm here to kill the pig," he said. Amá led him into the yard where Paco was lying in his usual place in the shade.

Polo forced Paco up from the ground and led him into the yard of tia Lupe where he would cut his throat.

None of us wanted to see Paco dying and the tears were beginning in mi mamá's eyes. Moy wanted to make sure that Paco had a dignified death because Polo was known for killing pigs very brutally with a bat. So this time the butcher carried a knife, making it clearly visible to us because Moy had specifically instructed him, "None of this baseball bat crap. You will kill our pig with a knife."

Polo was a terrible butcher but was afraid of my cholo brother, Moy, so we were sure he would follow the order.

We watched from far away and listened. We could hear Paco screaming. Polo kept stabbing him in the neck as Paco screamed for his life. A good butcher should give a pig only one stab to the heart, but Polo was the only "butcher" available that day and he wasn't even a real butcher. He stabbed our pig a bunch of times until poor Paco was bleeding badly.

Fago and I watched the knife going in over and over. But

Paco didn't die.

And then we watched as, in the end, Polo grabbed his weapon of choice, the baseball bat, and finally finished Paco when he hit him on the head for the ninth time.

In this way, our Paco died. Brutally and horribly.

When a family pig is killed, the butcher cuts the meat into strips and makes carnitas and chicharrones. So as soon as Polo had finished killing the pig, he bled the carcass and put the blood in a big vat. He heated the blood in the vat, cut the pig into strips, and cooked it.

Paco's death was filled with sadness; it felt to me like someone had killed the dog my family had had for years. If it were your family dog, could you eat it? I had just watched Polo not only kill but destroy my pig and I was mad. I was disgusted and I was heartbroken that my Paco was gone. And I wasn't a little boy anymore. I was seventeen years old and I wanted to beat up the butcher. And I probably could have since besides being my pig's killer, he was also a drug addict.

If it had been my choice, I would've kept Paco. I would've bought a pig already cut in pieces—a pig that I didn't love. But Paco's death had not been my choice to make.

On the day of the quinceañera, while everybody else was enjoying their carnitas, my mom refused the food and I admired her for it. She had been true to Paco. For a few hours, I hadn't eaten anything.

But all day, Fago had been going on and on, saying "Oh, this is so good!" and my other friends kept saying, "You're such a menso, Chispa. Just eat the pinche carnitas!" When Fago finally brought me a little plate of Paco, it looked and smelled so good. And I was so hungry. So with all of my friends around watching, I ate some.

I betrayed Paco. The carnitas were tasty, but I couldn't stop thinking about my Paco who had given his life so that I could enjoy the flavor of a little food.

5. *PROBLEMAS* y *SOLUCIONES*
PROBLEMS and SOLUTIONS

Torito

At sixteen I was still very tiny when my dad found me this job with his friend, Señor Carlos. It was my very first construction job. A lot of grown-ups didn't last at the job because we were working in one hundred and fifteen degrees under the oppressive summer sun. My dad had predicted even I wouldn't last more than two days.

Some friends from my neighborhood had tried to do the work. One by one, they had been hired for the job and one by one, they had quit. Every day, under the hot sun, we dug deep holes in the dirt with shovels for the bridge posts that would be inserted to expand the highway. We were digging the holes that hold the posts for the rails that prevent the cars from going into the river. (Here in the U.S. an auger would do what we were doing by hand.)

There I was on the third day, working and now that everyone from my neighborhood had quit, I knew no other workers.

I was kind of lonely, until along came a group of rancheros, a bunch of guys from the boonie town called General Trias who arrived every day on a special bus used specifically to carry them to the bridge. These small town "cowboys" were hard workers so the contractors sent a bus to their town every day and picked them up for work.

Something about farm boys—they're tough and don't want to look like wimps. These rancheros were tough and ever since the day I met them, they made my life a hell on earth.

The leader of the rancheros was named El Torito (the little bull). He was big and muscular. Every day he wore an unbuttoned cowboy shirt so that his bulging chest and abdominal muscles were easily visible.

He was buff and he was also a bully. So much so that one day he actually forced me to give him my lunch. To me he was a grown up, probably between twenty and twenty-two years old; I was a sixteen and a half year old kid and only five foot two. How could I possibly have been in a worse situation?

I was so tiny and this huge guy, Torito, didn't like me at all. Every time he saw me, he hit me on the back of the head. What was I going to do? Torito and his cousins were horrible to me.

One day I had had enough, "You are very abusive, Torito," I said. "I have been telling my older brothers about you and they say they're going to come over and kick your ass one of these days."

He just looked at me and laughed. "You're like a little rooster," he said, "hot blooded. Do you want to fight with one of my little cousins? I will bring one to you."

In the back of my mind I thought, "Oh, great! I'm so dead." There was no way I would be fighting against anyone remotely close to my size; the guys from General Trias were all huge compared to me.

A few minutes later, without my having any choice or

anything to say about it, Torito brought a guy over to where I was working. "This is my cousin, Demétrio," he said. Demétrio was much taller than me and much thicker. I thought he must be older than me because he had a little beard and thick curly overgrown sideburns. He was already glaring as if he was extremely pissed off. He looked like he wanted to kill me. I couldn't figure out why.

"I heard you were talking smack to other people about me. You said I looked like a joto?"

I hadn't said anything about the guy. I didn't even remember seeing him. Torito had lied to him.

"Did you really say I looked like a fag, you little bastard?" He yelled it at me.

I told him again I hadn't said anything. Still, he refused to believe me.

By the time I was sixteen, I had been in so many fights I thought who cared if Demétrio believed something that was not the truth. I guess it was time to fight. There was no more talking for me to do.

"Let's go," I said as I looked up at him and took a deep breath, trying to shrug off my fear.

He grunted at me, "I'm so gonna kick your ass, pendejo. You're dead." When he said it, I knew he believed it. I saw it in his eyes, but still I didn't show any signs of cowardice.

Ever since I can remember, my older brothers had told me, "Whoever hits first, hits twice. If you have heavy hands, two good punches and the battle will be over." I always thought of those words so I could stay mentally prepared for any given fight at any given moment.

But the guys in my neighborhood were close to my size—maybe just a little taller and a little thicker—not like Demétrio and the guys from General Trias.

Even now, in my mind, I can see Demétrio's arms.

In most human forearms, the ones I had seen before that day, the veins popped out a little when the muscle was flexed. This guy flexed showing veins that were thick and green, like a body builder's.

At the time, I thought he must lift weights, but I didn't think about General Trias being close to where the Menonites lived. Demétrio was whiter than other guys I had seen and thicker and probably of German descent. These guys were the offspring of big Germans, which would explain why Torito had green eyes.

Demétrio attacked first.

The whole time Torito stood fifteen feet away and he laughed so hard. He couldn't wait for his cousin to destroy me. "When you get him in the clinch, just take him down," he yelled, grinning. "You can take this little wimp down so easy," I heard him say. "When you get him down, pound the crap out of him. Then make him cry and ask for forgiveness." I could hear Torito's coaching the whole time that Demétrio was running toward me, then grabbing onto me, attempting to wrestle me to the ground.

In those same moments, I knew I should focus on the fight, not listen to him. So then I did just that—tuned out his words and focused on my actions.

Before too long, there was a crowd of dozens of workers surrounding us. For the first time, I thought of all of the kids I made to fight each other in my neighborhood. I empathized with them.

When you are surrounded by people and you know you're going to get your butt kicked, get ridiculed and beaten, it's an awful feeling. My stomach was in knots and I had to keep swallowing to diffuse the gigantic lump in my throat. I watched everything and everyone around me move in painfully slow motion.

I scanned the crowd of people, searching for help and saw some familiar faces, but to my great disappointment, no one came to rescue me. No one wanted to get involved. I realized as I endured the beginning of my beating that they were all too afraid of Torito.

Torito had been in about six fights in the last week and he

had easily beaten everyone.

"Whoever hits first, hits twice." I was doing my little boxing dance while Demétrio laughed at me. "Whoever hits first hits twice." I tried to focus hard on what my brothers had said.

Soon I ran in toward Demétrio and kicked him in the thigh with everything I had. His thigh was so hard, at the moment of contact, it felt like I was kicking a tree.

He recovered and grabbed onto my neck. He held my tiny neck in his thick left hand, pressing deeply into my windpipe and choking me. As he held my neck, he punched me in the head. It was strange. When he punched me, I didn't feel pain, but I saw black for about three seconds, then gray, then yellow.

Moments later, when I came to, I lay dazed on the ground. Demétrio was on top of me in a full mount, and then, from out of nowhere, came Carlos.

Señor Carlos saved me. "This is totally uncalled for," he said, as he lifted me up from the ground. He glared at Demetrio. "This is an unfair fight." He knew that Demétrio was much older and much stronger than me. "Demétrio, you are now on probation. You are going home for a week."

Carlos then turned to me. "Chispa, why were you fighting with this big guy?"

"Señor Carlos," I said. "I'm sorry, but this guy's friend, Torito, has been harassing me for over a month. If I was larger I would've taught him a lesson. But look at me." I motioned so he would really notice just how small I was. "I asked Chentito to come over and beat him up for me, Señor, but he hasn't been here yet."

Torito, who seemed to shrug it off as nothing, laughed until Señor Carlos looked deep into him and said he had heard about all of the fights. "This is a reputable company. If you don't stop it, you're going home, too." There was no play in his voice, just business.

Torito became purple with rage, but he didn't talk back to

Señor Carlos. Torito could not talk back. In Mexican culture, you never talk back to your elders or superiors. That is, if you want to keep your job.

At the end of that day, when the bus was ready to leave to take the guys back to General Trias, I saw Señor Carlos talking to Torito and his friends. "I don't want you boys messing with anybody. You understand?"

After he gave his warning, Carlos walked away, and Demetrio came up to me and whispered to me, "I'm gonna kill your skinny ass."

I said, fearlessly, "Why don't you try it?" For the first time that day, I noticed that Demétrio was limping a little. And I was the one responsible.

He started to limp away, and then, as I thought about how I had the power to hurt a huge man like Demétrio, I got brave, "Next time you try to hurt me, I'm gonna kick you hard, right in the nuts," I said. I know he must've heard me, but he never turned around. He just continued walking.

Torito had been heading toward the bus when I had yelled to Demétrio. I guess he had heard me; now he walked up to me. "Remember this, you little bitch. If Señor Carlos fires my cousin, I'm personally gonna kick your tattling, fuckin' ass. I know where you live, puta madre." I knew that was a lie. There was no way Torito knew where I lived. He was just trying to scare me.

"Why don't you come to my house then, puto? Yeah, that's a good idea. My brother is looking for you... he's a professional baseball player. I can't wait. Why don't you come this weekend?" Now I was the bully.

Because of everything that had happened the day I fought Demétrio, Torito was very angry. He didn't talk to me for about a week. Every time I walked by, he would mumble nasty comments about me. And every time, I wore a big smile on my face and waved. That made him even more furious.

Then Demétrio came back to work, but he and Torito never touched me.

For about two weeks everything at work was calm. Until the Saturday my friend Tica came.

Tica was my best friend; he was about 18. That day, he was selling popsicles from a little paleta cart. It was Saturday and he pushed his cart onto the construction site at lunch time so I purchased an ice cream on a stick and stood hanging out, talking to him.

As Tica and I talked, I noticed Torito and a couple of his cousins point to the paleta cart. They walked over and grabbed some paletas off from it. They didn't pay for them, they just took them.

Torito must've realized that Tica was my friend because he said, "Come on. Get a real job, wuey. I can't believe you are selling paletas. You are such a girl."

Then he ripped open the wrapper of the paleta he had grabbed and stuck it in his mouth. He bit off a chunk and spit it out. "These paletas are terrible!" He made a horrible face. "I can't believe your friend just sold me a bad paleta, Chispa. You two are a couple of rip off little girls!!"

Tica just looked at him, shocked. I think he couldn't believe that someone could behave like such an asshole. "I'm not paying for this crap," Torito raised his voice to Tica. "It's no good!"

"Are you Toro? I've heard about you." Tica looked up into Torito's face. He was calm.

I knew from the moment that Tica set eyes on Torito that he knew. I had been telling Tica about him—how Torito was such an abusive bully. Today, Tica had come to check it out for himself. Although Tica was about my height, he was thicker than me, and, of course, a little older.

"Are you the guy who's been giving Chispa so much crap?" Now there was fire behind Tica's eyes. The fire that I had seen many times when my friend was ready for a fight. Tica was not from the city originally. Like Torito, he was also from a little rancho called Rancheria. Tica was familiar with the ways of the country. And he was tough.

Tica was the best fighter I had ever seen and he, like me, always hated abusive people. Even though there wasn't much I could do about Torito bullying me, I knew I had a friend who could help me. I was excited. Tica had come to talk to Torito face to face, man to man, to set things straight between him and me.

"I heard you've been abusing Chispa. He's my best friend. And you know what? If you mess with my friend, you mess with me. I'm going to ask you politely to apologize to him for what an asshole you've been."

Torito laughed hysterically. He must've thought what Tica said was the funniest thing ever.

But when Torito laughed at Tica, Tica's face got red.

Tica pulled his shirt off, like I had seen him do several other times. I knew when he pulled off his shirt and let it fall to the ground that he was hot and there was going to be a fight. Tica then looked at me and said, "Chispa, can I take care of this business?"

I nodded.

Then he turned to look Torito in the eyes. "I warned you, Torito," he said, " I really don't like to fight, but now you've crossed the line." Tica, without his shirt, charged toward Torito, punched him under the chin, and knocked him down. Torito moved into a sitting position on the ground. He wore a look of surprise. Torito had been taking his shirt off, and when Tica noticed Torito wasn't looking, Tica had used the moment to his advantage.

Torito tried to stand up, but as soon as Tica saw him trying to lift himself from the ground, he pushed him down again and began to kick him in the chest and in the legs. All of the cousins stood nearby with their mouths wide open in shock.

They couldn't believe someone like little short Tica was getting the best of Torito and by this time, a crowd had formed.

Tica was sort of on the chubby side, but he had such heavy hands that Torito now had a bloody nose. Torito had been knocked down not once, but twice. Tica was now beating the crap out of him.

It was a fair and square, one on one fight and Torito's cousins could do nothing about it. I looked away from the fight into the crowd

There was Señor Carlos. He wasn't mad any more. He was just watching with interest, watching my friend deliver a good beating to Torito. In fact, even though he said nothing, when he saw me looking his direction, he winked at me. I was surprised.

Señor Carlos was really enjoying the fight. Torito was such a bully and had beat up so many people, now he was getting his due. Torito was an ass, but he was a good concrete worker. I guess that's why Señor Carlos didn't get rid of him.

I looked back at the fight. Tica had a full mount going on Torito. Torito continued bleeding, now even harder from the mouth and nose and it appeared he had suffered a cut above one of his eyes. He was almost unconscious when I leaned over and said to Tica, "That's enough."

Tica stopped the rain of blows he had been throwing in Torito's face, stood up and stepped away.

Señor Carlos walked over. He moved in between the two.

I thought for sure that in the next few seconds Torito was going to try to get back at Tica, but I was wrong. Torito stood up, looked at my friend, and said with respect and awe, "That was a really good fight. You are a good fighter. No one has ever knocked me down before."

After the two shook hands, Torito limped over to me and said, "Chispa, I'm sorry. I didn't realize I had been so bad to you. I think you are a good boy and I didn't realize I was being such a jerk."

I couldn't believe what happened next. All of the cousins came over, too. They shook Tica's hand and complimented him. "Good fight," they all said. And then, "You are a very good fighter."

Next they apologized to me, as Torito had done.

"I never imagined this little guy could do this to me," Torito said, looking over at Tica. Torito was really bloody and his nose looked broken. "Tica, is that your name? You have proven me wrong. You have my respect."

On that day I realized that Tica was a great friend to me. I also realized that although rancheros could be jerks, these small town guys had one exceptional characteristic, they had honor. I had never seen cholos apologize the way these rancheros did and had never ever seen someone in awe of and respectful to the one who had just beat him in a good fight. But I was impressed with this way of being. I actually wanted to try out this new idea that Torito had shown me.

Drogas
Drugs

I was talking to my neighbor girl, Marisol, in the back yard of her house with Fago when her papá sent her to the store for some tortillas.

The yard was beautiful like Marisol and like none of the others in my neighborhood. It was filled with fruit trees and had a tiled path.

As Marisol's father talked to me, I noticed he was messing with something in his pocket. Moments later, he pulled out a cloth and held it to his nose, then offered some to Fago and me. "Do you want to smell it?" he asked.

I was standing across the yard from him and could already smell it; it smelled deep, dark, and putrid, like acetone. A moment later, he walked closer until he was beside me and shoved the cloth up onto my nose and mouth. The smell was overpowering like nail polish remover. I felt the damp of the cloth against my face and, careful not to inhale, jerked my head away.

Then he moved to Fago, but Fago didn't resist. He breathed the chemical in deeply.

In that moment, I didn't realize my friend was getting high from the cloth. But the thing had a horrible smell and in order to feel the buzz, he had to sniff it deep. It was such a disgusting smell, I couldn't breathe it, but I could see how it might be enticing and Fago didn't hold back.

Within minutes, Fago was smiling and happy. When he started acting like that, I realized that the cloth held something bad. Watching Fago made me forget Marisol and I urged him, "Come on, Fago. Let's go." He followed me back through the house and out the front door.

Thirty minutes later, Fago complained that his head was going crazy and there was loud whistling going on in his ears.

The drug is like poison to your brain. When it hit Fago's, he was laughing and saying incoherent things. I had seen so many people acting funny like him. Now I realized that all those people I saw on the corners holding rolled up cloths to their noses, their eyes all out of focus, were getting high. Until that day, I had never known what they were doing. And with my new knowledge, I decided to take Fago to la huerta, hoping no one was there and I could keep him away from his family until his terrible high subsided.

A few months passed. I was by myself in Cleofas' store. As I was looking around, I noticed Lyoba, this chubby Chihuahua Indian-looking guy. Lyoba had long black hair with bangs that almost completely covered his eyes. He was about eighteen, six years older than me. I noticed that he went to the shelves and grabbed a jar of baby food, then bought it. I had heard about what he was doing from my friends. They said that Lyoba would buy a jar of baby food, then ask any random kid to eat it because all he wanted was the little jar.

He said thanks to Cleofas and the door banged behind him as he walked outside.

A minute or two later, Lyoba came back inside the store and came up to me. "Hey, Chispa, do you wanna eat this Gerber? It's peaches. If you don't eat it, I'll just throw it away."

"Sure," I said, hungry. "I can eat it real quick."

"Hurry, then. I've gotta go," Lyoba said, rushing me.

I devoured the peaches from the jar. They tasted great. Then I went outside with Lyoba and gave him the little jar. He hurried to the nearest water faucet and rinsed it out.

Then he dried it with his own shirt. Next he reached into his pocket and pulled out the Resistol 5000. It was thick, yellow rubber cement glue. He poured it into the jar, filling it up only a quarter full and then poked two holes in the cap and twisted it back on.

He started inhaling through one of the holes and within a matter of about two minutes he was acting high. All of the cholos in my neighborhood carried knives, but this time Lyoba carried a different weapon: a fork with two ends, like what you flip your meat with on a grill. He was playing with it with one hand and holding the glue jar to his mouth with the other. He twirled the fork around his body as I sat on the ground and played marbles on the sidewalk in front of Cleofas' store. No one else was around but us.

"Hey Chispa, come here," he said to me. "You wanna sniff a little bit? You wanna try it? You're just staring at me so I'm thinking you want some. Do you?"

"No thanks. I didn't mean to stare at you. Sorry." I pulled my attention back to my marbles. I hadn't thought I had been staring. It's just that so many kids I knew had talked about eating the baby food from the little jars for Lyoba that I wondered what he was doing exactly. I guess I was just really curious even though, at the same time, I had no interest at all in trying it for myself.

"No. You've got to smell this," Lyoba said, looking at me, unable to focus on my eyes or on my face, even. "This is the best thing you will ever smell in your life."

"No, Lyoba. I don't like it," I said.

But he kept insisting. "This is the best. Come here. You have to smell it."

"No," I repeated, but because I was afraid of him, I went closer. I sniffed about six inches away from the jar. The smell wasn't disgusting.

"No. Not like that, Chispa. You have to smell really deeply. This is the good stuff, better than thinner."

"I don't want to try drugs. I know it's bad for me." There

was a knot in my throat. I was beginning to get scared now and I wished I could run, but my fear held my feet to their spot.

"Who told you this thing, 'Drugs are bad'? Resistol, it's the best. I've been doing this for five years now and it's my favorite thing to do."

"No thanks, Lyoba." I just wanted to walk away, down the street, to my house.

But Lyoba grabbed his big fork from beside him, and held it out toward me. "Sniff it! I said do it! Are you a joto?"

He grabbed my head and I sniffed a couple of times as he held me close to the jar. I was trying not to breathe in. "Breathe it in, you little faggot!" Lyoba yelled at me and tears rolled down my cheeks as I inhaled. I felt sick to my stomach as I succumbed to the power of the reeking fumes.

About one minute later, I felt a huge buzzing in my ears. Then he let go of me and since now I had a little chance, I ran away. I felt like I was running so fast, but I was actually running stupid and Lyoba caught up with me the following block.

"You little creep," he screamed. "Don't you ever run away from me again." He called me a bunch of other weird names and then lifted the fork and brought it down hard into the back of my neck. He gave me a little stab just to punish me.
Blood bubbled from my neck. My ears were still buzzing like the hum of a fluorescent light bulb, but louder, in a more annoying way. I just wanted the buzzing noise to stop. I was experiencing for the first time what drugs could do to a person and I didn't like it. Not at all.

I ran away to la huerta and hid in the trees. A couple of hours later, I came home and lay in my bed. I didn't talk to anyone until that night.

A few days later when my mom saw the two stab marks on my neck, she made me tell her what had happened, but I didn't tell her the truth. I only said that we were playing and Lyoba stabbed me. I didn't want to tell mi mama anything at all. In fact, I didn't want to tell anybody; I was afraid of what would happen. I thought it was safe only to tell her that Lyoba had stabbed me, playing. But I didn't tell anybody that I had sniffed. They all would've killed Lyoba if they knew he had forced me to do it.

My biggest brother Chentito went after Lyoba when he learned that he had stabbed me.

"I didn't stab your brother. Why would I stab him? He's just a kid." He tried playing with Chentito, tried to make me look like a liar, but Chentito would have no part of it. Chentito beat Lyoba right there in front of Cleofas' store.

Later that weekend Lyoba told his cousin Fish that Chentito had beaten him up, and when Chentito and Moy were on their way out of the house on Saturday night, Lyoba, Fish and Oso walked up on the sidewalk in front of our house. Fish confronted Chentito. "Why did you beat up my little cousin?" he demanded.

"That puto was high and stabbed my little brother with a fork."

They all started to fight. Fish was a big guy, bigger than Chentito. Fish hit Chentito first, but Chentito was winning anyway. He jumped on top of Fish, ready to beat the crap out of him.

"Ya estuvo," Fish said, "no more."

So Chentito offered Fish his hand and helped him to his feet, but as soon as he got up, Fish threw a vicious punch in Chentito's face and ran away. Julian and I watched the whole encounter from the sidewalk in front of Cleofas' store. I was so happy watching my brother kick two guys' asses for me, but at the same time I couldn't believe Fish was so gutless that he would punch and run, especially after Chentito was nice enough to help him up.

At that same time, I had some friends—J.J. , Che, and Nando. Even though the three of them weren't really close with me, for some reason they always wanted me to hang out with them. I wondered if I should because they were always hiding from the adults. There were many hang-outs in the neighborhood where there were no grown-ups allowed. Las casetas (the baseball dug-outs), el rio (the river), and at la huerta by the nut trees.

Every day after school the three of them, J.J., Che, and Nando, who were a little bit older than me, would hang out at one of those places. They were doing stupid stuff like sniffing glue and sniffing the cloth dipped in acetone. I knew it was wrong so I didn't try it, but when you're a kid it's fun to hang out with other guys that do bad things in secret. Unfortunately, smaller kids think it's cool to try to imitate the older ones. I never thought those guys were cool. I actually thought they were dumb, but, at the same time, I thought it was kind of fun watching them get messed up. To me, it was funny.

Those three and some of their other friends sniffed stuff and they smoked pot, too. And seeing all of it was kind of normal to me. Mostly all of the older guys in the colonia did those things. I know one of my brothers smoked pot; maybe the others did, too, but they never did it around me.

Everybody in industrial did something—weed or whatever drug. But even though I thought they were all dumb, the main reason I didn't do it was because I was terribly afraid of my dad. It was tempting to do what they did because it looked fun. But I'm so grateful that I was so afraid of my dad—of both his discipline and of disappointing him. My dad didn't even drink in front of me. In fact, he didn't drink, smoke, or do anything disrespectful in front of me. His example was really powerful.

My closest friends were still Tica and Fago. The three of us never smoked pot. I was also fortunate to have a friend like Tica. And my brother, Bombin, was fortunate to have for his friend, Gegos, Tica's brother. Bombin and I were the most studious of all of us, and we were the ones with the high-quality friends.

One day, Tica and I and some other kids were hanging out far away from our colonia in the hills by the river in a place where no one could see us. We liked to go to the hills to hike around and kill animals. At least Tica and I did. The kids with us that day were kind of popular in the neighborhood and when we sat down to rest in a hidden spot, one of them pulled out a little ball of marijuana.

"Cool. You brought it, Pablo. This should be a nice place to smoke it," one said.

Tica and I had made a deal that we weren't going to do any drugs. But we sat down with the guys anyway. We were all sitting around and these eight other kids were passing the joint to everyone.

Whenever we were with the guys and the joint got passed, Tica and I never did take a hit, but we always sat there with them. The first few times we hung out and just sat there talking and watching, the other kids tried to pressure us to smoke. But no more.

In the hills so far away from my house, I thought for the very first time, "I want to feel what they feel." I had all of a sudden become curious about what getting high felt like.

Unlike the three guys I usually sat around with, I admired these different, popular kids and because these guys like Pablo were "cool" and they did it, I thought there must be something cool about smoking. So I quickly scanned the area to make sure one of my brothers or cousins wasn't around, and, when I knew it was safe, I asked for the joint.

They all looked at me, kind of shocked and then passed it. Tica and I took a couple of hits each. I started to laugh and I felt the weirdest and the stupidest that I had ever felt. After we smoked, all of us ran around trying to kill lizards with a sling shot, and we couldn't kill anything. Tica and I were laughing that we couldn't shoot straight. We were actually laughing like crazy at ourselves because we couldn't hit anything at all.

Soon I noticed that I was laughing at everything, and I thought, how stupid. This is stupid. We were laughing like dumb asses. I had sucked the smoke into my lungs and now all I could think about was how completely stupid I looked. If my dad saw me smoking a joint, he would be so disappointed. What would he think of me? Would I be able to look him in the face ever again?

"Isn't it the best thing you've ever done in your life?" one of the "cool" guys asked me about an hour after I had taken a few puffs from the joint.

"No," I said, completely honest. "I think it's stupid. This is the dumbest thing I've ever done."

I can't believe I told him this, outright. But before I smoked with them, I thought they were cool guys and I liked them a lot, and now, since they had initiated me into the world of marijuana, it might seem strange, but I didn't admire them anymore.

I think it was necessary for me to smoke with them that one time because the experience caused me to realize a lot of things. I developed a theory which goes like this—people with weak minds are the ones who fall into drugs. Most people will follow the crowd and join in. If someone comes from a neighborhood where there is widespread drug abuse, it is likely that he will become a drug abuser himself. There are only a few people who are strong-minded. Those people will do what they think is right no matter what they are exposed to, no matter what they see. I had a very strong-minded father who taught me right from wrong. And I wanted to be like him, not like these weak-minded boys.

A few moments before I had taken my hits, these guys had said to me, "Don't worry. If you do this, we won't tell Moy." This had been reassuring because I really didn't want my brothers to find out.

But now it didn't matter if these guys told or not. The following day, I still felt disappointed with myself. In my neighborhood, once you tried one thing, you did it all. If you had no goals, you would do the drugs again and again and you'd get hooked little by little. But I had goals and I learned very young, through those three experiences, that there are really no benefits to drug use. Trying drugs to be cool is always a bad thing, and in response to all the drug users in my neighborhood, I didn't mind becoming a nerd.

I always liked my brother Moy's friends. Lalo el cacheton treated me like a little brother and he didn't do any drugs. I wanted to be like him. I admired my brother because he was popular, but Lalo was clean, and today he has a good job—he's a supervisor for the Coca-Cola Company in Chihuahua.

The friends that I used to hang out with that were clean have good jobs. And the kids who did drugs—many of them are dead.

We called my friend Juan "Juka"(Yu-ka). He was a full-blooded Tarahumara Indian who had moved to my neighborhood directly from la Sierra Madre when he was about twelve. He had a brother named Gregorio who we called Goyo. Goyo was a few years older.

Juka and Goyo were always being picked on by the cholos because they were different. They had red skin and long, thick, black hair like the Sioux or Pawnee or any other Native American Indians. They looked different and stood out and for this they suffered. But we had all been picked on at one time or another.

For a while, Juka hung out with Fago, Tica and me and he was one of us. He was a good kid who went with us to the hills to kill birds and lizards. He joined us to throw rocks in the colonia and throw rocks at the trucks that passed by on the highway. Juka had always been clean. But at fourteen, he succumbed to the bullies. He started hanging out with his eighteen-year-old cousin Cruzito sniffing glue and he stopped hanging out with us. Sometimes I would see him and ask him to go to the hills or the rooster fights with us, but he always said no. He wasn't interested in doing things with us "kids" anymore.

Juka went from being a clean, shy kid to a druggy who was wasted all of the time. He became a good example—a good example of why not to use drugs. Within a year, his interests had dwindled to only two things—drugs and stealing, which he did with his older "friends".

In the beginning, when Juka started sniffing and smoking, he had tried to talk us into doing it with him. And he soon became the kind of friend that I would not call a true friend. The kind of guy who only wants his friends to do the bad things he does, not someone who wants the best for his friends. "I don't like your new friends, Juka," I had said to him once. "I don't want to hang out with people like them. All they do is get high and steal."

"Come on, Chispa," he kept saying. "They're cool. You'll see." or "Come on Chispa, the drugs are cool." or "Don't be such a baby, Chispa. It's fun. Come sniff with us. You'll like it, I know."

And every day or every other day when he'd see me, Juka would ask me to go with him and try to push me to use the drugs he used with his friends and I would have to say no. After a few weeks of this, I started avoiding him. I had to stop talking to him because he was very insistent with me about trying his drugs.

At age fourteen, Juka had started hanging out with older kids and now, at fifteen, he was spending most of his time with grown-ups. I never understood why he was so obedient to older people. And these were not respectable older people. They were the kind of people who may have been older but were not worthy of respect.

Before, when he hung out with the eighteen-year-olds, he was sniffing stuff and then smoking weed, but now he was into heroin.

One time after Juka became a druggy, his older brother, Goyo, was sitting with Lyoba down by the river. Tica and I were at the river that day hunting doves when we saw them. We often took our sling shots to the hills or down by the river to kill doves. We would take them home and ask my mom to cook them for us.

In the quiet of the river, we saw Lyoba leave to go who knows where. Goyo pulled out some syringes from his pocket and filled them with what appeared to be heroin.

Goyo had been kind of a nice, clean guy when he moved into my neighborhood, but he soon started to hang around with the wrong people and he had changed, too. From where I was standing with Tica, I could see Goyo examine the syringe and then push the needle into his arm, injecting the drug. We commented to each other that we were shocked to see him shooting up. When Goyo saw Tica and me looking at him, he called me over. He was insistent. "Come on, Chispa. Come shoot some drugs with me. You too, Tica."

"No, Goyo," we both said over and over. Heroin was definitely not a part of our plan. "We don't want to do that, Goyo."

We knew this disgusting drug was the worst thing you could do. One guy in my neighborhood had maggots growing in a sore on his arm from an infection since he was shooting up so much. Others had scar tissue growing on their arms and chests from so many needle pokes. "Wimpy kids," he said, "you should appreciate that I'm gonna give you some." He would not stop talking about us trying it.

I looked over at Tica. His face had changed. He had been smiling and now his jaw was set and his eyes had become fixed and intense, the way he looked before a fight. Before I could say anything, Tica punched Goyo. Then Goyo and Tica started fighting. Goyo was a grown-up, like twenty-two, and we were teenagers. But Tica must've been irritated at how all of these older kids were always trying to force drugs on us; I know I was. So I raised my fists and joined in. About two minutes later, Goyo lay on the ground, bleeding from the nose and even from the eyes. Tica and I walked away and Goyo said nothing more to us about the drugs, forever after.

That was the last time in a long time that Tica and I went to the river.

A couple of years after I broke ties with Juka, he started hanging out with Rafa. And then I knew something terrible was going to happen to him. Rafa Pajarero was in his thirties and had killed my sister-in-law's uncle ten years back with a tomahawk. In Mexico, if you had money you didn't go to prison for life. You went only for a few years, even if you killed someone. Rafa's parents owned a lot of land so he served two years at the most.

Rafa was probably the worst person in my colonia. He always carried guns and knives and he wasn't afraid to use them.

He didn't have a job, he did all kinds of drugs, and all he had decided to do with his life was steal and hurt people. Rafa (Pajarero as we called him) used to go to the store and on the way there he would assault the kids in the middle of the street if they didn't give him money.

Many times he had scared me so much, I gave him money out of fear.

We hated him and his friends so much that we would gather rocks in our shirts and climb onto the flat rooftops in our neighborhood.

Late at night on the weekends when all the druggies sat or laid around wasted out of their minds in the streets, we would pelt them with the rocks. You could hear the rocks smash on the heads of those zombie-like humans. Rafa would pull out his gun and shoot aimlessly in every direction. But he was so far gone that he had no idea where the rocks were coming from.

Rafa had not only been in prison for killing Tere's uncle. He had killed others. He would be in prison for a little while, he'd get out, and then he'd kill someone else and go back.

And his stupid parents always bailed him out, no matter what he did.

One night, some people in my colonia saw Juka with Rafa walking toward the river. The following day I found out that Juka was found dead at the river. It is said that Rafa gave him some drugs and later pushed him in. Juka was only seventeen.

I was sixteen. Drugs were not an option, I already knew. I wish that Juka had known the same.

6. *GALLOS Y GALLINAS*
CHICKENS AND ROOSTERS

Gallinas
Chickens

Roosters are such cool animals. I loved their way of being. I was always amazed and in awe of their wild nature and it seemed some roosters were just born to fight.

I understood that fighting roosters wasn't the nicest thing to do, but I just loved to watch them. When the roosters got angry, the feathers that ringed their necks and chests stood on end. The brilliant colorful fluff framed their heads and added to the luster of battle. When their galleros let them go, the roosters ran at each other and in a flurry of motion and feathers, they kicked at each other so rapidly it was hard to see the knives attached to their bright-colored legs where the talons had once been. As they hovered inches above the ground, they slashed and slashed at one another over and over again; they were so incredibly fearless, so brave that they seldom gave up. I admired how they fought beautifully and ferociously and to the death.

It was a big adrenaline rush—the winner survived and the loser died or was maimed. When one of my roosters was beating on another rooster, the moment was gripping and intense. And it was a lot of work, too. By the day of the fight, I would've worked so hard training my rooster to win, as if he were a professional fighter. I would've spent hundreds of hours training him.

Also, being the youngest gallero in my neighborhood made me famous all over my part of Chihuahua.

My obsession with roosters led me to study them carefully. I read books about them. I learned that roosters got chicken pox, measles and mumps and they also got the flu. I would feed them lime through the beak to cure the flu. Eight drops per nostril.

One other thing I learned from being a gallero was how to cure roosters' wounds. Pancho taught me how to stitch up their open wounds with fishing line. There was a really old gallero from another neighborhood who taught me to use toques de violeta (a purple liquid like methiolade) to cure their wounds.

But I wasn't always fighting roosters because it all started with chickens.

Every day after school, I went to la huerta to feed my chickens and every weekend, I hunted for cucarachas. I would rig up boxes with honey bait and deliver them to my neighbors who would place them in or near their houses to collect their unwanted roaches. After a day or two, I would return, collect the overflowing boxes, and run back to la huerta. There, I would pour the cockroaches out of the boxes and the chickens would chase them everywhere.

On the weekends, I would collect friego, leftover food now growing maggots, from my neighbors. For every bucket someone gave me, I would trade ten eggs. Everybody won. The neighbors enjoyed eating the fresh eggs and my chickens enjoyed eating the friego just as much as they enjoyed the cucarachas.

The chickens ate from a small tire that I had found in the trash. I had spent a couple of hours a day for three days cutting this tire in half with a very sharp machete. When I fed the chickens from it, I filled one half of the cut up tire with friego and the other half with water. The tire worked great and the chickens ate and got fat.

Many people in my neighborhood didn't take good care of their chickens and little bugs called corucos would collect in their feathers. The bugs would spread easily and, if I had bad luck, my chickens would get infested with them, too. So I would quarantine my sick chickens by making special houses for them. To cure the quarantined chickens, I would dust traces of mouse poisoning under their feathers.

Another problem I had was this one—some of my chickens ate their own eggs, although an egg-eater was a very bad chicken to have because as soon as she laid her egg, she ate it. There are two cures I know of for a chicken who eats her own eggs. You can use a lighter or match to burn her beak a little bit. Chickens' beaks are very sensitive so when they peck at the egg with a beak that's been burnt, it hurts, and they stop cracking the eggs open and eating them. Sometimes a chicken won't stop eating her eggs even if her beaks is burnt. For her there is a more drastic cure. You can crack her beak with a hammer.

I hated to do this so if I tried to crack a beak and it didn't work, I would take the chicken to my grandma, Mamá Maria and she would crack the beak. Or sometimes, if our budget was tight, my grandma would grab the egg-eating chicken by her neck and spin her around like a lasso until her head fell off. Then the chicken's body would run like crazy, bumping into everything—outside walls of the house and bushes. As the body ran, a fountain of digested liquid food spewed from the neck.

My little brothers and cousins ran after it, trying to catch the headless body. When a child grabbed the body, the chicken spun around in his hands. When he felt the chicken spinning, the child screamed and ran away. But then, even more children came and chased the chicken, screaming and yelling, until she stopped moving and fell over, dead.

When my grandma killed the chickens, I couldn't watch. Instead, I walked over to Tia Lupe's house and waited inside until I heard all of the screaming stop. Once the chicken was dead, Mamá Maria walked the two blocks to get mi mama who joined her at la huerta where she and my grandma boiled the chicken and pulled out all of the feathers. Then mi mama would gut the chicken and cut it into pieces. After that, in my grandma's kitchen, mí mamá would make the best chicken soup in the world.

Many times when I won chickens, I wouldn't win very pretty ones. If a chicken was beautiful I would keep her; otherwise, I would give her to my mom and she would make the chicken into a tasty soup or fried chicken.

I supplied eggs for the whole family and for friends, too. At one time I had thirty-five chickens, fifteen roosters and about eighty-five chicks.

Even though my chickens lived mainly in a house, many of them laid eggs in nests somewhere else. I knew which egg came from which chicken by its unique color and shape. The very young chickens laid smaller eggs with drops of blood on the shells while the older chickens laid big, beautiful eggs.

I would send my little brother Pedro and some of my little cousins to find the eggs, and once they were found, I would identify which chicken they came from and, if necessary, tell my brothers to go search for more. If I was missing the eggs of a specific chicken, I might tell them, "Go find some long white eggs, the eggs of Gertrudis."

If a rooster reached two months old, I would usually sell him. I could get one-hundred fifty pesos for a rooster; that would be the equivalent of two-hundred dollars today. This was a great benefit to my family because when I sold a rooster, I would give the money to my parents.

During all of the time I had my chickens, I'll bet I sold twenty roosters. I didn't sell a lot of chickens, because we ate them.

Other galleros ate their cowardly roosters, the ones who ran in a fight. I never ate a rooster. I preferred to retire him or trade him.

Rambo

Almost every year my brothers and sister travelled with mi mamá to Sinaloa to see my grandmother, Mamá Chiquita. I never went with them because I loved to be with mi papá who stayed behind in Chihuahua to work.

About an hour before it was time for the train to leave, Apá and I would take my five brothers, my mother, and my little sister across town to the train station. The train was not like an Amtrak train, the kind you would've seen in the U.S. in the late 1980's. This was an old-fashioned train, the kind that you see hauling grain and coal.

In the oppressive 110 degree heat of a Chihuahua summer day, we would drive to the train station and pile out of my dad's little truck, adults exiting from the cab and kids from the truck bed. Inside the big office room of the train station, my dad would buy the tickets for fifteen pesos each and each child would carry his own suitcase and board the train. My dad and I would go outside with the rest of my family to hug and kiss them before they walked up the few steps and got inside.

Inside the train there were people, chickens, and pigs. And the cars were like a big bus with old seats. Once my mom, brothers, and sister went inside the very rough cars, we sat and waited for the train to leave. Within an hour, the train and its noisy whistle pulled out of the station in a cloud of black, stinky smoke. At the time, I thought the smell of the burning coal was nice so I inhaled deeply as the train moved out of station, taking my family along with it. My heart beat with excitement; I would be alone with mi papa for two whole weeks.

In those two weeks, my dad would cook for me, take me to the baseball games and buy me barbacoa every morning for breakfast.

Every week day, my dad would take me to work with him. He had a dump truck he had named el Rebelde (the rebel). My dad's friend, Solo Vino, had painted a desert scene on the back tailgate with the name of my sister, Flor Elena, in large brilliant letters in the middle and all the brothers' names, including mine, painted smaller in brown around the edges. Solo Vino was the neighborhood painter. And he was nicknamed Solo Vino which means "he came alone" by my dad, because he always came alone.

My dad drove his dump truck every day. When it was baseball time, the back of the dump truck was loaded with children; my dad had something like a bus route and he would pick up all of the neighborhood kids, even those who were only going to watch the game and even some of our opponents along with several grown-ups. My mom, Doña Andrea, and my dad would ride in the front. Fifty to sixty kids would fit inside the box where we would travel. There was a special ladder built and welded onto the side of the truck by Camanáy, the neighborhood welder, so that we could get in and out of the dump box with ease. Standing inside, we bounced around as we rode because there were no springs. Unlike a car suspension, the dump truck was made to carry tons of dirt, not tons of kids.

People loved to see my dad driving through the streets, so much that mi papá was once pictured in the newspaper with his el Rebelde, carting loads of kids around Chihuahua.

During the week, my dad used el Rebelde for work. He picked up orders from construction people for gravel to mix with their cement and then drove out to the rivers to collect it. At the rivers, he would back his truck up into the water and would shovel gravel into the back.

Bico, Chota, and Cuco, neighborhood guys in their twenties, were his helpers at the time. Bico was a funny, adventurous guy who rode his weird bike everywhere. Chota was much taller and muscular. He always had a big head and thought he was a pimp with the ladies. Cuco was the youngest of the guys. He was always talking about his girlfriend to everybody. He told us how he went to the forest alone in the car with her and how the two of them would be there until the next day.

My dad only took two guys at a time in his truck. Two was all he could fit so he tried to divide the work up evenly between the three.

For those two weeks, I enjoyed my time with my dad. Then the day came that everyone would be coming home so we returned to the station to pick them up.

The year that I was ten, my brother Moy stepped off of the train holding a beautiful red (Colorado) rooster. It was love at first sight for me. Moy held the rooster in his arms in the back of the truck as we drove home. When we got back, my brother installed the beautiful red rooster in the chicken house at la huerta and I named him Rambo.

Rambo was amazing-looking. He was about ten months old with intertwined red and black feathers and white legs. He had come from the Sinaloa rancho where they bred high-quality, expensive roosters. My uncle, who produced roosters that fought in the palenques, had given Rambo to Moy. I couldn't believe that he was ours. But my brother must not have felt the same.

Moy fought Rambo right away. But he only fought him against his friends' roosters. None of them knew anything about fighting the gallos. Moy would just strut around carrying his rooster in his arms, showing Rambo off to his friends. But he never took care of him. I fed him, made sure he didn't escape from his house and protected him from rival cholos who wanted to steal him. I would go over to la huerta at night to check on Rambo and would see cholos walking around. I would ask, "What are you doing here? You're not here to steal Rambo, are you? I'll tell my dad if you do."

Those words reminded the cholos to stay away since I knew most of them by name.

Within a month, Moy lost interest in Rambo. He was too busy with his cholo friends being popular.

I had fed and guarded Rambo for three or four months when I went to mi papa. "I've been taking care of Rambo for this whole time, Apá. Moy hasn't taken care of him at all. Can he be mine?"

"Sure," my dad said. "If Moy is not taking care of him, you bet he's yours."

Now I just had to talk to my brother and tell him that I was taking Rambo. He said that was fine with him as long as he could fight him whenever he wanted. But my brother fighting my rooster was not OK with me.

"You need to let me fight him," Moy argued.

"No. You don't even know how to fight a rooster."

"Yes, I do. And you're just a kid. How can you tell me I can't fight my own rooster?"

I just thought it was wrong. First, Rambo was too young to fight. Second, Moy didn't even train his rooster so Rambo was out of shape and unprepared.

We continued to argue. I finally asked my dad to talk to my brother. Mi papá backed me up. He told Moy that fighting Rambo was not an option. He needed to leave that rooster alone. "He belongs to Chispa now," he said.

Right about the time I took over ownership of Rambo, there were a lot of rival galleros from other neighborhoods sneaking into our colónia early on Saturday and Sunday mornings to kill our roosters. My Rambo was safe because even though Moy had fought him, he had only fought him against friends in our neighborhood so the people in the surrounding neighborhoods didn't realize we had him.

Pancho La Bruja, the main neighborhood gallero, was one of the few people who knew I had Rambo. He had been showing me how to train him and what to feed him. Amá and the neighbor ladies had been saving their strained red chile from their blenders and I would feed the leftover ground up seeds and skins to Rambo since Pancho had told me that the chile would make him brave.

It is common practice to cut off a fighting rooster's crest along with the barbs hanging from the neck so that his opponent can't grab him, hold him, and easily cut him in a fight. But the cutting, if not done carefully, can be dangerous for the animal. Pancho taught me that I needed to be extra careful cutting Rambo's crest, because a rooster's jugular vein is very close to the place where I must make the cut. If I cut into that main vein, my rooster could bleed to death. Pancho had also taught me a long standing tradition known only to the rooster fighters. "After you cut the crest and barbs off the rooster, dice them into little pieces. Then feed the pieces to your rooster and he will become very brave. He will never run in a fight."

So I did like Pancho said. We cut the crest and barbs and fed them to Rambo, which I later did with all of my roosters. It probably sounds crazy, but they loved to eat the meat! And I don't know if they indeed became more brave, but it didn't matter because just thinking it was true was enough for me.

Pancho explained to me that when chickens are in danger, they cluck and roosters have a natural instinct to protect their chickens. Roosters who are trained to attack protect the chickens from all the animals that run at large. And a lot of animals ran at large in Mexico and most of the chickens did, too, so we needed tough roosters in order for our chickens to stay alive.

With the ideas Pancho gave me, I trained Rambo. I would chase him for fifteen to twenty minutes at a time until he could barely walk to build his stamina; I would grab him by the tail and hold him in mid-air while he tried to run for five minutes at a time; and I would hold his face up to a mirror and pull him by the skin of his neck until he became very mad which made him aggressive, so aggressive that he would peck violently at any hand that came near him.

Roosters are such cool animals. I loved everything about my Rambo; I was always amazed and in awe of his wild nature and of how willing he was to fight. And I trusted Pancho since he never told anyone that I was now the owner of a beautiful bird who we had been training.

It wasn't long before Pancho began to hint about me fighting Rambo for our neighborhood.

He and his gallero buddy, Oso, had never bothered Moy about it because Moy was a tough cholo and Pancho and Oso were a little intimidated by him.

The hints continued for a while, until one day Pancho came out and said directly, "You should fight your Rambo, Chispa. The galleros (from Rancheria Juarez) have humiliated our neighborhood and we don't have any more fighters." Pancho and Oso Yogi had each lost three roosters in fights against Rancheria. Both of them owned other roosters, but the roosters weren't yet trained and ready and would have met certain death. So my neighborhood needed me. After a few weeks, I agreed to fight Rambo. I was nervous, but thought it was a decent idea since I had been training Rambo so much.

After I said yes to fighting Rambo, I took the two guys to la huerta to see my black and red beauty. When Pancho lifted Rambo, he commented that my rooster was ready. His leg muscles were tight and hard and he was even the correct weight.

"You've done a good job of training this boy, Chispa," Pancho said. Then he said to me, relieved, "We really have a chance." His huge bruja nose wrinkled slightly as he beamed at me.

The day Pancho came for Rambo, Diego, Fago, and I were sitting on the ground playing marbles. We got up from our game and led Pancho and Oso to where Rambo was waiting.

Fago and I had been working with Rambo all that week. Since this was my first fighting rooster, training him had actually been part experimental. Rambo had been relaxing without any chicken contact for a couple of days. We had also tied a little cloth over his eyes for a week. We would take it off only to feed him. That got Rambo so mad, he would peck at our hands like he was possessed. He had even pierced a hole in Fago's hand. We decided that in two days, we would remove the cloth to see what Rambo would do.

When we arrived at the chicken house, Pancho could see that Rambo was really angry and he said excitedly, "This bird is a good fighter. He's pissed."

He continued, "I shouldn't say this, but I promise you your rooster will not even get a scratch, Chispa."

Don Chuy, who owned the brutal opponent, Ráfagas, was also sure of his rooster. He had said, "If for some crazy reason your rooster wins, I will pay you two to one in chickens. For every chicken you bet, I'll give you two."

Ráfagas and Don Chuy were from a fancier neighborhood so Ráfagas was more valuable than the over-fought, tired roosters from my neighborhood. He was bred well for fighting and had won more than twenty fights.

But Don Chuy knew nothing about Rambo.

My Rambo was now almost two years old and his daddy had been a fancy palenque fighter. My tio Mario had traded a sheep for four chicks that were about a month old, and only my gallito Rambo had survived. While Moy was visiting Sinaloa, he had fallen in love with the young rooster so Mario had given Rambo to him. He knew that Moy was a troublemaker. "I'll give the rooster to you if you straighten up," Mario had told him.

But the rooster didn't change anything for Moy. Moy didn't care much about Rambo and he didn't straighten up either. Rambo was now my rooster and now he would be fighting for real, with knives. But Pancho needed to assure me that my rooster would be alright.

I carried my beautiful, shiny Rambo nervously the couple of blocks into Oso's back yard. I felt special since there were only grown-up men there that day. Fago and I had never been to a grown-up rooster fight. There were knifeless fights which included men, a few women, and kids. Then there were others that a few boys went to where roosters fought with knives, but there were no drugs. And then there were grown-ups only fights where people smoked weed and a few shot up heroin into their arms and chests.

The fight today was one of those adults only fights. The Rancheria men had come from the other side of town, many to buy drugs while others were there just to enjoy the sport of the roosters. And rooster fights had been going on between the two neighborhoods at least three times a year for four years.

This particular fight was a big one. There were at least one-hundred grown-ups in a "big" back yard, which really wasn't that big by American standards—people were packed in. I could see everything that everyone was doing.

I looked around. It was exciting, but at the same time it was intimidating. This was one of the fights that my brother Moy loved to attend, but this time, thank God, he wasn't here. Good thing, because he would've turned me in if he had seen me fighting Rambo.

As we walked across the yard, I noticed many people staring at us. The whole neighborhood was eyeing my rooster now; he was no longer my secret. I knew everyone thought that my rooster and I would let Oso and Pancho down. The whole time they had thought that Panchito and his rooster would be representing us, not mine. Panchito's rooster had been a really good fighter but was now very old. An old rooster is strong because the meat gets tougher with the years, but roosters tend to get slower as they age so, although people thought he was the rooster of the day, Pancho never even considered fighting him.

The spectators looked shocked to see me. I had told many people and promised mi papa that I'd never fight my rooster with knives. He was strictly going to be a semental (or a breeding rooster). But not now.

I saw Don Chuy eyeing my rooster. I thought I heard him say, "This is going to be a good fight." It was. Rambo was the real thing. He was fourteen pounds with a maniacal face and a violently angry beak. Rafagas was a dark burgundy and black Colorado. He had white legs and was just a little larger than Rambo.

Before every cock fight, in order to introduce the roosters, the galleros hold them out in the air and let them peck at each other. When Rambo and Ráfagas were introduced, they went crazy trying to attack. The feathers of each rooster stood up like a lion's mane. But now I was no longer scared for my Rambo. I was ready for Pancho to let Rambo loose.

Once free in the yard, the two fought violently. Usually, the one who attacks first has the advantage. Some roosters, like the high quality Palenque birds, will run from ten feet away and attack each other. Other roosters mess around a lot; they don't run immediately at each other and seem to avoid fighting. But these roosters never let up attacking and kicking. After the third attack, I noticed that Ráfagas limped and fell down onto his side. He had been cut in the leg.

"Yes, Rambo is winning!" I yelled, excited. Along with the others from my neighborhood, I was cheering like crazy. My rooster was going to win!

Ráfagas couldn't get up from the ground now so Rambo ran toward him and went for the kill. Rambo cut Ráfagas in the jugular vein. Blood spurted everywhere, even onto the nearby spectators. Ráfagas was dying, but he kept pecking and trying to get up. I watched and waited for the moment when he would make his comeback. Sometimes a rooster miraculously comes back from near death and kills his opponent. We called this the lucky ending. In a rooster fight, it doesn't matter which rooster goes down first—whichever dies first loses.

Today there was no miracle, no lucky ending. This time, Rambo attacked and attacked until Ráfagas no longer moved. I smiled with a kind of pride I had never felt before. My rooster was a champion!

After the fight, Rambo was going crazy with adrenaline. Pancho tried to grab him by the tail but he pecked violently.

Pancho finally covered Rambo with a shirt to calm him down.

The day of that fight, Rambo became highly respected. I got many offers for him. Oso Yogi was one. He offered two-thousand pesos (the equivalent of two-hundred dollars). But I wouldn't accept it; I refused to sell Rambo.

Moments after Don Chuy picked his lifeless Ráfagas up from the ground, the guys from the other neighborhood filed out of Oso's back yard. On his way out, Don Chuy grabbed Pancho la Bruja by the shoulder and said, "This rooster is the real deal. He's not for sale, is he?" Pancho looked at me, and I said, this time to Don Chuy, "No. Sorry."

Don Chuy left, carrying his dead rooster. "Ráfagas fought strong in twenty-two fights," he said. "I guess it was pay day for him today."

A few days later, Chuy contacted Pancho to make another offer for Rambo."If this kid Chispa sells me his rooster, he will be a pure semental on my rancho," he told him. When Pancho told me, I was tempted. I liked the fact that Rambo would be safe since I still wasn't very turned on to fighting my rooster.

But I kept him as my fighter.

Rambo won six more big fights and he earned several scars on his chest.

Pancho la Bruja borrowed Rambo to "make chicks" once, but I found out later that he had fought him. Since Pancho had helped me a lot, I didn't get mad and I never mentioned it.

The Pinto

I was just about to turn thirteen when I decided that I wanted my chickens to have some more baby chicks. But I was frustrated. Most of my chicks were dying before they reached adulthood. I needed to come up with an idea. I dug through the trash in my neighborhood and found old pieces of wood, mattress springs, the webbing of screen doors—all kinds of pieces that I could use to fashion my own chicken houses.

Houses in Chihuahua have flat, concrete roofs so I would build my chicken houses where I knew my chickens and roosters would be safe—on my roof.

After I built the houses, I put Rambo the rooster in one with three chickens and Mendigon (Bad Ass) in the other with three more chickens. I was excited to have lots of baby chicks now that each rooster had three girlfriends.

One day when I was feeding my roosters, I noticed that Rambo was missing an eye.

I ran down the stairs, furious. I yelled to my older brothers, Moy and Chentito, "I know you were fighting Rambo." Moy and Chentito had their own roosters and they fought them, but this time I thought for sure that they had fought my Rambo. My brothers denied it, but through it all, I didn't believe them.

Immediately afterward, I marched up to my dad who was outside next to his truck, preparing to leave for the day. My face was red hot. "Apá, Moy and Chentito are fighting my rooster!"

Mi papá confronted my brothers and, again, they both swore they weren't fighting Rambo.

"Your brothers are not the ones to blame, Chispa," he said.

"Something else must've happened to that rooster. It's very strange, but I don't have an explanation for you." If it wasn't my brothers, some other people must've messed up my rooster. I was sure.

I felt helpless. I loved that rooster.

Plus, I was a gallero and Rambo was my prize. Now that he had lost an eye, he would no longer be able to fight. So I decided to move Rambo. I didn't want him hurt again. If he lost both eyes, he would probably die.

I took Rambo over to la huerta where he would be safer.

When I returned home, I reconstructed the chicken houses on the roof, tearing apart the two to create one. Since Rambo was no longer there, the rooster Mendigon moved into the single rooftop chicken house with all six chickens.

For the next two weekends, I spent many hours on the roof, hiding underneath some boxes. I patiently waited for the someone responsible for Rambo's missing eye to come around. On the second day of the second weekend I got tired of hiding under the boxes on the hot roof. So I went downstairs to my room to cool off and take a short break in the relative coolness of our cement block house.

I had been down there for almost an hour when I said to Bombin, "Time to go back up to the roof." He looked at me like I was crazy spending so many hours up there in the heat. But I hurried back up the stairs. I only got to the second or third step when I heard something that sounded like roosters fighting. How could this be?

I ran the rest of the way up to the rooftop. I was shocked and infuriated at what I saw. There was Mendigon, caught in the netting of the cage. He was caught in those pieces of old mattress springs and door screens I had woven together and he couldn't get free.

Oh dios mio! Mendigon's head was stuck and there was my neighbor's rooster, Pinto thrashing Mendigon with his talons and mauling him with his sharp, yellow beak. Poor Mendigon. Imprisoned inside his cage, he couldn't even retaliate. It was such an unfair fight; in human terms it was like punching someone who has his hands tied behind his back over and over again. And Mendigon was still a baby—not even a year old.

"Pinche gallo!" I screamed as I rushed in to grab my rooster. My scream and my presence startled Pinto. He looked in my direction and turned, but not before slashing and pecking violently at my legs. I grabbed a stick and whacked him. We fought for a few minutes. I hit him again but he continued to tear at me. So I took more swings at that ugly old rooster. "Go away you stupid puto!" I screamed.

The Pinto finally hopped away. He flew from rooftop to rooftop back to his home at Martha Morado's.

Now, with ripped pants, I turned back to my Mendigon. "Oh, no!" I was shocked when I saw him. "What did he do to you?" Mendigon's head was still caught in the net and he was missing an eye, too. The tears started. "NOOOOOO!" I cried out.

I hated that ugly Pinto. He had blinded my two favorite roosters. I would get my revenge. But I would be patient.

I planned my strategy and took action. Every day before school, I went up to my roof to hide. I left Mendigon up there, but I fixed the netting so if there was a next time, his head wouldn't get caught. But the Pinto did not come back.

Not yet.

The following weekend I threw some corn and friego out on the rooftop and made chicken noises. Some chickens came first and then...there he was, the Pinto. He was flying up to my roof. What a lucky day!

My eyes blurred a little from the excitement and I could taste revenge in every corner of my mouth. This time I was not alone—Fago was with me. He had helped me to sprinkle out a little road of food and to rig a trap.

"Fago, look!" I whispered, watching from my hiding spot as Pinto and his chickens moved directly into our trap. The trap was like a reja (a giant wooden box). And so, when Pinto and his chickens stepped in, Fago and I acted quickly. We ran over, closed up the box, and captured them. Then we let the chickens go one by one.

Once the chickens moved away, I grabbed Pinto by the legs. That rooster fought with his feet and tried to peck at us. But Fago grabbed Pinto's body and even though he flailed around, we held on. Together we managed to trap him inside a big flour sack. I grabbed the bag by the top. With the rooster pecking around inside the bag screaming, "Awk!" we ran to la huerta.

"This rooster is dead!" I screamed, smiling as I ran holding the heavy bag with that bitch Pinto inside.

At la huerta, I dragged the bag to the big tree and flung it twice at the trunk. Then I opened it up and grabbed the disoriented rooster by his legs. I quickly tied them together with a long piece of twine and secured the other end to the tree. Fago and I went home, but we left Pinto there. He hung from the tree branch. Pinto hung there from that afternoon until we returned the next morning.

Earlier that morning, I had met with my buddies Fago and Tica. Still filled with anger, I had told them, "I'm going to beat up that puto! He's getting the baseball bat!"

"You can't do that, Chispa," Tica said. "That rooster isn't yours." But I still thought about it.

Instead, I ran and grabbed my blinded roosters from the chicken house to take care of their own unfinished business.

Rambo was first. He pounded on Pinto for a while, but Pinto wasn't crying. He was fighting with his legs tied. After about a half an hour, we decided to give Pinto a rest. But later that day my friends and I would return with Mendigon.

Pinto still hung from the tree, bloodied and exhausted when I brought my Mendigon over and tied a knife where his talon should have been. Then I let him loose. He ran to Pinto with feathers fanned out around his head and slashed at Pinto with his knife. "Kill him!" I yelled to Mendigon as my friends quietly watched.

And Mendigon fought. But Pinto, in his exhaustion, fought,

too. Soon I realized that I had placed the knife wrong, and it never cut Pinto, but Mendigon was bloody. He had cut himself instead.

Watching Pinto as he fought, my anger turned to surprise. "Look at Pinto!" I shouted to my friends. "He got two horrible beatings and he still wants to fight. What a warrior!"

In awe of Pinto and his bravery, I carefully untied the rope from around his legs and brought him into the chicken house where I fed him and cleaned his wounds. And then I noticed, really noticed the Pinto for the first time. He was large and muscular. The feathers of his body were interesting, red with white spots. He had mainly long, black, shiny tail feathers with a few white feathers woven in among them. Pinto looked like a special breed. "Pinto is a REAL fighter," I said to myself.

That was Sunday. I kept Pinto safe and hidden in the chicken house at la huerta for that whole week. The following Saturday I fed him really well. Along with friego, I gave him a lot of chile so that he would be brave. El Oso Yogi and I had already scheduled a fight with a rooster from the next neighborhood over.

Ever since Pinto had fought back so hard with my two roosters, I had been spreading the word of his fighting spirit and everyone from my colonia was excited to see him fight. Because such a tough rooster was fighting, a bunch of people from my neighborhood had gone over to la Hacienda de la Flor a few days before and had put together a big bet. I bet four chickens and fifteen pesos. Some other people bet two to three chickens and ten pesos or fifty pesos, whatever money and chickens they could afford.

Pinto's owner, Martha Morado, had no idea all of this was going on. And Pinto had never fought so he was rested. Our roosters fought every weekend so they were worn out; even my own roosters were exhausted. But Pinto was fresh.

Pinto had already earned his reputation for being tough when I tied him to the tree that day. And when we practiced him against Fago's roosters he showed his spirit again.

It was three days until Pinto's debut. Fago and I took him over to Pancho la bruja's house so we could try him out with a rooster other than Fago's.

When we arrived at Pancho's, he was on his porch like most evenings, smoking and watching his chickens. Pancho knew about the upcoming fight, but this was the first time he had actually seen Pinto the rooster. When he examined him, he was clearly pleased. "That's a good rooster. A real Espanol."

"I want to see what he's got. Let me get my Colorado out and let's fight them very briefly. Then I can tell you what I think about it." Pancho took us into his backyard. There, in the yard was his beautiful red rooster with green legs, slightly smaller than Pinto. He was Pancho's best rooster; he had won five fights and Pancho was very confident in him.

Since I was still mad at Pinto, a big part of me hoped that Pancho's Colorado would win the contest.

Pancho picked up his Colorado from the ground. "We're going to have a very quick fight. I don't want to hurt Pinto because I know he's not yours."

When we let the roosters go in Pancho's back yard, Colorado attacked Pinto quickly at first. Then Pinto got so mad, he ran to Colorado and beat him horribly with his talons. In less than one minute, Pinto pounded Colorado. And poor Colorado got so scared, he looked nervously from side to side and I thought he would run.

The moment the two roosters moved apart, Pancho hurried over to his wounded Colorado and lifted him. As he examined his rooster, I saw it. Pinto had also pecked out the Colorado's eye! Now Pancho's champion was missing an eye, too.

"I'm so sorry," I said. I felt so bad. "I didn't mean for Pinto to hurt your rooster. I didn't ask to fight them against each other, but you insisted. Your poor rooster. I'm sorry, Pancho."

But Pancho, who was never quiet, was speechless.

After a minute or so he asked, "Who is the owner of this rooster? If he is for sale, I'd like to buy him." Pancho had this childlike look of wonderment in his eyes. I knew he was in awe of the rooster Pinto and his skills. He was so impressed he wanted to trade all of his roosters for the one Pinto.

I told him the whole story, about how the Pinto had pecked out the eyes of two of my roosters. About how I was trying to kill Pinto, but he fought back and I respected him because he had proven himself so brave. There was no way I could kill him. Now I just wanted to fight him.

I felt great that Pinto was such a good fighter, but, at the same time, I was surprised that Pancho's rooster couldn't even touch Pinto.

Pancho, a father, was now going to join us kids in our deception, fighting Pinto our borrowed rooster. In three days, the big fight with the rooster of la Hacienda de la Flor was coming up. A few weeks ago, a rooster from that colonia had killed one of my friend's roosters. So, we, as a collective group of neighbors from Josefa de Ortiz, were going to do everything in our power to keep from losing again.

We knew that Pancho would serve us well. He would keep Pinto overnight to prepare him for the fight, giving the rooster massages on his legs and body to relax him since he knew all of the techniques required to achieve optimum performance.

Today was Friday, the day before the fight. Fago and I walked over to Pancho's house to get our fighter. After collecting Pinto, we proudly walked back through our colonia showing off our true warrior.

Pinto was agitated. I tried to gently touch his feathers and he pecked at my skin. "Ow!" I yelled out as he tried to rip a piece of flesh from my hand. I knew that inside, he was like dynamite igniting. If you got him going a little bit, he would get very angry very fast. Pinto had a very short fuse. And that was exactly what we needed from our fighter.

When Saturday came, we were ready. Pancho would be the one to place the knife because he actually knew what he was doing. But in order for him to do this, he would need to first cut the talon. We were a little apprehensive because when we returned Pinto to Martha, it would give us away. But I was young and excited so without another thought of being found out, I gave Pancho the go-ahead to cut the talon and place the knife.

When we got to the house of Pinto's opponent in la Hacienda, a couple of guys opened the door. "Cool rooster," they laughed and pointed at the red bulky gobbler on Pinto's chin. "Toda la gente is back there." The guys led us to the yard. I walked through the house carrying the Pinto in my arms. He was strong. I still remember how hard the muscles of his chest and legs felt as I held him.

Some kids in the back yard pointed at Pinto and laughed. "Look at that rooster. That's one ugly crest!"

But I wasn't listening to them. My mind was already completely occupied with the fight to come. "Wow!" I thought when I saw the big orange-red Colorado standing with complete confidence across the yard. He was beautifully proud and intimidatingly large. I was in awe.

Then I looked down at the rooster in my hands and I recognized it. Pinto was equally large and muscular. Pinto appeared to match up evenly with the rooster he would fight, but he was at a big disadvantage with that big awful red crest; the Colorado could grab him, hold him, and maul him with the knife on his foot.

All the same, this was going to be a very good fight with two equally matched fighters. And it was close to starting time.

The Colorado's yard was big and full of people; the fifty or sixty spectators surrounded the roosters, Pancho la Bruja and the Colorado's owner in a big organized circle.

Pancho was in charge of letting the Pinto go. He had placed the knife, and, today, would be Pinto's gallero. Colorado's gallero was a forty-year-old man who looked to be more like eighty. A long gray-black patchy beard covered his whole face and grew almost up to his eyes. Unclipped pitch black hair hung out of his nostrils. Although it was rumored that he was a drug addict, he was a respected gallero in the region anyway.

Pancho and Don Pelos stepped apart until they were about ten feet from each other, crouched down and let the roosters go. The fight had begun. Spectators from both neighborhoods chanted for their respective roosters, "Kill him, Colorado. Finish him!" It was noisy, but La Hacienda had drawn a bigger crowd than my colonia.

Despite the shouting, the roosters fearlessly ran to each other. Pinto immediately took the initiative and attacked first. The Colorado and Pinto flew in the air in a frenzy of kicking and flying feathers. I was so worried that the Colorado would grab onto Pinto's crest and maul him. But I was wrong.

During this exchange, Pinto stabbed the Colorado in the jugular. When they landed, blood was spewing violently from the Colorado's neck. "Ohhh..." could be heard through the crowd. The people from la Hacienda were in shock. Pinto's legs were covered in blood, but the rest of his body remained clean.

I was also in shock, but for a different reason. "You are for REAL," I shouted. "Pinto is a fighter!" Pinto had been my neighbor rooster for six or seven years and every time he came over I would send him on his way. I thought he was a regular stupid, annoying rooster. Besides, he looked incredibly ridiculous with that gigantic crest.

After the fight, I took Pinto, who had come through unharmed, back to my house. On the walk home, Pancho la Bruja and Oso Yogi tried to talk me into selling him. "We'll give you two-hundred pesos for him," Pancho said. That was three times the going rate for a fighting rooster in my neighborhood. Adults in my neighborhood earned two-hundred pesos for a whole week of work and a good rooster usually cost between sixty and one hundred pesos.

"I can't," I said. Pinto was not mine.

I brought Pinto back into the chicken house. I had had the

rooster in my possession for almost two weeks.

The next weekend I would fight Pinto again, against the rooster of another well-known gallero. This particular rooster had won fifteen fights and had killed at least one of Pancho la bruja's roosters.

This fight drew a much larger crowd. I bet several chickens and 100 pesos. The roosters came at each other five times, madly. During the fifth attack, the opposing rooster got wounded in the leg, deep in the nerve. He couldn't get up because Pinto had cut him from behind. Pinto had won again. This time, Pinto had sustained a couple of wounds in the chest, but after the fight, Pancho la bruja stitched him up and he was fine.

I hid Pinto in the hen house for another week after the fight. But by then Martha Morado must've noticed her rooster was gone.

I saw Martha at my house one day, talking to my mother in the hallway. I knew why she was here, so I stayed hidden in my room. "Have you seen my rooster?" she asked mi mamá. Martha knew I was a gallero. Mi papá was sitting at the kitchen table reading the paper when he overheard my mother talking to Martha, so he got up and walked into my room. "Chispa, have you seen that rooster?"

"What rooster?"

"The rooster of Señora Morado."

"Oh, that rooster," I said. "I haven't seen him for a while."

"Really? And you have no idea where he could be?"

"No," I lied.

"Are you sure he's not at la huerta, in the chicken house?"

Mi papá knew. He had to know. He had found me out. My heart beat fast, I felt a lump in my throat and my mouth grew more dry by the minute. "I..I.." I tried to speak but didn't know what to say. I was in so much trouble. I could already feel the sharp, burning pain of the switch on my skin.

"I already know," he said. "Many people in la colonia have been talking about how you are fighting a very brave rooster.

I've heard of your success with 'Pinto'." He paused for a moment. "Chispa, if he is the one who hurt your roosters, do you think fighting him is the way to solve the problem?"

"Go get the rooster," mi papá commanded. "You will return him to his owner along with a sincere apology. In the next hour."

So I left for la huerta to collect Pinto and deliver him back to Martha. As soon as I returned home, I was ordered to go and stand facing the wall of the house. Forget about the switch. Mi papá hit me over and over with the belt. I felt the tears in my eyes, this time not only from pain, but from shame. The shame of disappointing my father.

But, although I felt guilty for my dad's disappointment, I didn't feel regret. I would've done it all again, everything from tying the Pinto to the tree to fighting Pinto two different times in two different neighborhoods.

My father was finished. "Go inside, "he said, still calm. "If I ever hear that you are fighting a rooster that is not yours, I will take away all of your roosters and chickens, and you will never have any more of those animals as long as you live in my house! You should've known better, Chispa."

A month later, Pinto got kidnapped from Martha's yard, after his reputation for fighting had had time to spread around.

This time, when Martha came to ask for the Pinto, I truly had no clue what had happened to him. I asked around the colonia and nobody seemed to know anything, either. But a few months after Pinto's disappearance, there were stories. Stories of how Pinto had won several fights. And, as the stories go, he turned out like all the rest. His owner over-fought him, neglected him, and he was killed by a "fresher" opponent.

Not long after that, I noticed el Oso Yogi, one of my rooster fighting advisors, was no longer driving an old, rusty Datsun. He had recently purchased a beautiful 1974 Chevy Nova with a high-quality stereo system.

Here's the history of the Pinto: five or six years earlier, Martha Morado, had traded a car for a bunch of animals—one rooster and some chickens and pigs. The owner of the animals had told her that Pinto was a very special rooster. He said, "If you mate this rooster with your chickens, you will have some money in the long run, because you will produce some very expensive fighting roosters." He claimed that he got this rooster's father from a palenque fight.

Only the really fancy, expensive roosters fight in the palenques. So Pinto had come from a very high-quality parentage. His father had been bred by the wealthy rooster farmers for the express reason of fighting in these stadiums. Pinto was indeed something special. He was the type of rooster someone in my neighborhood could never afford. He could only come to us under some type of special circumstance.

Anyway, the story goes that Pinto's father was mortally wounded in his last showing at the palenque, but this man brought him home. Instead of killing him like the fancy galleros do, he worked hard to cure the rooster since he was so beautiful. The rooster lived long enough to mate with one of the man's best chickens and the only rooster that came out of the union was Pinto, because shortly after Pinto's birth, his father died.

And Pinto...poor Martha Morado. I'm sure she loved that rooster. And she had taken care of him, too. For five or six years she had kept him to protect and breed with her ugly chickens. Until the day that Pinto decided to peck out Rambo's eye. That day Pinto's life changed forever and so did mine. Martha lost her rooster and I gained my reputation as the gallero who had fought Pinto, the rooster who was of the same caliber as the special roosters, the roosters who fought in the palenques.

La creacion de un luchador
Creating a Fighter

My grandma knew I loved chickens so she had recently given me two of the most beautiful she had. For a year, every morning, I had run the block over to her house to find eggs for her. My Grandma had seven chickens who ran around outside and their nests were hidden in bushes or in other remote areas. It was a challenge to find the eggs, but it was fun. Once I found the nests and collected the eggs, mi abuela thanked me, gave me a kiss and some eggs for our breakfast, and sent me home.

Now that I had two chickens, all I needed was a rooster.

Pancho la Bruja owned a huge rooster. He was stunning-looking, beautiful with a red body and orange feathers around the head. Rojo was a Colorado, meaning he was red, but this particular rooster was unique with bright orange feathers mixed in with the red and bright green legs.

Pancho's son Panchito was my friend so one day when I was over visiting with him at his house, I commented, "Pancho, your rooster is beautiful."

Pancho looked over at his Colorado and shook his head in disgust. "This rooster was my fighter until a couple of weeks ago. He got cut in a fight and bled a lot. Then he ran. That rooster is a coward. I was going to kill him, but I just couldn't. I don't know what to do with him."

Most galleros killed their roosters that ran, but Pancho didn't have the heart to do it.

When I told Pancho that I was given two chickens and needed a rooster but could only afford to pay five pesos for one, he offered Rojo to me for free. This was unbelievable. An average fighting rooster weighed thirteen or fourteen pounds, but Rojo, who was the biggest rooster I'd ever seen, was more like twenty-five pounds. He was a freak of nature.

I proudly carried Rojo to la huerta that day and re-baptized him Cuerpo de Okis (big body, good for nothing).

It wasn't long before my chickens laid a lot of eggs. I was going to have baby chicks and I couldn't wait. Maybe one would be a gallito who could fight!

I moved the chickens from the chicken house at la huerta to the roof of my house to more easily guard their nests.

La Negra, who was smoky black with a purple face, nested on the roof. About one month later, I heard some tapping from the inside of one of her eggs. I ran fast to get Fago and we watched. When the chicks were hatching, they would first peck out a perfect little star-shaped hole in the shell. And then the hole in the egg would grow and grow. These were the first chicks that would be born to a chicken that was exclusively mine.

La Negra laid nine eggs, but only eight chicks were born. Eight little beautiful chicks. They were different colors; some were black, some were yellow, and some were white. All of them were furry and puffy.

Sadly, we never knew how many boys or girls there were because they all died before reaching maturity. When my other chicken Gertrudis had babies, all of her chicks died, too.

All of the baby chicks were gone. "I'll never breed a rooster I can fight," I worried.

Philamena was my beautiful white chicken with black wing tips and a black tail who had come from the rancho in Sinaloa. She was my most productive chicken and would lay anywhere between twelve and fifteen eggs at a time. Philomena and my black fighting chicken, Gertrudis, mated with Mendigon and Cuerpo de Okis. Gertrudis laid about five eggs and so did Philomena. That was great, but when I noticed that Philomena and Gertrudis were not sitting on their eggs, I became concerned.

I watched my ugly chicken, Patas Peludas, sit on her nest faithfully. I knew she wouldn't produce any beautiful roosters. So I gathered Gertrudis' and Philomena's eggs together in a bowl and waited for Patas to leave her nest in the bushes next to mi mama's nopales. As soon as she got up from her nest to eat, I gathered up her eggs and replaced them with the eggs of the other two chickens. Patas sat on her nest with eggs that weren't hers for the full twenty-eight days. Out of these eggs, hatched three boys and five girls. Since roosters were worth so much more than chickens, I was really interested in the three boys.

As the boys grew, I could already see that two of them were going to be beautiful. One was a cute little black chick with red dots on him. The other was white with a little bit of bright yellow and black.

The one that was clearly Philomena's chick became a white, yellow, and black rooster that I named Waffle. Gertrudis' chick, Mendigon Jr., was a red-orange Colorado like his daddy. As he grew, he developed a mixture of red, orange, and black feathers on his body and dark green legs—he was easily the most beautiful rooster I had ever seen. The third boy, who was not as beautiful, was a Colorado, too, but he was eaten by a skunk when he was two months old and only eight inches tall.

After the gallito died, I stayed around la huerta every day for a few hours to throw rocks at the dogs and cats who tried to eat my other two baby roosters. I noticed that since Mendigon Jr. and Waffle hung out together. They would play fight, but Mendigon Jr. was clearly the leader.

A faster rooster kicks harder and will grab the other rooster first. Mendigon did this with Waffle when they played. As I watched them, I dreamed of how Mendigon Jr. would be a great fighter, a killing machine when he grew up. Waffle was beautiful by this time, too, white and bright yellow with a black tail. When they were eight months old, I cut off both roosters' crests and started training them separately. But Waffle wasn't performing well as a fighter.

I had never been attached to Waffle like I was to Mendigon Jr. so when a ranchero came to my house and asked to buy him, I said yes. He offered me big money—the equivalent of two-hundred dollars plus five of his chickens. With that kind of money, I could buy just about anything I wanted, but instead I gave most of my earnings to Ama who used the money to pay off some kind of debt.

Now I had only one rooster to fight—my beautiful Mendigon Jr. By the time he was ten months old, I had been practice fighting him against the neighborhood roosters. "Vamos a topar los gallos," someone would say, "Let's fight the roosters," and we would let our roosters go into the circle for a practice bout. We tried Mendigon Jr. out on Fago's rooster and on Pancho's roosters. We would practice them with each other for a few minutes each day. Mendigon Jr. was good; he would win every time, even though he was so young. He was an excellent fighter even though he weighed only ten pounds.

It was all Oso Yogi's idea. This rooster from Hacienda de la flor had been killing all of the Josefa Ortiz roosters. He had killed a couple of Pancho la Bruja's and a couple of Oso's. "Come on, Chispa," Pancho said. "He's beating our roosters every time."
"Yeah, fight him, Chispa," Oso pressured me. "Your Mendigon Jr. is ready."
"But he's so young. I don't want to fight him yet."
Mendigon was just a baby and he was my only rooster so I had hoped to save him until he was mature. I knew he would gain probably five more pounds. Most roosters didn't reach their full adult weight until they were a year and a half. And at only ten months, I felt wrong fighting Mendigon Jr. I had lost too many roosters already, and he was too young. Plus, I was very attached to him. I couldn't bear to think that my baby

rooster might lose an eye or be injured, let alone be killed.

"But your rooster is like a professional fighter. It doesn't matter if he's so young," they assured me. "He's so beautiful and fast, like the roosters in the palenques." Wow! What a compliment. To think he was the caliber of the roosters at the big fighting rings in the center of the city where people bet huge money.

I was only fourteen years old and impressionable, and, through all of his praise of my young rooster, Oso Yogi convinced me to let him take my Mendigon home to train him "professionally".

The day of the fight came and I felt jumpy, more jumpy than my rooster. When the men cut Mendigon Jr's talon in order to place the knife, the space was too small and the knife couldn't fit. A rooster's talons aren't fully mature until he reaches about sixteen months. Mendigon Jr. was so much younger so Pancho and Oso had to rig up something else. Normally, we would put a botedór (like a tiny cast) over the talon to secure the knife. But even the bump on Mendigon's talon was too small. Someone cut off a little piece of his shirt so Oso could wad it up between the leg and the knife to give the knife a place to rest.

Oso Yogi didn't worry too much that the knife was not placed securely. I guess he was anxious to fight my rooster. Everybody was anxious. There were at least eighty or ninety people in attendance that day, eager to see the fight and watch Josefa Ortiz get its redemption. "Let's do this," Oso Yogi said, eager for his own redemption, even more anxious than the rest.

The rooster Maton (the killer) was famous all over Chihuahua for winning over fifteen fights. Chuma was the owner and gallero. He was young like me and was a student of Don Martín, one of the greatest galleros in all of the surrounding colónias.

Someone yelled, "Time to fight!" so all eighty people formed an enormous circle. My rooster was already trying to fight; he was strong and enraged from all of the chile I had fed him earlier that day.

Then Pancho yelled "suelten los gallos" and Oso and Chuma let the roosters go. The roosters engaged and somehow Mendigon Junior, in a flurry of feathers, landed on top of Maton, kicking and kicking at him. During the fight, my rooster flapped up to the top two or three times. Usually, the top rooster will inflict a mortal wound on the bottom rooster during the first engagement. So I wasn't worried. I thought, "This is going to be great. My rooster is going to win."

But Chuma's rooster was tough. That rooster never gave up. Three times he ended up on the bottom and came away not even bleeding or limping, nothing. Each time, he came back ready to fight even harder. Then I heard Pancho yell, "Look at the knife of Mendigon. It's out of place." The roosters were at a natural break so the fight was stopped to re-place the knife on my Mendigon's tiny leg.

I looked over at Maton then. He wasn't injured but was still angry, pecking and looking ferocious. When the fight resumed, he grabbed Mendigon Jr. He cut my rooster in the chest and then Mendigon went limp. We stopped the fight again.

In a rooster fight while the roosters are engaged, no one can get in the middle. Only when they take a natural break can people stop the fight. But stopping a fight is dangerous and in some cases, galleros get cut by their own roosters.

During break, I looked Mendigon Jr. over. He was bleeding from his red, black and orange feathers. He had been such a breathtakingly beautiful rooster. The most beautiful of all. And now he looked like he might not make it.

Pancho fastened the knife again, looked at the wound and shook his head. I panicked. "Can we quit?"

He told me, "He still has a chance to win, but this is a mortal wound, Chispa. He's going to die anyway."

I felt horrible like never before. I should have never fought my beautiful Mendigon Jr. Because of my stupidity, he was now going to die. "What will I do?" I thought. I worried. I wanted to scream out and cry all at the same time.

But I was a gallero; feeling all at once great love and extreme pain was part of the deal. In this moment, I was overwhelmed with my sadness, but my anger kicked in, too. My anger at Oso. Oso hadn't placed the knife right. I really believed in my heart that my Mendigon would've killed Maton that day if Oso had taken the care he owed me to place the knife correctly.

Then my thoughts came back to the moment. It was time. He will die, I thought. And I will watch it all.

Oso and Chuma let the roosters go again and I stood half hiding my eyes as they engaged in two more fighting motions. My heart raced with joy when I saw Mendigon cut the other rooster badly, but sadness overcame me when I saw Mendigon get hit again. This time he fell to the ground. And he lay there still trying to peck at Maton. He was so very brave, even when so close to death.

The tears came as I watched my rooster still attempting to fight as he lay there dying on the ground.

Pancho moved to where Mendigon still breathed and unwound the knife from his tiny foot. "I'm sorry, Chispa," Pancho said quietly as I lifted Mendigon's bloody feathered body from the ground. I walked without turning, my head hanging, as I carried my dying rooster home. He flailed in agony and stopped moving on the way.

I reached the front of Cleofas' store. Mendigon Junior's head hung limp. I couldn't go to my house.

I didn't.

I hung out across the street from Cleofas' with my friends for four hours. For four hours, I cradled my bloody dead rooster in my hands.

Fago came over. "Your rooster, he's dead," he said and he cried with me for awhile. Other friends came and said, "Lo siento, Chispa." They were truly sorry. They all knew I dearly loved my Mendigon Jr.

Before I left that night, I hid my rooster's little body in the space between two buildings. Then I went home. But every night for four nights I went back to the corner to visit my rooster. The fifth night, Mendigon Jr's little rooster body was gone. Some animal must've eaten him.

My parents knew something was wrong with me. I would talk very little and I didn't smile much. One day about a month after Mendigon Jr.'s short life had ended, mi papa asked to talk to me.

"These are the chances you are taking when you fight these beautiful animals, Chispa. You can win or you can lose. If you're fighting with knives, most likely the loser is going to die. And fifty percent of the time, the loser will be your rooster."

I thought a lot about what he had said.

After losing my Mendigon Jr., my feelings about fighting roosters changed completely. I still bred roosters but sold them only to people who were not going to fight them. When my buyers came over, I asked them a lot of questions to make sure they would not fight the birds.

I'm sure you're wondering what happened to Maton, the rooster who killed Mendigon Jr.

One story claims that Maton died a couple of days later. The other goes like this: Maton won a few more fights and then he died, a winner. But I believe the first version to be true since I never witnessed him fighting again.

And I didn't ever talk to Oso much after that fight. I had once admired him for being a good gallero, but no more. My Mendigon Jr. was dead, and I would never again fight a rooster with knives. At only fourteen, my days as a gallero were over.

7. *LAS GANGAS*
THE GANGS

Moy

When my brother Moy was sixteen, he decided to go to Los Angeles to work. So my parents arranged everything for him; in L.A. he would stay with my father's sister, tia Lencha.

There Moy worked as a busboy and saved up enough money to buy the car of his dreams and some nice clothes. Like most of the guys who leave Mexico to work in the U.S., he wanted to show everyone in his colonia how successful and sharp he could become.

After staying in Los Angeles for one year, my big brother, at age seventeen, was returning to Chihuahua.

We were all excited to see him. Especially me. I had missed my brother. Before he had left for California, he had been a good brother, always taking me places and spending time with me.

That day in 1987, everyone stopped what they were doing and stared as Moy drove through the dirt streets of my colonia in his white 1977 Monte Carlo. When Moy parked in front of our house in his car, all of the teenaged guys in the neighborhood gathered around and praised him. "You look so cool, Moy," one said. "Horale homes, you're a real cholo now."

"Hey, bro. Nice ride." I could see that they were impressed with how he was dressing so nice like a real cholo. He wore black shiny shoes, extremely baggy dickies pants, and a hugely oversized white button-down shirt with a tank t-shirt underneath. The car he drove was also beautiful—nicer than any in my colonia, even the cars of the adults.

He was so fancy. What a cool brother I had!

Even though all of the kids thought my brother was cool, my dad wore a look of disappointment when he saw my L.A. cholo brother. I watched mi papá examining my brother and his car and then pull my brother to the side.

"Be very careful who you spend your time with. Some of these boys do a lot of drugs," he said softly. He was referring to the neighborhood cholos, the kind of teenagers who were sure to look up to Moy now that he was a well-dressed L.A. gangster, the gun-wielding icon these Chihuahua cholos could only be in their dreams.

As the days passed, I noticed that my brother had returned a "new" person. Even through my twelve-year-old eyes, I could see that he was different. But at the time, I didn't realize that the U.S. had changed him in a way that could potentially scar him for life.

Now that Moy had his very own car, his friends were always riding around with him. In fact, almost every day the whole barrio went cruising around in my brother's car. When Moy and his buddies took off down the dirt street in front of my house, the metal of the white Monte Carlo's back bumper dragged on the ground and threw sparks just like the low riders did. But the sparks didn't fly because the suspension was lowered. Sparks flew because the car was sagging under the weight of the fifteen cholos riding inside.

Surely my brother Moy was the most popular guy in my neighborhood and in all of the surrounding neighborhoods, too. I just couldn't wait for the day that I could ride around with him and his friends in his beautiful white car.

Whenever I saw him put on fresh clothes and shave, I ran out the door ahead of him and sneaked into his car. I was small for a ten-year-old, so I could lie down on the floor of the backseat and hide and he would never find me until we were already driving down the road.

I would be hiding in the back seat when Moy would get in the car with a couple of his friends. The two of them would be talking and listening to loud oldies tapes. They'd drive a few blocks and then one of the friends would turn around in his seat and see me. "Pinche Chispa's here," his friend would say, annoyed but laughing.

"Pinche, Chispa."

Moy turned the car around and drove home. As soon as we pulled up in front of the house, Moy would open up the driver's side door and fold the seat over so that it fell on the steering wheel. "Get out," he would say.

"Can't you please take me?" I pleaded.

But he would always answer, "No, pinche mocoso. You can't go with us."

I trudged back inside the house or left to look for my friends. Since his cool return, my brother never let me go with him.

Before, I had always been close to my brother Moy. When I was a little kid, three years old, my two biggest brothers Chentito and Moy would take me all over with them because I'm sure they thought I was really cute and tiny, and I would say silly things that would make their friends laugh. But I was closer to Moy and he took me with him the most. He took me around with him for an hour or two almost every day.

When Moy came back home to Chihuahua, I just wanted to be with him. I had always been proud of him. He always had been a cool guy, and everybody had always liked him. But now he was muy chido. If I could just go everywhere with him, then all of Chihuahua would know that he was my brother.

But this didn't happen the way I planned. Once Moy came

back from L.A., he didn't pay much attention to me at all. And not too long after that, he pretty much only hung out with the Puesto 1.

The Puesto dudes went every weekend to what they called La Liber. This street was a main downtown street where the cholos cruised. Cruising meant driving La Liber, West to East, East to West. They just drove and looked for trouble. My brother and his friends often got into fights at La Liber. There they would meet up with smaller groups of cholos from other barrios to fight.

On the weekends if they didn't take the car, they rode the Chihuahua buses to pick fights with rival gangs. Puesto 1 was one of the most intimidating barrios of the era and I was proud of Moy for being so popular and for being such a bad ass. When Moy fought, he was almost always victorious and this was lucky because victory was an important part of the cholo lifestyle.

A few years before Moy came home in his Monte Carlo from the fascinatingly unknown world of L.A., he and my older brother, Chentito, had been hanging out on la avenida. The two of them had attended secundaria (junior high) in another neighborhood. Only a few kids who went to the school had come from our tiny neighborhood, Josefa de Ortiz, because it was so much poorer than the neighborhood that fed the school. The other students were rich kids in comparison and they made fun of my brothers, calling them "Sucios", "Mugrosos" (Dirties), and "Ratas"(Rats).

The other kids laughed at our neighborhood and said that our parents drove their "old, ugly cars on dirty, rat-filled streets" and our barrio smelled "dirty like the black water river." At school, my brothers got into fights with cholos from la Miller, las canchas, and la ferro neighborhoods. These cholos had more money and wore fancy clothes. But the guys at school weren't even cool. And unlike my brothers, they weren't even real cholos. They were what we now call wanna-bes.

But it didn't matter. My brothers still got tired of being made fun of every day and by seventh and eighth grade, Moy and Chentito had been kicked out of school for fighting so much.

At this time, my friend Rene's mom, Martha, had a store on the avenida where my brothers hung out. Martha's little mobile metal store was like a long bed truck with a camper top. From her mobile store, Martha sold candy and cigarettes. We referred to Martha's store as the Puesto.

Martha had two older sons the ages of my older brothers. Both of her sons had also quit secundaria, so, with no jobs and nothing else to do, they spent a lot of time just hanging out at the puesto with Moy and Chentito. The four of them started calling themselves Puesto and within a few weeks, my brothers and the other coming-of-age Josefa de Ortiz cholos were calling themselves Puesto 1. The name stuck like chicle and later became the name of our neighborhood gang.

My brother Moy was not the only cholo I knew who had spent time in Los Angeles. Many of the guys in my neighborhood had also been living in the U.S. for a period of time. When they returned from the U.S., from L.A. specifically, they brought the barrio gang idea back to Chihuahua.

The barrio gang was a huge family circle of cholos. There were many elements to the barrio gang code. If there was a fight and your fellow cholo got in trouble you would defend him, no matter what, even if it meant that you got harmed. Once you were part of the gang, you were expected to defend everybody else with no exceptions. If anyone asked you, "De donde?" it was mandatory that you claimed "Puesto 1"; if a fellow gang member found out you said something else or refused to answer, you would get your ass kicked later.

Guys who failed to claim the Puesto or ran when it was time to fight got beat up and kicked out of the gang and they were harassed by the gang members for as long as they lived in the colónia. There was no choice; if you lived there, you were expected to claim and serve the Puesto.

So in 1987, when Moy and his friends created a gang like those of Los Angeles, the Puesto 1 morphed into one of the first barrio gangs in Chihuahua.

My brother Moy ran exclusively with the cholos. And the cholas, too. Moy had many girlfriends: all cholas from the barrio Lerdo.

The cholas often visited our barrio to hang out with my brother and his friends. I would see them sitting on the curb, talking in front of my house. These girls wore huge hoop earrings and their hair was dyed pitch black. They wore lots of make-up, too. Eyeliner that made them look Chinese and bluish or reddish eye shadow. They painted dark lines around their burgundy red lips and their dazzlingly bright red tops were tucked into tight black dickies pants that showed off their curvy hips. Sometimes they wore all black clothing.

What beautiful girls! I couldn't wait to get close to them and talk to them. My brother is so lucky, I thought.

But a lot of guys, especially the cholos from the surrounding neighborhoods, felt intense hate for Moy now. He was really popular and he always got the most beautiful ladies.

Moy hadn't always attracted so many girls. Tere, who lived next door, and my brother Moy had been boyfriend and girlfriend off and on since they were in primeria. But right now they were broken up. When Moy went to L.A., she got mad, and they hadn't been together since. But I could tell she still had a thing for him.

Tere had never been a gang girl, but now, all of a sudden, I noticed that she started to dress like a chola, too. She wore the black eyeliner and big earrings. And Tere was very smart. Tactically, she told Moy's friends, "I'm seeing a cholo from Lerdo."

When Moy learned this, deep inside of him, jealously started to trigger. I knew my brother; he had never stopped loving Tere, so, although he didn't show it to other guys his age, I knew he felt incredible jealousy. He wanted Tere for his novia again.

When Moy approached Tere, she refused him saying, "You lost your opportunity. Go hang out with your chola friends. You don't need me."

Now, every night, Moy went out partying and fighting with the Puesto 1.

One night during the summer he turned eighteen, Moy entered to the barrio Lerdo walking his girlfriend home. Her name was Mari, and I thought she was the most beautiful of all the cholas. Mari was about five foot seven and one hundred forty pounds with a really nice body. She walked so tough and confident and her hips swayed as she moved. She was very sexy.

After dropping her off, he left her house, still walking. Sometime after midnight, somewhere in the barrio Lerdo, fifteen of the Lerdo cholos ambushed Moy and beat him. They pounded him and jumped on top of him as he lay bleeding in the street. Some older ladies from Lerdo saw how my brother was being brutalized, and they ran into the street.

"Leave him alone, montoneros!" they screamed and pushed the cholos away off of my brother. Out of respect for the older women, the cholos de Lerdo moved away from Moy and walked up the street as the angelic ladies tended to my brother and called an ambulance for him.

The ambulance took Moy to the hospital. He was hurt in many parts of his body. He had been stabbed in the back and in the buttocks, both of his eyes were blackened, and he wore bruises everywhere.

He was briefly treated at the hospital, my parents were notified, and they left in a hurry to bring him home. Shortly after they came in with Moy, Tere walked through the door. "Where is Ramon?" (That's how Tere always referred to my brother, by his middle name, Ramon.) "Is he alright?"

After that, she came every night and helped my mother to cure Moy. Mi mamá and Tere put bags of ice over Moy's eyes and salve on his wounds. Every night they changed the bandages covering the place where he was stabbed.

A few months later, after Moy was healed, he sold some cholo clothing he had brought home with him from L.A. and used the proceeds to buy a gun. Now, he definitely wasn't the same brother I had known before. It seemed to me as if something had changed inside of his head. He rejected me. What little attention he had paid to me before was even less now and I was heartbroken.

But if I could've looked inside of my brother's head, I would've learned that he was unable to think about me. In fact, he couldn't think of anything except how he was going to exact his revenge. One by one, day after day, Moy and his four best friends were working to hunt down every single one of the lerdo cholos who were responsible for his beating.

My brother didn't kill anybody, but as he located each of his rivals, he beat each one. He jumped every one of those cholos unmercifully until they cried and asked for his forgiveness.

Moy had a plan. Along with each of these beatings, he would thoroughly interrogate each cholo in his quest to find out who had stabbed him. He tortured each one until, finally, he learned the names of the guilty. Now that he knew who they were, he searched out the two guys responsible for his stab wounds; for the two of them, he was ready with a really nice surprise. He hoped they would like it! Moy couldn't wait to use his gun on them. So when he found them on one warm, dark Chihuahua night, he shot them both. He shot the two of them with the 22 caliber pistol he had bought, but he never shot to kill them. Instead, he shot each of them square in the ass, where they had stabbed him.

Because of the revenge Moy had slowly, carefully, and diligently exacted on the Lerdo cholos, my brother earned his reputation in the Chihuahua area. He was now a warrior. He had always been known for being a noble guy, but now, he was a true bad ass. He was the kind of guy you would never want for your enemy; but on the other hand, he was the kind of guy who was indispensable as a friend. With Moy's reputation among the Chihuahua cholos, bad consequences were sure to follow.

One night, there was a fight. The Puesto 1 was involved.

That night, except for my dad, all of my família was at home. That night, even Moy had stayed home; he didn't go out because my brother, Chentito, had just come back from the U.S. and Moy wanted to spend time with him.

At eleven o'clock, Apá was still gone, playing pool somewhere with his friends. Amá, my little brother and sister, Chentito and I were sleeping in the two adjoining bedrooms and Moy and my brother, Bombin, were sleeping in the bedroom across the hall. The hall was not like a typical hall way. Our house had two parts divided by an outdoor passageway. The two bedrooms where most of us were sleeping were on one side of the passageway. On the other side of the passageway was the other bedroom where Moy and Bombin were sleeping.

I've never been a very sound sleeper so I woke up when I heard some commotion outside.

I heard someone yell my brother's name.

Then I heard the door across the hall bang open.

Looking out the window, I watched three shouting men armed with huge assault rifles in the passage. They must've awakened Moy and Bombin from their sleep. They were dragging my brothers in their underwear toward the front door of the passage.

"We got you, killer," one of the polícias yelled. "You're done. You're going to prison for a long time."

They laughed at Moy in his underwear and made fun of him. They didn't tell my brother what he had done to warrant his arrest.

I sat up in my bed, confused. My little brother and sister were looking around with sleepy eyes in the dark, also confused. My mother was pregnant at the time. With eyes full of surprised fright, she jumped up from her bed and ran out the door to help my brothers.

"Mis hijos," she cried. "Why are you taking them?" She moved toward my brothers in the darkness and drew close to them. I saw her move toward Bombin. "Jesus," she pleaded and tried to lunge for him, "Why are you taking my sons?"

Chentito had stayed in the bedroom with my little brother and sister. He acted like he didn't want to come out, and now I know that he was hiding so he wouldn't be taken, too.

"No! Stay away!" one of the judiciales barked at mi mamá. "We're taking him. He's under arrest."

The polícia judiciál (Mexican FBI agent) pushed my mother down as he dragged my brother by the back of his shirt. My mother, big and pregnant, fell to the cement.

"Pinche puta! Look at you. You just keep on making more criminals!"

I ran to my mother and helped her pull herself to her feet. Mi mamá, pobrecita. She was crying and whimpering as she followed the judiciales outside. "Mis hijos. No! Why are you taking them from me? What have they done?"

I looked down the passage after the judiciales as they rushed my handcuffed brothers toward their unmarked police car and pushed them into the back seat.

Why were they taking my brothers? I didn't think they had done anything.

There was my pregnant mother chasing after them and sobbing, unable to do anything to save my brothers. I ran after her into the street as she fought to get my brothers back. "Amá," I said. "Please calm down. Apá will come home and we can go get them."

I knew mi papá could make it better. He knew people in the government and he would know what to do.

We didn't find out until the next day why the police had taken them. My dad asked around and learned that the cholos from the Puesto 1 were fighting with the cholos from las canchas. Somebody from Puesto 1 had shot a guy from las Canchas in the head. After he was shot, the cholos from my barrio had jumped him, unaware that he was already dead.

When the police learned that one of the cholos from Puesto 1 had shot a las Canchas cholo, they rushed into my neighborhood and grabbed random Puesto cholos who they saw on the streets. The police detained these cholos in their cars and questioned them.

"Who in Puesto 1 has a gun?" They questioned several Puesto members.

All of them said, "Nobody."

But after the police forced mineral water up their noses and beat them with their fists and the butts of their rifles, one of the cholos admitted that my brother, Moy, was the only Puesto cholo with a gun.

"Did he do this?" they asked.

The cholo said, "We don't know who did it. We only know that he has a gun."

But since the Chihuahua police knew who Moy was and they knew also of Moy's reputation for violence, they assumed he was the killer. The police contacted the judiciales, who were the ones who broke into my house and took my brothers into custody.

That night, Moy and Bombin were in the backseat of one cop car, two other Puesto cholos were in another car, and there were two cholos from another neighborhood in the third car.

Once at the police station, the judiciales confiscated my brother's gun. They punched him in the face and in the stomach, trying to get him to confess. They threw him, already injured, to the hard floor and smacked him again and again, all over his body, with the butts of their rifles. Of course, Moy was not going to confess to anything he didn't do.

So for the second time in only a few months, Moy was in bad shape. He had two black eyes and a broken rib and he was bruised everywhere.

The judiciales released fifteen-year-old Bombin the next

day, after roughing him up a bit. They wanted him to say his brother Moy was guilty for the killings. But Bombin couldn't confess to a lie; his brother didn't do it.

Often, in Chihuahua, the judiciales would beat someone into submission to get a confession, even if the confessor was actually innocent. A confession would make it appear that the killer had been found and the judiciales would look good.

But this time was different. The police were dealing with strong minds and hearts and this time they would never get the credit for a job they didn't do. If they could've seen a few days into the future, they would not believe just how bad they would look to the entire city of Chihuahua.

After two or three days of interrogating Moy and beating him three times daily, the body of the dead cholo from las canchas was finally examined. Once the autopsy was complete, the police were notified. To the judiciales' surprise, the fatal bullet had come from a 22 caliber rifle, not the bullet of Moy's 22 hand gun.

And after all of the beatings and interrogations to obtain a confession, the judiciales, now aware of Moy's innocence, were forced to release him. Now after everything Moy and Bombin had gone through, the Chihuahua judiciales came to my house and made only a tiny apology to my brothers and the rest of my family.

Mi papá, enraged at the way his two young sons and pregnant wife had been brutalized by the polícias judiciales, was fuming. Although he was full of anger, he would not exact his revenge in the same way Moy had done. Instead, he wasted no time in contacting the local T.V. station.

T.V. reporters came to my colónia with their cameras the next day and make a news report. That evening on the news, they showed pictures of Moy and talked about the police brutalizing him. The interview was shown on the six o'clock news all over Ciudad Chihuahua.

The newspaper people came, too. They interviewed Moy and asked him questions for a feature they published in el

Heraldo de Chihuahua. Now the whole city of Chihuahua knew about what the police had done.

Moy's charges were dismissed since he was clearly innocent.

Following the news report, the judiciales came back to our house to make a more formal, appropriate apology. "We are sorry for taking your sons into custody," the taller one said to my father. "It was a mistake. All of the evidence pointed to your son, Luis. He has been heavily involved in gang activity and according to the other gang members was the only one with a gun in your colónia."

"It was our mistake," the other one said, "and we are very sorry."

Mi papá was still angry and clearly wanted to respond, but he held his tongue. I know he thought that it should not have taken a negative news report to extract an apology. But my father was honorable, so he accepted their weak words.

Afterward, they returned Moy's gun and left.

A weak apology may have appeased my father, but it failed to appease the rest of the city. Following the news report, the people of Chihuahua protested and put pressure on the police, so, one day, the chief of police came to my house and offered to pay for all of Moy's medical bills. In Mexico, you can't sue the government so the government felt no obligation to offer anything more. .

Moy's arrest and beatings brought an end to his career as a cholo. Moy could now rest, since he had taken revenge on the cholos who beat him. At eighteen, in a period of a few months, my brother had suffered a horrible beating by some rival gang members and a second by the police. Even after the news report, many people in our barrio and the surrounding barrios still thought my brother was a killer. But I knew the truth.

Cruzito

It was Saturday night and my brother Bombin and I were hanging out with his friends Che and Jimmy at Lico's house. We hadn't eaten dinner so by nine thirty we were getting really hungry. After a little discussion, we all decided to go to la avenída and get some tacos. Tonight, even though I wasn't feeling very well, I didn't want to miss any action so I went along.

We walked the twenty blocks to la avenída; there we found a lunchera and we bought some horse meat tacos and tortas for dinner. After I ate my taco, my stomach started to hurt even more, but still I said nothing.

After dinner, we headed over to la cantina el Capulina, the bar across the street from the taco truck. I wasn't old enough yet to get into the bar, but since the owner knew my older brother, Chentito, he let me in with my brother Bombin and his friends. It didn't hurt that by then Chentito was famous in my neighborhood for being a professional baseball player. We each ordered a caguama, like a forty ouncer, because the caguamas were cheap, seven pesos each (about seventy cents). The waitress brought us our beers, but after three or four sips of mine, my stomach was killing me.

I felt this vertigo in my stomach, like when you get extremely nervous and you want to throw up. I really didn't want to be a wimp, but on the other hand, I didn't want to throw up in the middle of the cantina and embarrass my big brother.

"You should just go home, Chispa," Bombin said. "We can hang out next week. Go home and get better."

We were going to play soccer the next day so I listened to my brother and went home. I went to sleep early that Saturday night. What a waste! Saturday night was supposed to be for drinking and having fun and here I was going to sleep in my bed.

I woke up the next day and felt like new. But something was wrong. That morning when I went to Cleofas' store to buy some bread and milk for breakfast, there were a lot of police cars driving around my neighborhood. The policia seemed to be looking for something or someone. I figured that something bad had happened the night before.

Remember, my little neighborhood Josefa Ortiz and the larger colonia industrial was the roughest in Chihuahua in the late 80's. So rough that the cholos ruled. The cholos in my neighborhood would gather on the rooftops as the police drove by and would throw rocks at the windshields of the police cars, shattering them. Now that the police were outnumbered by the cholos, they only came into my neighborhood when someone got hurt or lost or when something tragic happened. And they often brought four or five patrol cars at one time—safety in numbers.

When I got home with the groceries for Amá, I went to ask Bombin what had happened last night. My brother told me that something went wrong. Shortly after I left the cantina, some cholos from a nearby neighborhood waited outside the bar to fight with Bombin and the guys. The owner of the cantina alerted my brother, "Don't go outside. They are waiting for you. You are only four, and there are around twenty of them."

While Bombin and his friends were inside having fun talking with a couple of old bartenders and some cute ladies, the rivals were hidden outside the bar, waiting to ambush them. At two a.m., Bombin and the guys walked out the door of the cantina and they scanned the area for the rival cholos. Luckily, five other guys from our neighborhood were passing by in the street. "Some cholos from El Cayejón are looking for you.

They're around here." El Cayejón was twenty blocks from Josefa. The guys in Cayejon were almost as tough as the guys from my colonia. And there were more of them.

Bombin and the other guys decided it would be better if all nine of them went home in one group so they would be safe. They didn't want to fight with the other cholos. They just wanted to go home. It was late.

When the guys had walked together about three blocks, the cholos from El Cayejón appeared, walking, from out of the darkness. Their faces were stern—they wanted power. In their quest to hurt the Puesto, the El Cayejón cholos attempted to surround Bombin and his friends. They closed in from the far corners of the dark street. This time, they brought with them even more guys; in all they numbered around thirty. The cholos in their baggy jeans and mismatched t-shirts, walked toward Bombin and his friends. They held weapons in their hands: rebars, and sticks. Some even twirled metal belts.

Bombin said, "When we saw so many cholos from El Cayejón, we freaked out and ran. The pinche El Cayejón guys yelled, "Stop!" but of course we didn't listen. We ran toward Josefa to avoid a beating! There's no way we were staying there."

"All I could think of was my bed and how I just couldn't wait to sleep. I was tired, wei."

To the cholos from El Cayejón, it didn't matter what Bombin and his friends wanted. So, relentlessly, they followed my brother and his friends through the dark, deserted streets. Now they pounded the Josefa guys with rocks they found as they ran. Pounded them on their heads and on their backs, and when Bombin's friend, Che, turned his head to look behind him, a cholo from the other neighborhood threw a rock like a fastball, and the rock gashed Che's forehead. "Blood was going everywhere," Bombin told me. I guess Che tried to run then, but he stumbled and almost fell. When Che's friends saw him bloody and dazed, they came to help him, walking quickly as they surrounded him to protect him.

"Hijo su puta madre! Let's try to get him home," Lico had screamed. "Vamanos."

"We hoped the other cholos would retreat," Bombin said, "But those putos still followed us. They weren't giving up."

Che was injured. They were pissed. Hot blood pumped in their veins and they ran against the group of El Cayejón cholos. Bombin and his friends ran with anger and energy and were able to push the El Cayejón cholos back. They continued to run through the Chihuahua side streets, shouting and breathing heavy.

As the cholos ran in the other direction, Che walked quickly toward our neighborhood. He got home and went to bed.

A few minutes later, the cholos from El Cayejón regrouped and came back, chasing Bombin and his fellow cholos again. And this was how we fought, chasing back and forth until one guy was captured and beaten. Tonight, the cholos from El Cayejón, came within one hundred feet of capturing a guy from my neighborhood. Bombin and the others from Josefa were scared—they realized now that since they were totally outnumbered, they'd better go home.

"We decided to chase the Cayejón guys away again," he said. "We were fucking tired."

But it worked. Now, gassed out and in need of sleep, they were ready to walk home.

And then a cholo from my neighborhood came out of the darkness with an idea. His name was Cruz, but we called him Cruzito. Cruzito was about five foot five and a very athletic semi-pro boxer. But he liked to inhale glue.

Tonight Cruzito was under the influence of the Resistol, so he was crazy pumped up. "Let's go chase them again. All I need to do is capture one of them and beat the shit out of him."

Here was Cruzito, feeling strong from the glue.

"They started it, esos putos, so they're gonna get their wish."

My brother and the other guys begged him, "Let's just go

home, Cruzito. We've chased them down now, and they've got to regroup. Chingon, Cruzito! We're fuckin tired. Let's just go home."

But Cruzito insisted, "Let's run at them just once more. I'm going to capture one and pound his ass." His voice was full of bravado...for him there was no turning back.

"Let's go home, pinche Cruzito." Several other guys said, knowing that they could not easily dissuade him.

But Cruzito refused to listen to the guys. He ran off down the street alone, into the darkness.

It had been about thirty minutes since Bombin and his friends had left the bar and only a few minutes since Cruzito had run off when the police sirens began to wail. This was the signal to run. Bombin and his friends now knew they had no choice. They couldn't follow Cruzito. They had to run toward home. They knew they had no choice because the police would chase all of the cholos. It was way past curfew. Everyone ran the quickest route toward his cantón.

"At about four A.M. we all met up by Cleofas' store. Everyone was there but Cruzito," Bombin told me. "We think Cruzito got arrested. That menso should've run home. We told him but there was no changing his mind."

Bombin finished his story and we sat around talking some more inside our room. Maybe an hour had passed when I heard my next door neighbor, Berta, crying. She walked down the passageway next to our room. Bombin and I heard her sobs and we started to worry. Berta was Cruzito's tia.

Berta was in the kitchen talking to my Mom. I got up from the bed and walked over by the door to listen.

"He's dead, Nena. He was horribly beaten."

Then she told mi mamá how Cruzito's face was bruised terribly and his body was gashed all over with knife wounds.

In shock, Bombin and I pieced all of the details together. When the police came, everyone ran away because it was after curfew. But when Cruzito had gone after the other guys, he didn't realize he was on his own. He could've captured one rival cholo, but no one had been there to help him. The other cholos from el Cayejón must have surrounded him, beaten him, and stabbed him.

Since Cruzito was a very good fighter, he was over confident. And he was also high from inhaling the glue.

We stayed in my room, in shock. Neither one of us wanted to confront Berta. On some level, we were to blame for Cruzito's death. But so was the glue.

Now I know that sadly, when we're young, we don't realize that substances like drugs make us feel like super men. Cruzito was high and he thought he was invincible, but the glue affected his ability to think straight and at the same time slowed his reflexes.

Cruzito, like other substance abusers, thought he was ten times tougher than he really was. The mind is very powerful. Under the influence of drugs, the powerful mind can be equally self-destructive. And it was the over-confidence of Cruzito's powerful altered mind that destroyed him.

Julian and la Miller

When I was about fifteen and a half, I bought my very first car with my own money. It was a 1976 Dodge Super Bee: a muscle car. I named it "Motoraso" which means big ass engine. My car was amazing; I was one of only two teenaged guys in my neighborhood who even had a car. Not even many adults had cars.

When I got the car and started driving, my reputation among the girls in the surrounding neighborhoods skyrocketed. But it was the opposite with the boys. With them, my reputation went down the hole. So much so that when I drove through the neighborhood, guys my age threw rocks at my "Motoraso". Immediately, my relationship with my friends changed. A lot of people started harassing me, they threw rocks at me, and they scratched up Motoraso's paint with nasty nails. Some guys pushed nails into Motoraso's tires and, as I drove, the nails lodged deep into the rubber and the air slowly leaked out.

After a while, I learned. So many tires had been punctured that I would scan for nails before I went anywhere. What a mess. Having something nicer than the rest in a poor neighborhood caused envy to surface among my friends. It was a bad situation—I really liked my car. I wanted my car. I had always wanted one. But the acquisition of my car caused a lot of problems in my life.

The summer before I got Motoraso, my cousin Panchita came from California for vacation. One particular day, Panchita and I were hanging out at la huerta just talking. It was kind of late at night. My friend Raul had just returned from living with his brothers in Texas. Raul was proud that he had learned some English and was anxious to practice with Panchita. Although he was a nice-looking dude, he was very arrogant. Apparently, he had always liked my cousin so he told me that he wanted to talk to her alone.

I asked her, "Do you want to be alone with Raul? He says he wants to be with you."

"Don't leave me alone with him," Panchita's eyes pleaded.

Raul got mad. He started calling me Panchita's babysitter. He was talking a lot of smack about me, trying to piss me off.

"Why don't you go to Lulu's while I calm him down," I said to Panchita. Lulu was our cousin who lived next door to la huerta.

Now that Raul and I were alone, he started to yell.

"Why don't you leave her alone?" I asked.

"I'm going to kick your ass, puta madre," Raul said, his jaw set.

"Que tu quieres, pinche Raul." Raul had been my friend. I didn't want to fight him. But my prima was important to me; this couldn't be avoided.

We decided to meet at Cleofas' store. But as we walked there, twelve other cholos came down the street in a big swarm ready to team up with Raul against me. I could see one guy named Rica in the group. He really hated me. He was about twenty years old, a little older than my brother, Bombin, and I knew he was jealous of how I was getting girls.

The guys threw insults at me, "We don't like you, cabron. You have no cajones. You think you're too cool for us, pinche puto."

"Bring it on pinche Chispa, right here, right now," Raul said.

"No," I said. We would've been in front of tia Lupe's house, and she would've told my mom.

So we walked up the street to the corner, to where we had originally planned to fight. A moment later, Gato came out the door of his house which was across the street from Cleofas' store. He did not slink out the door as his name might suggest. He sauntered out, like a regular guy; Gato was never a sulky, complacent cholo.

Gato was in his early twentiess and was kind of short and muscular with long seventies hair. He knew my brother Moy. A few years before, Gato had had a lot of problems in my colonia. He had come from a different neighborhood, and moved into Josefa as an adult. He was never fully accepted and was always fighting with the other cholos his age.

"Are these cholillos going to jump you, Chispa?" Gato asked me calmly. "If more than one steps in, I will help you."

As I stood next to Gato in front of his house waiting for the fight to begin, I told him the whole story of how Panchita didn't want to hang out with Raul. "That's a fucked up reason to fight," Gato said. "I would do the same for my prima."

Moments later, in the street in front of Cleofas' store, Raul and I fought. I again remembered what my brothers had told me—whoever hits first, hits twice. So I hit Raul first, and he kind of backed off. I was so angry, I managed to throw him to the ground and there, I kicked him over and over in his back. When he got up, I attempted to deliver a high kick to his head, but I only tapped him with my foot, lost my balance, and fell to the gravel of the street.

Seconds later, Raul jumped on top of me, but, surprisingly, he didn't hit me. Instead, he said in almost a whisper, "I don't want to fight anymore, cabron. Let's quit."

When Rica saw his friend giving up, he moved toward us, wanting to hit me from behind, but as he came closer, Gato must've read his intentions. Gato grabbed Rica and wrestled him down. He twisted Rica's arm behind his back, "Don't you ever do that to him, puto estupido. You're older. If you touch Chispa, I'll fuck you up bad."

Moy had always liked Gato, but after I told my brother how Gato had aided me in that fight, Moy rushed over to his house and told him he could count on Moy whenever he had a problem. Since Gato lived on the corner, he heard guys talking about him all of the time, and he fought with people a lot. He really needed Moy.

After that day, Moy and Gato became friends and Gato was much better off in the neighborhood.

Before Motoraso, a lot of girls liked me, but after the car, a lot of girls wanted to go on dates with me. A lot of girls would even ask me for rides.

My favorite girl to ride around with in Motoraso was Gato's sister.

I first saw her at the baile. That night when the dance was over, me and my friends were walking behind she and her friend. Some guys were bothering her, yelling "Hey, Chiquita!" and were asking her if they could take her home. I was with my friend Julian, the seemingly handsomest guy in the neighborhood, Javier, and the wannabe handsomest guy in the neighborhood, Nando. The girls liked Javier for his green eyes, curly hair, and white skin. Nando had a very dark, solid unibrow. He was one of those ugly guys who was really picky and was disrespectful to girls. He thought he was the greatest just because he had wealthy parents.

The four of us saw and heard what those other guys were saying to the girls so we rushed ahead to protect them. I knew the chubby girl, Angelica, and she introduced me to her friend, Monica, trying to score points with me. Angelica had a pretty face, but she was too chubby so I didn't find her very attractive.

But Monica was different. I immediately thought she was the most beautiful girl I had ever seen. She was very tiny, only about five feet tall, very slim, with a cute body, a beautiful face, light skin and light brown hair. She had striking hazel eyes. Monica wore these big, beautiful gold hoop earrings and beautiful make-up—dark brown and pink eye shadow and the eyeliner the cholas wore with the line that extended slightly out from corner of the eye toward the edge of the hairline. This made her look kind of Asian and, therefore, somewhat catlike or exotic.

Usually, Julian and I wore our baggy jeans, cloth belts, and oversized shirts—our cholo clothes—but tonight we were dressed as cowboys with our tight jeans and sweatpants underneath to show more ass, snakeskin boots, button-down shirts and our cowboy hats. I was glad we were dressed so nice.

As we walked toward the girls, the two "cute" guys were arguing about who was going to "do the cute one first". They assumed she would be into them since they were real cowboys, and the girls in Chihuahua supposedly loved cowboys. Javier and Nando had such big egos and they were older than us and closer to Monica's age. From the way they talked, they must've really thought they had already won.

We caught up to the girls. "Go away," I said to the guys bugging them.

"These girls are with us," Javier said.

The two girls had smiled, like they were happy to see us. They stopped talking to Javier and Nando.

Now we walked together in a group, Julian and I next to the girls and the two "real" cowboys behind. Monica started a conversation with me. "Maybe she thinks I'm nice," I thought. But then the cowboys immediately started trying to impress her with the price of their boots and their fancy clothes, how well they could dance, stupid stuff.

Angelica must have seen me somewhere earlier, driving. She asked, "Where's your car parked at, Chispa?" and Monica looked impressed.

By this time, those fancy cowboys were becoming really annoying. We had been walking for about twenty minutes when they pulled us off to the side. "Hey, guys," Javier said. He used a really bossy tone. "You know we like these girls. We're going to go take them to eat some tacos so you guys need to get lost. As you see, they really like us, and you guys are just kids. The hot one, she's like twenty-one years old. You're just a couple of mocosos. Chispa, you keep talking to her, but you can see she doesn't want nothing to do with you."

"Just leave," Nando said.

We returned to the girls. I asked them, "Are you girls going to go have dinner with these guys? They told us to leave so they could take you to dinner."

"Please don't leave us with these mensos," Monica said to me, quietly.

"Julian and Chispa are going to take us to dinner," she then announced to the cowboys.

Javier and Nando looked down at the cement. They stayed a little longer, but the girls now ignored them completely so after walking about four or five more blocks, they made nasty faces at us and walked away.

I had only ten pesos and Julian had only five so the girls took us to dinner. Monica didn't let us pay. She paid.

After dinner, we walked the girls home. "How come you didn't drive your car today?" Monica asked me.

"I don't really like to drive the car to show off. It's pretty much to use for work. Earlier Julian and I were driving around in the car. But I didn't bring the car to the baile because I didn't want people to think I was showing off and then have my car get vandalized."

"Oh, that's pretty cool," she said. "Any other guy your age would've brought the car tonight."

But Monica didn't know I was only sixteen. I had told her I was eighteen. Sixteen...I wouldn't have stood a chance.

Angelica asked me, "Is it true that Nando has a car?"

"Not that I know of. I don't think he does."

Angelica said Nando had been telling them that he had a car and a really good job. But he didn't have either. He just had wealthy parents, by far the richest in my neighborhood, so he didn't have to do any work.

The following day, the cowboys saw us in the colonia. Nando reminded me, "She only wanted to be with you guys, because she wants a ride in your car, Chispa." Maybe that was true, but I didn't really think so.

Later that same day, I was driving around in the car with

Monica and I made sure I drove by both of their houses. They were so mad. They clearly couldn't believe I was with her

Monica told me later that her brother Gato told her how I had helped out my cousin. That I had defended her honor to a guy bigger and older than me. She was impressed with this. She was also grateful that I had told Moy how Gato had helped me and had effectively improved the quality of her brother's life in my neighborhood.

Cholos from my barrio and others were pissed off at me because I was dating the cutest girl around. Although Monica's brother liked me because I protected his sister and drove her friends around in the car, a lot of cholos were pigs when it came to females, so I didn't let any of them ride around with us or have a chance at Monica or any of her friends.

At about the same time that I had bought my car, my Puesto cholo buddies and I were having nasty fights with la colonia Miller. Things were changing in the barrios. The gang life, which was cool before, was now getting very frightening. We used to attack each other with rocks, punch with bare fists, and kick each other with our metal boot tips. Not too many got killed in this manner and the odds were better, more even, actually kind of fun. Being a cholo wasn't all that bad.

But the guns were different.

Now there were people being shot. When I realized other cholos were carrying guns and the violence was becoming more deadly, I didn't want to be a cholo anymore. But by that time, I was way too deep into the gang. My whole colonia was filled full of cholos. My brother was a hard core founder of Puesto, and because of my family ties and my Motoraso, I had received about six beatings in the last year. After each beating, my cholo buddies had helped to avenge me. The Puesto always protected me, and, for this reason, I guess you could say I was indebted to my barrio. Since the Puesto cholos had helped me so much in the past, it would have been dishonorable to just up and quit the gang.

By the middle of 1991, two of the Puesto cholos had been the victims of gun violence. Gegos got shot when I was twelve, and Frankie had recently been shot and was just lucky to be alive. Even though he hung out in the colonia and lived a seemingly normal life now, Frankie would forever deal with a bullet lodged in his neck. The doctors said if he were to get surgery, there would be a good chance that he wouldn't walk again. As far as I know, Frankie still has the bullet and it is travelling inside his body a few millimeters each year.

Martin was one of my best friends and Frankie was his thirty-year-old brother. I remember when Frankie was shot... what a horrible feeling it was to see your friend lying there in a pool of his own blood. We didn't know if he was dead or dying or what. Although Frankie survived, I thought he was going to die right there in front of my eyes.

The guys from the Puesto were not the only victims. I had also seen one of the cholos from la Miller get shot; when an older cholo from Puesto 1 shot the Miller dude in the head, he fell to the ground and the guys from my barrio beat him as he lay on the ground, probably already dead.

Because my brother Moy was such a popular cholo, I was popular by association. It is very cool to have a famous brother, but when you realize that people from other colonias hate you because of who your brother is, it becomes disheartening. I had no future living in my colonia without the gang as long as my brother Moy was around.

One Wednesday night, there was a funeral at the neighborhood catholic church, Perpetua Socorro, for a guy who had died a few days before. Pepillo was his name and he had been shot near my neighborhood. He was from a rival neighborhood and an older Puesto cholo had ended his life with a 22 caliber rifle. None of my family or friends were there when Pepillo died. Only some of the older cholos, who liked to rob people of their money and take lives, stealing them away in cold blood.

Julian, Fago, Tica, Panchito, and me walked past the lit-up church on our way to la avenida. We often went to la avenida to use the pay phone and call our friends because we had no phones in our houses. In fact, very few people in the whole neighborhood had telephones. The first to get one was my next-door neighbor, Doña Andrea. But we didn't want to ask Doña Andrea to use her phone since we called a lot of people and we would talk for hours. On the nights we went to use the phone, we didn't take Motoraso; we usually walked.

We passed the church and we knew that with Pepillo's funeral going on, the rival cholos would be there, so we sneaked quietly around the block. We went to la avenida and made our phone calls, but when walking home, talking and laughing, we noticed that somehow the cars at the church had mysteriously disappeared. For this we grew quiet, and, for our own safety, we decided to go the long way around. We walked down the street by my old elementary school; the street resonated with an eerie darkness. All five of us agreed that we felt something strange, that something was wrong. We didn't remember the street being so dark. Often the light poles were bad and the lights would burn out, but this time it was unlikely the lights had gone out on their own.

When we had walked halfway through the block, we heard what sounded like a stampede of angry bulls running toward us. I glanced behind me and saw the street completely filled with cholos, about thirty in all. I had recognized some of them. They were Pepillo's buddies. Since their friend had been shot and killed by a cholo from my colonia, and because of our association with him, I knew they were after revenge.

So it was our turn to run. We ran so fast, we flew. Eight blocks we ran, eight more blocks away from our barrio, and then it got silent. It was still very dark and we had gotten separated.

We called out to one another by whistling through the

darkness. That was our sign to gather together. But by the time we all found each other, the night had grown frightening. We were exhausted and, at the same time, were entering into another neighborhood. We thought we were in Santo Niño, a neighborhood with no cholos, a neighborhood of pacifist teenagers.

"Let's go home," Tica said. He was the oldest and the wisest.

"I'm tired," Julian said. "Can we stop and rest?"

We decided to stay in what we thought was safe terrain and catch our breath, then walk home.

After about ten minutes, when we were almost ready to quit and walk back toward colonia Josefa Ortiz, we heard whistling. Then more running. Then more whistling.

"Fuck! Hurry! Let's get out of here!" we yelled to each other, at various moments within seconds. Then we ran. A half a block later, in a well-lit part of the street, I saw two cholos from Ferro. I recognized their faces in the light.

Ferro was right next to la Miller.

We were in Ferro territory!

The Ferro dudes and the cholos from la Miller had formed some kind of an alliance. So it was the Miller cholos who chased us, along with their buddies from Ferro. We were pretty much screwed at this point.

"These guys are from Miller!" I screamed. "Run!"

The Miller guys chased us, a street full of them. They took up the whole width of the street.

About ten Ferro dudes had joined the thirty Miller dudes. Somehow my friends and I, the six of us, broke into two groups.

Now forty dudes were chasing us. I knew if I fell or got hurt and couldn't run, I could be the one shot or killed. It was one of the scariest nights of my life. We were certain that somebody was going to get beaten close to death...at least if we split, maybe some of us would make it out alive. So I ran with Fago and Tica and Julian ran with Panchito and Lico.

I ran so fast, I felt sick from exertion. My lungs were caving in and I could barely breathe.

When Fago, Tica, and I were about two or three blocks from our neighborhood, I heard Panchito screaming in the distance, "They got 'em." We guessed that the Miller dudes were beating Julian. We all turned around. There, on the next block, they were in a big circle around our friend. They had been beating him for about a minute when we ran to him. Five other Puesto dudes joined us from out of nowhere, it seemed. The ten of us closed in. We threw rocks at our rivals from Miller and Ferro. We were about ten feet from Julian when more Puesto cholos came. The Miller and Ferro cholos finally ran away.

Julian lay bloody on the ground. Tica and I lifted him but he didn't move. So we carried him, running, back to our neighborhood as blood gushed from his nose and mouth. He was heavy and unconscious and he breathed hard. As we ran with our bloody friend, I heard the whistling of bullets speeding next to my ear. Bullets shredded through the leaves on trees above me. Little pieces of falling leaves touched our heads on their way to the ground as we rushed by.

I realized in those few seconds while carrying my bleeding friend on my back that I didn't want to live this life anymore. I was so young...I wanted to have a family. I knew that living like this, I could die. Here was Julian. He was only seventeen. And in fifteen, maybe thirty minutes he would probably be dead. Next, it could be me.

So many times we had fought these stupid gang wars with the guys from la Miller and Ferro and las Canchas, and why? Why did we all hate each other so much? Until the bullets started flying, I never really thought about what the gangs were doing to me. But now, this time, it was my friend who was dying and it was so close it finally mattered.

And more than just me dying, I didn't want my younger brothers to be doomed for life because of the stupid gang. I was doomed because of my older brothers. My ten-year-old brother had just been beaten up because of me. I didn't want all of this violence happening to him, too.

And Julian was dying.

What were we going to do?

We carried him. He now seemed amazingly light.

Only one block further, a man stood outside his front door. "Is he hurt?" he asked. "Bring him inside." The good Samaritan opened the door—the other cholos were chasing us still. Quickly, all ten of us rushed inside the house. We could see through the window about thirty of them outside. Two of them had guns. All of them had some kind of weapon. They were right outside the house, but thank God they couldn't get to us now.

When we lay Julian down on the floor, he choked on his own blood. The kind man washed Julian's wounds and, still, the bleeding didn't stop. He grabbed coffee grounds from a trash can and rubbed them inside the wounds. Like a miracle, the bleeding lessened and then stopped. Then the man and his wife filled a bucket with water, and they used a rag dipped in the water from the bucket to clean Julian's wounds. When they were finished, the water in the white bucket was blood red. It smelled like iron death. The man lifted the bucket and carried it away. Then he got on his phone and called an ambulance. Julian coughed up a lot of blood and started to wake up a little bit.

We all waited. It took an hour for the ambulance to arrive. But, in the time we waited, the Samaritan managed to keep my friend awake and he saved his life.

Julian was in the hospital for a while. The doctors thought he had blood clots in his head. It was sad, because Julian's brother had just left for Utah, and his father was no longer around so he was supposed to be el hombre de la casa, the man of the house. The one who worked and provided for the family. He wasn't able to work to support them; instead he lay in a hospital bed, close to dying.

Later I learned that the good Samaritan happened to be an off-duty policeman. Because of his position, no one threw rocks at the house or tried to break in.

Julian's beating had a big impact on me.

I had received so many beatings, but I was always able to defend myself a little bit. I had only been beaten by two or three guys at once, and I could cover my head and defend myself until someone jumped in to help.

One time in my dad's store I had gotten kicked in the face by this guy Vicente from la Miller and his cholo buddies, Jimmy and Mario. The three of them beat me until some of the other merchants along the block heard the yelling and fighting and came to my aid. The merchants were the age of my father and wanted me to report the guys, but I would choose to take justice into my own hands. I knew the repercussions would be greater for me if I reported those cholos to the police.

In Mexico when you get jumped, you shut your mouth and are patient and, if you can, you take your own revenge. I knew where these guys hung out.

One day I found Jimmy walking his girlfriend to her house. Again Julian, Tica, and I were walking to la avenida to use the phone, but we stopped and I talked to Jimmy. Jimmy was the cousin of another Jimmy who lived in my colonia. The Jimmy from la Miller was older and he was much bigger, tall and really thick. He wanted to fight me but I said, "No. But you can fight with Julian or Tica, whoever you choose." Jimmy chose Julian, and so they fought, right then and there, and Julian really messed him up. After he got beat by Julian, Jimmy retired from being a cholo and became a good sheet rocker.

Another guy that had jumped me in the store that day was named Mario. The Puesto cholos found him drinking outside his house. He was going to get it. It was just a matter of time. On that day, the Puesto cholos messed him up so bad that he had brain damage and after that he was kind of retarded. Had I been there, I wouldn't have beaten him so hard. I would've just given him a lesson.

And Vicente? Two or three months after he kicked my head like it was a soccer ball, he tried to assault this regular, non-cholo civilian that worked in the factories and rob his wallet. Vicente and the factory worker got into a tussle and, in the end, stabbed each other. Vicente got stabbed in the back of the neck. He was taken to the hospital and something went wrong. He died a couple of months afterward.

When I told Monica about my friend Julian and what happened, she couldn't understand why I was still part of the gang. I told her I was planning on leaving eventually to come to the U.S. and that I thought leaving Chihuahua was my only way to leave the Puesto 1 for good. "You're crazy, Chispa," she said. "Why do you want to go away to los estados unidos?" I didn't need to to leave Mexico to be successful, she thought.

But Monica could never understand. She was from a wealthier neighborhood. She had a two year college education and was a supervisor in a factory. She thought she had a good life so she strongly believed that in Chihuahua I could do the same. Her life was good, as far as Mexico was concerned. She made fifteen or seventeen dollars an hour but never considered she would probably make this for the rest of her life. Yes, I could do the same, but if I came to the U.S., I might be able to make this kind of money at twenty-five and by forty-five be making more like fifty to seventy dollars an hour.

Monica had plans for me. Since she thought I was eighteen, she had introduced me to her parents and wanted to get married. She had a daughter and had had a guy in her life before me that she either lived with or was married to, but she had left him. So she really wanted to be married, just not to him.

When I told her about my plans to leave Chihuahua for the U.S., she said, "No." I said, "Yes." We went back and forth on it, and that was the end for me—the end of my three month relationship with Monica. Monica was neither a bad person nor a bad influence. But Monica didn't share my dream or understand that I couldn't end the chapter of my cholo life and begin a new chapter of success without leaving Chihuahua and starting fresh in the U.S.A.

8. *MIRANDO PARA FRENTE*
LOOKING FORWARD

Aprendiendo
Learning

Even though most Mexican children don't go to kindergarten, all of my brothers, my sister, and I went. In first through sixth grade I went to primeria or primary school. In my primary school in Chihuahua there were forty kids in a class. Students sat in rows and the teachers stood up in front and instructed, then students did work from a limited supply of text books. Students did not get extra help from the teachers like they do here in the U.S. and there were no special services for struggling students. In fact, there were only a few special treatments—the ruler or pulling of the ears or the hair. And if students didn't understand the work in the grade they were in, they just got held back. And held back. And held back.

Secundaria was seventh through ninth grade, like middle school and I went to school for welding, electricity, and carpentry. In secundaria we took all the other basic classes: math, science, English, Spanish, social studies. Many of the kids

I knew didn't even think about going to secundaria; actually, most of my friends didn't go to school past sixth grade and none made it past eighth grade. All of the kids in my neighborhood talked about how they couldn't wait to go to work and none of my friends ever even mentioned going to college. They just hoped to finish elementary school.

But my parents had different expectations for us. Mi mama was a country girl who only went through the second grade and could only print her first name. But that never stopped her from making us go to school. We never missed a day unless we were near death. And mi papa was the same. A very well-spoken, classy man, he wanted us to become educated just like mi mama did.

Preparatoria, or high school, was almost unheard of in colonia industrial. For one, there was and still is no high school in my neighborhood. We had to go into another neighborhood with kids who hated us. But my parents were so excited for two of their children to make it there, they never thought about the problems we would face. When I got accepted into my prepa, or bachilleres, there were no others from my neighborhood at the school although my dad did know the principal through coaching baseball. Still, I was on my own. Even though my parents had tried so hard to push us, out of seven kids, only one of my brothers and me had made it into high school. My brother, Bombin, went to a short career school for accounting, "the place to go" according to the older people in my neighborhood; I went to bachilleres, more of a comprehensive high school where I studied electrical applications.

When I was in first grade, my bully Chuy had been there for four years, and, at the time, he was already ten years old. He struggled the whole year and never made it past the second grade. And this was the case with many others, too. Most kids were lucky if they made it through primeria. Because so many kids failed so many grades, I remember being in elementary school with my brother Moy's friends who were six years older than me. My friend Frankie's brother was fifteen years old in the sixth grade when I was nine in the fourth.

I always had an inventor's mind. Toward the end of primeria, in about fourth grade, many of my toys were plastic or thin metal cars, hand-me-downs from my three older brothers. One day, when I was playing with one of them, I noticed the wheels no longer turned. So I pulled the car apart—sure enough, it was broken inside. What would I do? I didn't have the parts to fix it or another car to take the parts from.

After having examined it a little while longer, a thought came to me... rubber bands. Rubber bands were cheap, so I asked my dad for a whole bag of them. Since I had good grades, he brought them to me and I experimented with them. I broke more cars apart, attached the rubber bands to the wheels inside and powered the cars with them. The wheels of all my cars now worked even better than before!

Even today, I've never seen anything like those cars I made. My cars were strange, but I had fun making them work. And the rubber bands followed the same principle as the toy cars you pull back on; the friction of the wheels moving backward made the cars spin forward quickly.

That car was my first invention. But now that I was an inventor, I needed a laboratory. So I created my lab. When you walked in the front door of my house, you walked down a sidewalk, an outside hallway, that went all the way to the back stairs leading up to the roof. On either side of this main passageway were rooms. At the back of the outside hall were some plants and a small tree. Every day for a few hours, I sat in this tiny shady spot by myself with an old brown tool box next to me and worked alone experimenting and inventing. No one had to pass through my "lab" for any reason; I liked it there since usually no one bothered me.

I was so excited and couldn't wait to share my invention. Who could I share it with? All of the kids in my colonia thought I was crazy. They just couldn't understand why I would spend all of those hours inventing and figuring out if things would work.

Then I had a thought, "Oso Yogi." Oso worked at the newspaper office as some kind of lead person and he was very smart. I liked Oso because even though I was young, he had taught me to hook up stereos. He would say to me, "This is the ground and this is the positive..." He saw that I paid attention and he taught me. By the age of ten, I knew how to hook up car cassette players and was putting stereos into the cars of my neighborhood friends.

If Oso could hook up the stereos, I knew he would probably understand my cars so one day I brought him a little jeep. It was a Tonka-sized plastic jeep and it had a lot of torque. It even burned tire. I told Oso, "You know, this car right here. It runs. It gets propulsion out of a rubber band."

Oso said, sort of playing, "I can see how you can propel this car with a motor. But I just don't see how this rubber band is going to move this car." I pulled the little car apart and showed him how it was set up inside. He smiled and said, "Chispa, that's actually cool." He became one of the few people besides my dad who actually appreciated my experiments.

Later I made a little propeller that flew around ten feet up in the air and I "fixed" some more cars. Again, Oso Yogi examined the work I had done and I could tell he was fascinated by how I made things work. I enjoyed talking to him more than the kids my age, even though he was in his twenties. Other ten-year-olds told me I was just wasting time making cars and other toys work, but they could never stop me because I loved what I was learning.

I did experiments instead of doing the things my friends were doing to pass the time—shutting the power off in people's houses or throwing rocks in the colonia and sometimes breaking windows.

Since I had limited supplies, I learned how to recycle. On the weekends I would go to the dump by the river and scrap tape players, video cassette players—any electronic devices I could find. I would take these little machines apart. At the time, I didn't know why I did this. I was just curious about the mechanics of the machines and wanted to investigate how they worked.

I loved school, too. If my parents would've had the money, I would've gone to college for sure. I loved to learn, I always got good grades and my teachers loved me. That's probably why by the end of elementary school, in fourth through sixth grade, I no longer hung out exclusively with the kids from my neighborhood. By that time, one of my best friends was Jaime, called Jaimito, because he was tiny like me. Jaime was very serious; he didn't play around a lot. He was really into school, very smart and a very interesting person to talk to. We hung out at recess. When everyone else was anxious to take a little break, Jaime and I would talk about math.

"What do you think about problem number six? How do you find the answer?"

"You have to change this bottom number in order to add the fractions."

"You have to make the denominators the same?"

"That's the bottom number, right?"

After being stimulated by my high-level conversations with Jaime, I would go outside to hang out with my other less studious friends who would make fun of me.

"You're such a schoolboy, Chispa. I can't believe you were talking to that other puny nerdo in the school."

"I bet you were talking about school stuff with that mama's boy."

"Yeah, Chispa. When are you gonna get chido?"

O.K., maybe I wasn't cool, but Jaime was a hope to me.

One day I brought Jaime home to show him my new invention. He was the smartest kid in the neighboring colonia so I thought if I could have these crazy inventor thoughts and actually make things work, Jaime and I together could invent something amazing.

At the time, I was working on a helicopter that I had never flown. It was made out of Styrofoam with the motor from a tape player. I had made a little hole in the Styrofoam and had placed the motor inside along with a AA battery. I couldn't wait to explain to Jaime that "the coils inside the motor work" and "the polarities of the battery make the motor spin a certain way".

When I took him into my "shop", I showed him the Styrofoam helicopter. "So what do you think?" I asked.

He looked at me, totally lost.

I just couldn't believe it. He didn't understand? How could Jaime not like what I liked?

"How long have you been doing this?" he asked.

"I've been working three weekends on my helicopter," I said proudly.

"It doesn't even look like a helicopter," he said. "The propeller is moving all over the place like it's going crazy."

"I need to somehow put a stabilizer in it, so it evens out." I tried to explain, but it seemed like Jaime didn't have any idea what I was talking about.

My friend Jaime, in some ways, was just like the others. He couldn't understand the inventor part of me. After he left my house that day, I sat quietly in my "shop" alternately glancing between my helicopter and the floor. I so desperately wanted to talk with him about my experiments, just like we talked about school and math. But I realized that there really was no one who could deeply understand all that was going on in my head. I was alone.

My other friends took advantage of me by making me teach them school material that they didn't understand, but then would turn around and call me nerdo and give me a hard time. I never understood quite how that worked. Now, looking back, I realize that kids were probably mean to "nerds" because they were jealous. They always talked about how school was boring, but new concepts are always "boring" when you don't understand them.

Secundária was when most of my troubles started.

My troubles were never academic. Every night around six or seven o'clock, I sat on a concrete bench on the sidewalk in front of my house and did homework. It was always loud inside the house and I needed silence to concentrate. Unlike the others in my family who struggled academically, Bombin and I had good grades. But amazingly enough, although most of my brothers and sister never went very far with their education, I know that none of us ever failed a grade.

When I was in secundária, my dad knew the counselors, and since we didn't have a phone, they would call him on my neighbor Dona Andrea's phone and turn me in if I didn't do my homework. Throughout school, my mom really pushed all of us to do our homework, and we got spanks if we didn't do it, so my younger brother Pedro and sister Flor must've gotten a lot. They were horrible about doing homework, especially Pedro, who never picked up a pencil at home.

My brothers, Chentito and Moy, only made it to the second year of secundária, eighth grade, but they didn't finish the year, and my sister Flor somehow made it to the end of ninth. After Pedro's first year of secundária, the school dumped him. Several kids like Pedro that went to school just to have fun and not to learn got dumped, too.

My secundária was four miles from my house. My friends Panchito, Cocol, and Julian walked with me to seventh grade every day. I was twelve, Panchito was thirteen, and Cocol and Julian were fourteen at the time; I was younger than the rest of my friends because I was the only one of the four of us to make it to secundária without failing a grade.

From day one of our seventh grade year, we were chased by the Miller cholos on a daily basis. And then one day, I started having problems with my own Puesto cholos, because I was popular at school and had so many cute friends. These girls would come over to my house to see me, and because of my popularity with them, the cholos in my neighborhood were always giving me a hard time and calling me nerdo. It didn't bother me at all. It was actually fine with me. They could call me anything they wanted because the girls were coming to see me, not them.

When I was in grade nine, I had a lot of problems with kids in other neighborhoods on my way to school. In order to make money, some people had video arcade games on their porches and the kids went there, to the little fenced in porches with a few games, to play. One particular day I left for school a little earlier than usual so I could play the arcade games at la junta street on somebody's porch. I was playing the game there inside the little fence, winning and winning and advancing. I was really into it.

Then I heard, "Hey, Chispa. Can I have some pesos so I can play the machinitas, too?" When I turned around, there was Pepillo.

Pepillo was a short, thick guy with a lot of pimples on his cheeks and a few on his forehead. He was about sixteen at the time. I had known him since he was about nine because he had played on my baseball team.

I said, "No. Why would I do give you money? I only have a couple more pesos to play my own game."

He said to me again, "Come on, Chispa, I mean it. I need money to play. I want to play, too. I really mean it."

"I don't want to give you any money," I said.

Pepillo left, and, since I finally had some peace, I continued to play. In what must have been only a few minutes, there he was again. "I need some money to play the machinitas."

Oh dios mio, this guy was really starting to annoy me.

"No! Get away from me," I yelled at him. "Go find something else to do."

I looked over at him. With wide, surprised eyes I watched Pepillo pull a knife out, a big one.

"I want money," he said.

Of course now I knew he meant business, but I was so angry, I yelled, "NO!" and he grabbed my baseball cap.

Even though he was from a rival neighborhood, I had never even considered that he would try to hurt me. But I was wrong. He really was going to hurt me if I didn't give him something. "Come on, Pepillo, I'm Chispa. Did you forget that we played baseball together?"

"Yeah, I remember. But we were kids. We're not kids anymore."

As he talked, I noticed that he stunk like glue or thinner. He was dirty, too. It looked like he hadn't taken a shower in a while. He must've been under the influence so maybe he just didn't care.

Pepillo grabbed me and held the knife up to my neck. "Every day you come through my neighborhood, you will give me money for the machinitas. Or else."

"What?" I couldn't believe it. My heart was pounding. Shit, I was going to die. "I'll give you my pesos," I said. "Just let me go."

Pepillo dropped the knife to his side and released me. He refused to give my hat back.

"Leave the colónia now or I'll hurt you."

I hurried away from him, so jumpy that I didn't go to school that day.

The next day I wondered what I was going to do. Pepillo's colónia was on the way to school and the only way to get to school was to walk through it. I couldn't go around. I had a huge problem. Pepillo had told me I was supposed to give him money for the machinitas or I couldn't pass through. But he was not going to stop me from going to school. Many of my friends didn't finish school because they were afraid of walking through the other neighborhoods. This wasn't going to happen to me.

The next day I walked around Santo Niño but on the third day, I brought my friend, Tica. Short and chunky, no one ever thought he was a great fighter. But Tica could fight like no other.

When Tica and I got to la junta street, there was Pepillo, sitting on the corner. He wasn't going to school. He was just collecting money for his drugs. He saw me first walking ahead of Tica and he immediately started toward me to collect his money. He stared at me. Then he looked behind me. When he saw Tica there, I watched him stop and stand like a statue. I knew then that he must've heard about Tica's fighting ability. Oh, good! He was afraid of my friend.

"Hey,Chispa!" Pepillo said it now like he was my best friend in the world. "Where you going, Chispa?"

There was a reason he was so nice to me now that he knew I was with Tica. Tica had kicked at least three of his buddies' asses on the bus. So Pepillo was acting like there had never been any knife. "Hey, Tica. How's it going? Nice to see you." He said it so nice, like he was Tica's best friend ever.

"Tica, he's being nice right now, but he's been horrible to me ever since I started secundaria," I said. Remember, at that time I was in ninth grade. Pepillo had been making life miserable for me since eighth grade, since I had been walking alone to school. For a year and a half I had walked ten extra blocks which was making me late to school almost every day. "He always wants my money, and the other day he pulled a knife on me and held it to my throat."

"That better not be," Tica said, looking Pepillo in the eye. "Is that true, Pepillo?"

Can you believe it? Pepillo started to cry, "I didn't know what I was doing. I was high on the chemo (the glue)." Pepillo looked really pathetic with tears streaming down his face after he had pulled a knife on me.

"If you ever mess with Chispa again, I'm gonna go to your house and beat you so hard your mama will not even know you," Tica grabbed onto Pepillo's shirt collar. Tica looked so full of rage, like he wanted to kill Pepillo.

"No, Tica. Don't hurt him." Tica wanted to, but I didn't want any bad repercussions. Tica let Pepillo go, but clearly wasn't happy about it.

I smiled, relieved. I was so proud of how strong and brave Tica was. After that day, Pepillo left me alone and I realized again just how much I loved my friend Tica.

When Moy was eighteen and a horrible cholo, everyone wanted to hurt him; the rival gang members wanted to take out their hatred for Moy on me and my brothers, too. Bombin was fifteen at the time and he got chased most days, but he thought it was kind of fun because he played on good soccer and baseball teams and could run for a long time without getting tired. He would walk into the house, breathing hard, and say with a smile, "You'll never guess what happened to me again today." That was part of the reason he had earned his other nickname—Loco (Crazy).

"You got chased by Lerdo?"

"Yep."

He thought it was fun until one day.

Bombin walked up the street. This day he wasn't smiling. He was looking very angry. "What happened to you?" I asked.

"I've had enough," he said. "Today they chased me and threw rocks...and sticks."

At the time, Bombin was going to the short career school learning accounting. "It's enough. Tomorrow I'm packing a gun. Don't tell Amá and Apá," he said. He knew my dad would beat the living shit out of him if he found out. The next day Bombin left the house with his gun. And he took the gun to school for about three months. He told his friends, "I've got a gun now. I'm sick of this chasing shit. If they throw rocks at me again, I'll use it. I'm not afraid to shoot someone." And I'm sure he would've used it, too, because he was Loco.

My friends and I could never be sure, but we always thought that some of Bombin's friends must've told the Lerdo guys because every day from then on the Lerdo cholos left Bombin alone. They probably were afraid, because this was the

1980's, and until the 90's, a cholo carrying a gun in Chihuahua was very rare.

My brother Bombin was smart. Because he took matters into his own hands, he was able to finish his short career. Four of the most studious guys his age from the colonia went to the short school. Cremas and Jimmy were two of them, but the only one who graduated was Bombin because he packed a gun.

Prepa (high school) had its problems, too. Now I had to walk through two different neighborhoods to get to bachilleres. Bachilleres was a comprehensive high school that I had to test into. I tested into Electronic Applications while some who tested lower went to Carpentry, Corte y Confeccion (Sewing), Delicatessen, or Welding. There were more boys than girls in bachilleres since there were more trade classes of interest to guys. Occasionally, my friends walked me there, but, unlike me, who just wanted to hurry and get to school, they were hoping for action. They tried to pick rock fights with the cholos from the other neighborhoods along the way.

So I didn't like walking with them. I actually preferred walking with some girls who I had met in secundária.

I went to school the second session of the day, which began around 1:30. At that time of day, there was always a group of young cholos, about eight of them, who hung out on the corner by Cleofas' store. In order to walk to school, I had to pass by them. The store was at the end of my street, and the cholillos on the corner did everything they could to try and stop me from going.

None of those guys had jobs. They just mooched off of their parents. It was common that these guys would even steal money from their moms' purses.

"What do you think you're going to do with your life?" they would ask me as I passed. "Are you gonna be a lawyer?" Then they would look at me and laugh, knowing I would never be able to afford to go on to the university.

Many times one of them would grab me by the arm and refuse to let me go and I would be late. The drugged up, stinking cholo would say, "Stay, stay. Where do you think you're going?" I was a little intimidated because these guys were eighteen or twenty and I was only fifteen.

"Why do you waste your time? You're going to end up working at la obra (construction) just like your brothers, anyway. You'll be like all of the rest of us in the barrio." They were trying to hold me back and pull me down with them. That was not what I wanted. I wanted success and I knew school was important. Plus, I still loved to learn—I loved anything academic. Studying and gaining knowledge made me happy. Learning made me feel powerful, and though they held me by the arm and put me down with words, they could never take the excitement of learning away from me. I was already on fire.

Every single day they tried to stop me from going. But I had my own plan.

I pretended that I went to my tia Lupe or tia Cuca's house and from one of my tia's houses I walked in the other direction to avoid them. I always ended up walking a few extra blocks so those guys wouldn't see me leaving the neighborhood on my route to school.

Not only did those jerks try to hold me from school; they also gave me a bad reputation among the cholos. They called me coward and wimp because I walked around the neighborhood to avoid them. Because of the guys on the corner, day by day, relations grew worse between me and the rest of the Puesto cholos.

One day Chuy Mudito was hanging out with the cholos on the corner. When he and the crowd at the store figured out that I was going around them to get to school, they would somehow always find me and would playfully throw rocks at me. It was so embarrassing. I'd be walking with girls to school and then out of nowhere these stupid cholos from my colonia would show up. The guys would taunt me and the girls, too. Since the girls didn't know the cholos, they would be scared for me, thinking that the cholos were going to chase me and jump me.

Most nights when I came back from school between eight-thirty and nine o'clock these same guys would still be hanging out at the corner. One night, Chuy Mudito, my bully for life, was talking smack about me. "Hey, pinche Cheepa, you little asshole. You're such a chicken, pinche Cheepa." This particular day had been a very bad day at school, so I was not in a good mood.

But I'd been taking kickboxing classes. A couple of months before, I had decided to enroll in the classes because I was afraid that I'd be jumped by someone at school. My dad knew it was dangerous for me to attend school alone in a different neighborhood and he had encouraged me to take the classes so that I could better defend myself. But Chuy didn't know that.

Chuy playfully hit me in the head really hard and I responded passively. I did nothing, I only said, "Not tonight, Chuy Mudito. Not tonight."

Chuy continued talking more smack in his own special way. (Remember, Chuy was mute for a lot of years and when he finally learned to speak at age twelve, he sounded mumbly, talking with a deformed-looking mouth and he had terrible pronunciation.) " Pinchi Cheepa. Cheepa coolo."

That was enough for me. Pushed over the edge now, I tagged him in the head with my fist.

"Pinchi Cheepa. I wa keek ur ass," he said.

Chuy pulled his shirt over his head, ready to fight. That's what he did every time to intimidate people. He had a grown-up man body, short and thick, and I wasn't very much taller than him. Chuy Mudito was famous in a fight for only two things: biting and body slams. He had bitten chunks of flesh off of my body at times and he was so strong, he could pick up guys by the legs and slam them down on the concrete, knocking them out and winning fights. Just last weekend, Chuy had beat up Chucas, an old drug dealer. They had been fighting about some chemo and Chuy had lifted him up and thrown him to the ground, even though he was a two hundred pounder.

I thought, "Holy Shit, I could get slammed and that would be the end of me." But it didn't matter. I took off my button shirt anyway, exposing my white camisa de tirantes (sleeveless t-shirt). I was sweating already.

Then I started moving my feet, performing my dancing maneuvers in preparation for the fight while Tica stood behind me, coaching me. "Don't let him grab you," he said, not wanting me to get the famous body slam. But I never let Chuy grab me. I kicked him and kicked him in the legs and the arms and although I wanted to kick him in the head, I was careful not to kick too high so he couldn't just grab my legs and throw me.

Fortunately, this was the best fight of my whole life. It would feel so wonderful to beat Chuy's pathetic ass. This would be beautiful retaliation for all of the abuse I had taken from him since I was six years old.

Then, Chuy's biggest weakness showed itself. He was getting winded and was getting mad. "No kick, Cheepa. Ma Chigasos."

But Tica yelled, "This is a street fight, puto. He can hit you however he wants. You can kick him, too."

The truth was that Chuy was getting winded and I was loving it. Finally, he grabbed hold of me by the legs, but he was so tired he couldn't lift me off the ground. And I wasn't very big, either.

My brother Moy had been watching the fight from among the group of people who had collected on the street but when he saw Chuy try to lift me, he, along with Chuy's brother Chilo, intervened. Moy grabbed me around my torso and pulled me away while Chilo did the same with Chuy.

As Moy pulled on me, I tried to get free. I wanted so bad to go back in and finish Chuy. "Come on, let me go," I begged my brother. He did, and I saw my chance to finish Chuy. As Chilo held him, I ran over and punched him straight in the face with everything I had. Chuy swayed and then fell to the ground. Chilo grabbed his bleeding brother and helped him inside the house. I couldn't help but dwell on the idea that today had been a great day, one of the best in all of my fifteen years.

I had publicly shamed the neighborhood bully. So much that he didn't come out of his house for the next two weeks. Now I was loved by all the kids who Chuy had terrorized. I had done my job that day—paying Chuy back for all those years of meanness.

By the second year of secundária, I was on my own. My friends Cocol and Julian couldn't handle all of the harassment plus the schoolwork, so by early in our eighth grade year they both had decided to quit. Normally I walked at least part way home with some girls who lived in one of the surrounding neighborhoods.

But one day I left school walking alone. About ten of the Miller cholos chased me so far and so hard, I ended up in a place I had never been and I was lost. I could see them in the distance. I yelled to them, "Let's see if you guys can chase me tomorrow. I'm going to bring my buddies." For some reason they walked away and I managed to get home fine, but when I reached my house, it was very late. I had left school at eight and didn't get home until around ten.

I walked through the front gate, tired and sweaty.

"What happened?" mi papa asked. "Why are you late?"

I told him I got chased and got lost.

Then I went to talk to some friends and asked them to get some Puesto guys together to come pick me up from school the next evening. I couldn't sleep much that whole night. The next day at school, I tried to listen in class, but I couldn't. The whole day I mostly worried about whether or not my buddies would actually show up at school to help me out.

The bell rang, signaling the end of the day and I cautiously walked outside. A half a block away from the school building, I saw only Julian and Fago. "Where's everybody?" I asked them.

"Raul got beat up yesterday on the bus, and everybody had to go to his house," Julian said. All of the cholos hung out at Raul's older sister's store, so he took precedence to me. I couldn't believe it. Why were the guys from Puesto never around when I really needed them?

"I've been told that the Miller guys are close by, so let's go now," Julian said, and we hurried down the street.

"Did you see that?" I whispered to Julian as we walked. I thought I had seen the faces of some of the Miller guys around a corner, watching us as we walked. Julian agreed he had seen them, too.

As we rounded the corner, there they were. All ten of them. I had been so stupid. I had said some things earlier that I shouldn't have said because I thought all of my buddies would be there to help me fight. I had run my mouth in anger; I hated how the cholos always bullied me and I could never go to school or back home in peace.

The next moment I heard, "Hey, little Chispa. Where are ALL your buddies?" I said nothing and they ran toward us. We ran away but they followed.

For several blocks we ran from them and then Julian said to us, out of breath, "I'm so tired. Look at Fago." Fago looked like he was about to throw up. "Let's stop."

I guessed we would have to stop and challenge them to a fight before we got completely creamed. At that point, the fastest of them was within about twenty feet of us. "We know who you are and you're dead meat, Chispa," one said. "Next time you won't talk about ALL of those friends you have. And you won't call us fucking assholes, either, puto."

I said, "If one of you wants to fight one on one, I can kick any one of your asses."

Julian seconded me and said, "I think all of you can kick our asses right now, so let's just fight one on one. Who do you want to fight?"

The first one said, "Chispa. I'll fight Chispa." When it came time for each guy to respond, all of them picked me. Their leader had picked me, too. I knew his name. "What are you talking about Cesar?" I asked him. "You're as old as one of my older brothers. You should fight Julian," I said. Julian was a lot bigger and older than me—a better match for Cesar.

Through all of this Fago was smiling and calm. Of course he wasn't nervous. Not one person had mentioned anything about him. When everybody was picking who to fight, Fago had said, "Why do you all want Chispa?"

They all said they had nothing against Fago; they had it out for me. Fago, who was huge, dumbly said, "OK" and stepped far off to the side, away from me and Julian.

I looked at him in shock, unable to believe that my friend who I had helped through every problem would just bow out so quickly without a second thought and leave me alone to settle something that wasn't even mine. He was supposed to be here to help me—not just be here to watch me get creamed by ten guys. And my only crime had been that I wanted to go to school and get an education. It was just my bad luck that the school was in the Miller neighborhood.

Julian was cool with fighting Cesar, but Cesar kept repeating, "No, I want Chispa. He's a little smart ass. I want to give him a lesson." I knew fighting Cesar was a bad idea. That guy was a lot older and a really good fighter.

I was working it out with Julian when Cesar hit me in the back of the head. I turned around fast and we started to fight. Cesar, who was kind of short and thick, was also really quick. He whacked me a few times in the head.

When I retaliated, someone put his foot on the ground behind me and I tripped and fell backward. I was down. Now all ten Miller cholos kicked at me.

Julian got in the middle and started pushing people. He screamed to them, "That's enough. One on one is fair. This is not!"

When they started to chase us, we had been in front of the school. We were three or four blocks away from the school now and that's where we fought. Within moments after the Miller cholos started kicking me, I heard a girl's voice yelling. "Estupidos, putos! Stop it!"

Someone had pushed them away. It was Imelda, a girl from my school. She was pretty and very skinny. "Leave him alone!" she yelled.

I knew she was friends with them, but thank God she was also friends with my sister.

Imelda had two other girls with her.

"What else do you want?" One of the other girls screamed at the cholos. They moved away and looked back in my direction. "You already messed him up." Imelda was crying really hard and shaking her fists at them. I felt a tear fall against my cheek as the guys moved away, creeping in baggy pants down the darkening street.

While all of this was happening—the cholos kicking me, the cholos saying they wanted to fight me, Imelda saving me—Fago did nothing. "Why did you just stand there, Fago?" I asked, sort of dazed, as Julian helped me up from the street. I was bleeding from both my nose and my mouth.

Fago only said, "They didn't have anything against me."

Imelda and her friends escorted us for about ten blocks until we got back into our own neighborhood. I had a horrible headache and horrible nausea. I threw up under a car, trying to hide it from the girls.

When I got home and took off my clothes, I saw that I had some bruises, but overall I was surprised to realize that I was fine.

The fights didn't end between my barrio and la Miller, even though I wish they could've. There was too much fighting and struggle for someone who was trying to do something good with his life. I just wanted to go to school. But things aren't always what they should be. Thanks to Tica, Julian, the girls at school and Flor's friends for helping me. Sometimes we all need help. If I hadn't depended on the help of others, I wouldn't have made it so far through school. And I needed their help along with my own motivation so that no one could derail me from my goals.

Saliendo a Chihuahua
Leaving Chihuahua

There was a fight in my colonia every single weekend. This had been happening my whole life, from the time I was three years old. People got hurt or even killed—it was just a part of life. In a little more than ten years, I had seen countless beatings and stabbings, and a few weeks before, when I saw a very strung out Juan Pajarero shooting at Gegos at close range with a 38 caliber gun, I knew I had to leave Chihuahua. So many young men were either dying or in jail and I didn't want to be another one of the statistics.

It just so happened that about this same time, Fago's older brother Sigy and Rene's brother Javier Gamboa came back from the U.S. driving fancy cars, a light blue Buick Regal and a maroon Cutlass Supreme. They were Moy's friends and since I was always nosy and listening in to their conversations, I heard them talking about how in the states "you could sweep the dollars from the streets with a broom." Literally.

"Wow!" I thought. "That's so cool." I remembered the chiste or joke in Mexico about the dos Mexicanos who come to the U.S. and start sweeping the streets, and they are sweeping money! Piles of money! If it was so easy to get money, I wanted to be there, not here.

I know I was only fourteen, but I was ready to leave my home to find new opportunities and adventures. Maybe I could go to school in the U.S. Javier's little sister Aracely was going to middle school in Denver and he was always telling everyone about how great the schools were there. I had heard that in the

U.S. schools they had libraries with lots of books, beautiful buildings and they even fed students lunch. It must have been so different from Chihuahua. We had few books and old buildings overflowing with students. In Chihuahua, I had to fight my way to school and feel hungry all day until two'o clock came and I could finally walk home and eat lunch.

I really wanted to go there. So much that every time mi mama talked to her brother, tio Sigy in Washington state, I asked for the phone. "I want to come to the U.S. and go to school and find a part time job," I would say. "Can I come and live with you? Please, tio."

And every time he would say, "Chispa, you'd better give up on the idea of coming here. You're just too small. You're tiny. Kids will pick on you and you'll have a hard time getting a job." Can you believe that these words came out of a five foot four inch man?

It didn't matter. My tio's words were ineffective. My tio did not know me well at all. He thought his words would dissuade me. But he was wrong. His words could never cause me to give up—they could only push me harder to take the risk to start a new life in a new place and prove him wrong.

And, by this time, most of my Chihuahua friends were doing drugs. They were always putting pressure on me to try them out, too, to the point that I didn't want to hang out with those friends anymore. I was tired of the danger and pointlessness of my life. Not to mention the lack of opportunities. It didn't matter if my uncle didn't want to help me; I would find a way to get the U.S. and I would become successful, too.

So what if tio didn't want to bring me over.

Once I was sixteen, I had made up my mind for sure. I would get to the U.S. no matter what.

There was this very funny guy in my colonia named Cremas who was my cousin Chicana's first boyfriend. His family had moved to my neighborhood when I was four or five from a little town called Benito Juarez by the Mennonite camps. Juan was called Cremas because when he was a kid, he had sold Mennonite sour creams. He was my brother Moy's friend and his brother Fago was my friend. I knew Cremas very well.

Cremas was nineteen and had been living in los estados unidos for two years. It had to have been easy for him; he had had no difficulty getting a job, because he was always a very tall guy. And in the early 90's, the economy in the U.S. was booming and it was easy to cross the border. Since so many of the Chihuahua guys could travel in and out of the U.S. without much of a problem, they would come home to visit their families for a month each summer. That's what Cremas did. And right now he was back visiting.

Fago was in the U.S. now, too. He had left Chihuahua with one of his brothers when I was fifteen. I always thought about my friend and wished he would come home for a visit; every time his brothers came home, I would go over there and ask if he had come along.

When Sigy and Cremas were coming home, their mother would tell my mother. One of these times, I went over. "Did Fago come with you?" I asked Cremas when he came to the door, and he told me, no, Fago had not come.

"How is Fago doing over there?" I asked.

"He's doing fine," he told me, "and he loves it so much, he says he'll never come back." Over in the states, Fago didn't have a job and had no responsibilities. He just watched TV and slept, Cremas told me. Cremas and Fago both lived with their brother Sigy and his wife.

"Is Fago dating anybody?" I also asked.

"Yeah, the TV. He's always with the TV."

Fago didn't think of things to do on his own, I thought, sadly. When he was here, he always did what Tica and I decided. We kept him busy. But I guess in the U.S., no one made sure he was busy, so he just sat around.

I asked Cremas, "What do you do there?"

He was telling me about cutting rich people's grass. He told me that people would give you lunch or beers or nice tips if you worked for them. Later I would learn that these "rich people" were just middle class Americans, but to Cremas and probably to a lot of other Mexicans, they were wealthy.

Cremas offered me information that the rest of them always seemed to leave out. "If you want to make money, you have to work," he said. Until this time, everyone made it look like the money came easy. But I never cared if it was true or not. I had always been willing to work.

Cremas was the only guy who never brought a car back with him to Chihuahua, because, unlike his brother Sigy and Javier Gamboa, he didn't have papers. Javier and Sigy could drive over and visit in their fancy cars. But never Cremas. It was always more complicated for him to find a way in and out.

I asked him many more questions about the U.S. Of course, I did ask about girls, especially about blondes. I loved blondes. "What do the schools look like? Are there mostly brown people in the schools?" According to Cremas, there were very few Mexican kids. When he was driving by a school, he didn't see many Mexicans. He told me, "Yes, Chispa, there are lots of blondes."

Cremas seemed safe so I decided to tell him about my plans. How I wanted to come to the U.S. but my tio wouldn't take me, because I was "too short". Cremas said he thought that was messed up.

"You know, I think if you just wait one more year, because, Chispa, you are very short, next year you can come with me when I go back." Yes! I believed it would happen for sure because I knew that next summer, he would be back as always.

And I loved that guy. You could depend on Cremas. He was such a good fighter and he always helped the younger kids when we were in trouble. We would all come to him and tell him guys were bothering us and he would go and kick their asses. Without hesitation.

Cremas knew I was serious about leaving Chihuahua for the U.S. Everyone who came back from there knew. So much that when anyone returned to the neighborhood to visit his family, he would always tease me about returning with him. I would laugh and joke around with him. Even though I joked about it, I always wished deep down inside that I would actually be going along.

All that year, I couldn't stop thinking about leaving. I was so anxious. I prepared and continued to live my life. I quit school, I bought my first car, and I met the most beautiful girl in Chihuahua. But as it would turn out, the girl wasn't adventurous. And I had a dream that I knew Cremas would help me to turn into reality.

Every time I talked about leaving, my mom would cry. My brothers would say, "Be careful," and things like that, but I don't believe that they ever really thought I meant it when I said I was going with Cremas to the U.S. My sister was upset and my plans bothered my dad, too, but, unlike my sister, he never really showed it.

That year went by fast and my new girlfriend, Monica, when she heard of my plans, said to me, "Stay here. You can do everything you want in Chihuahua. You don't need to go away to do what you want to do." She was always looking so beautiful, smiling at me with her hazel eyes shining, her brown hair glistening, and I believe she really thought she could get me to stay. But I was sorry. Her beauty could not hold me. I had a plan. And with her inability to understand my dream, there was no way for her to deeply know who I was. I broke up with the girl, but she still looked for me.

And then the day came when Cremas came back. It was late July. On the day I went to see him, he asked me, "Are you still wanting to go?"

"Of course," I said. "I've been waiting for you to come back for me."

"You're sure?"

"Yes," I said. I had no reservations. None.

The second week of August, Cremas came over one night to talk to me. He needed to leave Chihuahua so he could get back to work. He would be leaving on the twentieth on the one A.M.

bus. "Are you still in?"

I told him, sure. I had all the money I needed—I had been saving it all year. I had been working a lot of long, hard hours for this.

That night, my talk with Cremas had sealed our plans in my mind, and, little by little, I told everybody, Monica included, that I would be leaving forever.

And then the day came when I was leaving! Early that morning, I woke up and realized that this was the last time I would ever sleep in my bed. As I ate breakfast in our little kitchen, I thought about how nothing would ever be the same. Today was the beginning of my new adventure. After eating lunch, I walked around looking for my friends, and one by one, I said goodbye to all of them. Then I went to find Monica for the last time. Very regretfully, I told her that I needed to let her go, and that she would have to find someone who shared her plans and who would stay in Chihuahua and be with her. I didn't share her plans and never would.

At about nine o'clock that night, I walked through the neighborhood saying goodbye to my tias and primos. Then I went home and packed my suitcase and went back out again to meet up with my friends and hang out with them on the corner for my last few hours. At a little before one in the morning, I went back home to grab my suitcase and to wake my parents and tell them it was time now. "I'm leaving," I said, tapping mi mama on the shoulder, waking her.

My mom sat up in bed, her eyes full of tears and I know my dad wanted to, but he held his tears in. I couldn't cry. I was filled with quiet anticipation that I had trouble holding inside. I hugged both of my parents and walked toward the door. Mi papa caught me by the arm and said to me, "Wait, Chispa." Then, he grabbed his wallet and opened it up. He pulled out seventy dollars. That was three weeks' worth of wages for him! "This is for an emergency," he said, placing the money into my hand. "If something happens and you're in trouble, you can use this to come home." I hugged mi papa again, shocked. My eyes started to burn now but I still held in my tears as I thanked him again and again.

I walked out through the gate. Without looking back, I walked to the end of the street. I had four-hundred dollars in my pocket—the money I had been saving for a year. This money should be enough to pay the coyote and live for about a month in the states.

Here I was at the corner. The corner where I had spent so many hours of my life...watching fights, fighting myself, meeting girls and friends and just hanging out. And there next to the concrete wall of Cleofas' store was the spot where Cremas should be. I crossed the street to wait where we would meet. It was now almost one o'clock, and he should be here any minute. At two, the bus would leave, and we would be on it heading for Agua Prieta, Sonora, where we would meet our coyote and head across the border.

One o'clock, one fifteen, one thirty passed, and still Cremas never showed. As I waited, I thought. Moy had given me advice about the U.S. He had told me that it really wasn't that easy. "Watch out who you hang out with," he had said. "There are a lot of black people and white people who don't like us." I was shocked. I thought that racism had been left behind in history, and I wasn't sure if what Moy said was true. But it worried me a little.

One-thirty-five, and where was Cremas? I walked to his house, very nervous, thinking he was running late. How could he be so late for something so important? What were we going to do? We would never make it to the bus by two o'clock; we were about thirty minutes from the bus station. When I knocked on the door, his mom came.

I asked her, "Where's Cremas? Is he around?"

"I'm sorry, Chispa," she said. "He left at ten."

He left without me? I couldn't believe it. "But I've been outside on the corner off and on since about eight," I said.

"Maybe he went the back way," she said, "The bus left at eleven." She looked at me, concerned. I could tell she felt bad.

"I don't think Cremas thought you were serious," she said. And so he had left me. I had been waiting all year for this and now I would never get to live my dream. Cremas probably thought that I was afraid and would flake out in the end, but why did he promise me? I didn't know what to say to her. "I'm sorry," she said as I fixed my eyes on the cracking concrete and walked away.

I was heartbroken in the streets. Wandering lost down the aging sidewalks, I ended up back in front of Cleofas' store. I would be stuck here forever on this corner to live out my life. A few of my friends still sat talking. When I looked up from the pavement and they saw my face, without any hint of my usual smile, they asked, "What happened?" A lump filled my throat as I worked to produce my answer.

"Cremas left...without me." Tears started in my eyes, but I didn't cry. And they never asked me again. My friends did not rip me apart; they were a support to me. We hung out on that corner for hours, just bull shitting about nothing worth remembering. We didn't drink. We just sat and talked to pass the time.

At around five in the morning, I came home with my torn-up heart and quietly knocked at the gate. When my mom opened it to me, she cried so hard. "What happened? Why didn't you leave?" Then her eyes lit up, full of happiness and relief. After a few minutes my dad came outside. He must've heard me talking to my mom.

He gave me a hug. "What happened?"

"Cremas left me," I said. The lump grew bigger, and I started to cry. The tears spilled out of my eyes now.

"That wasn't right," he said, hugging me. He let me go and looked me in the eye. "If Cremas thought you would be a burden to him, he should've told you," he said. "But remember, Chispa, that things happen for a reason. Maybe it wasn't the right time. Maybe something would have gone wrong."

The next day I didn't even go out in the streets. I didn't want to talk to or see anybody. The day after that, Patricia came to my house. Patricia was my neighbor, Jorge's mom; Jorge was my friend in elementary school.

Patricia had found out what happened and she wanted to talk with me. She wanted to ask me why I was so upset and why I wanted to come to the U.S. so badly. I told her everything about my plans.

"You know what Chispa," Patricia said, her eyes shining. "Alberto and I are going to Denver next month, but we have visas so we're going to catch the bus and go legally. Rigo is going to come to Juarez and pick us up. You're welcome to come with us, but you have to have a visa. Talk to your dad and see if you can get one."

As soon as my dad came home, I told him about what Patricia had said, and the very next day, he took me to the U.S. consulate. There, they gave us instructions to apply for a visa. Within three weeks, my dad was able to get me one. He also got a permit for me and, with the permit, I could be in the U.S. legally for six months. Because I was only seventeen and still a minor, my dad could obtain these documents for me. It was good I was leaving now. Had I been over eighteen, these documents would have been difficult or even impossible to get.

My dad handled many of the preparations for me this time. With my papers in hand, he went to talk to Alberto and Patricia. They had decided to leave at the end of September, so I went over to their house to talk to them a few days before. I was ready to go and I even had a permit. The only problem was that my permit was for California, not Colorado, because my dad had told the consulate that I had family in L.A. and would be visiting them. It was possible that a permit to the wrong state could be a problem.

On the day of our departure, we had planned to leave at four. That morning, I was at the corner in front of Cleofas' store again telling people that I was leaving. Almost everyone I told laughed, but this time I didn't care.

At four that day, my dad took Alberto, Patricia, and me to the bus. When we left, my mom still cried, but she felt better than the time before, because she knew that I would be safe.

Before we boarded the bus for Juarez, my dad comforted me with his words. "You can do it. You're very smart. Try to find a school for the evenings." I felt good because this time I had my parents' blessings to take with me.

We got to Juarez. Rigo was there to pick us up at the bus station with his friend, Javier, and they drove us across the border without a problem. It didn't matter. As we crossed into El Paso, my heart beat faster. In forty minutes we were at the first checkpoint, and, once again, there was no problem because we only needed to show our visas. None of the border patrol people would need to know that my permit was issued to California until we were at the second checkpoint. We were now about thirty minutes away from that checkpoint, which everyone always says is very tough. You have to have all of your papers in order or they will kick you out of your vehicle and deport you back home.

My stomach was starting to tie itself up in knots. I knew I needed to tell Rigo that my permit wasn't for Colorado. I had gotten through the last checkpoint without having to show it, but from the little I knew, I was sure the immigration officials at the next checkpoint would ask for it. Fifteen minutes passed and when there was a pause in the conversation, I finally spoke up. "I hope there's not a problem," I said. "My permit is for California." Rigo pushed the brakes and slowed the car the moment I spoke. He parked along the side of the road. The silence hurt and my heart was pounding. Would he kick me out of his car right now?

"This is a big problem," Rigo said. "Why didn't you tell me sooner?" He almost yelled. He banged his fists on the steering wheel. "What are we going to do?" he repeated over and over.

"Puta madre, you're a minor. People have been taken from cars and buses. La migra will think we have drugs or some other shit. Chingao. Pinche cabron!"

Now everybody in the car was nervous. Rigo and Javier were swearing and were yelling at me. "Pinche puto, why didn't you tell us? What can we do?"

"Turn around, cabron. Let's just take him back to Juarez. We can't risk it. Chinita."

I guess I could just go to California by myself, I thought, but I don't have any clue how to do it.

Patricia said, "No, Javier. In Juarez, Chispa will get his money stolen."

Then she went on, "I'll just pretend to be Chispa's godmother." Patricia and Rigo argued back and forth for a few minutes and threw crazy panicked words around between the front and the back seats. But Patricia eventually won him to her idea. I had been sitting there, not able to say a word, and now they were making a plan. What could they do to get us through the checkpoint and make it seem like we were not trying to trick la migra?

Patricia finally said, "O.K., O.K. I know. We will do this. We will tell the people at the checkpoint that Chispa's permit is for California because in a month I am taking him to California to stay with his tia."

Everyone agreed. This might work. But if not, I was going to ruin their chance of coming to the U.S. We would all get deported, sent back, and we would have to try this all again. All our preparations were going to be for nothing.

"It's a good idea Mama," Rigo had said to Patricia, "but I really don't think it will work."

I was so hoping it would work. I had saved a lot of money for this and had waited for years to make this dream real. We were so close. Life was just teasing us, and now we were part of a big, humongous joke. I would never be able to do all of the things I had hoped for...have a job where I could be successful and a chance to meet beautiful American women.

Rigo and Javier talked fast as the rest of us sat there, rigid, in our seats. I had been thinking the whole time and now I realized that I should stop hoping. And then there they were—

the signs for the checkpoint. Patricia and I now started to pray. "God help us. Please keep us safe through the checkpoint." We were both telling God many things I would do if he would help me. Over and over we both prayed muchos oraciones a Dios.

And there it was—the checkpoint.

We could see it off to our right. It was time.

Rigo said, "We can't get into it."

It was blocked off with orange cones. The people were there, but the checkpoint said it was closed. "I've been to Juarez so many times to pick you up, mama, and I've not one time seen this place closed," Rigo said. "I can't believe it." He sighed in amazement.

"Me either," Javier added. "It's a really strange thing."

Our prayers must have worked. My luck was amazing today.

"Well, we still have one more checkpoint," Rigo said, looking a little scared again. "But if they stop us this time, we can just tell them that the other checkpoint didn't have a problem with our papers."

We talked, we worried, and we hoped for about fifty-five more miles that the people at this last point of entry would believe our story. And now the last checkpoint was just minutes away. We were still edgy, because this checkpoint was much further in but not as legendarily assholish as the other one. Then we saw the signs. "Checkpoint in three miles." My knees were shaking.

Until we saw the next sign.

"Checkpoint closed."

It was so mysterious and strange, I couldn't believe it. I was really here. I could stay here. For an hour or so, I had seriously thought I was going back. That my plan of a new life would never become real.

I felt a joyful wetness come to my eyes. I was on my way. My God had helped me to make it happen. There were no more checkpoints and I was finally here, ready to sweep as many dollars off of the streets as I could.

ABOUT THE AUTHOR

Rogelio Bolivar is a business owner in Denver, Colorado. He lives his American dream with his wife, four children, three dogs and two cats. Some of his favorite things to do are to watch Pumas, his Mexican soccer team, work at his shop, drive his sports car, and hang out with his dog, Mikey. He and his family enjoy traveling, eating various ethnic foods, and participating in sports and outdoor activities together. Rogelio still loves to learn about science and invent things. He also loves telling stories about his various experiences in both Mexico and the U.S.

www.ingramcontent.com/pod-product-compliance
Lightning Source LLC
Chambersburg PA
CBHW051647040426
42446CB00009B/1017